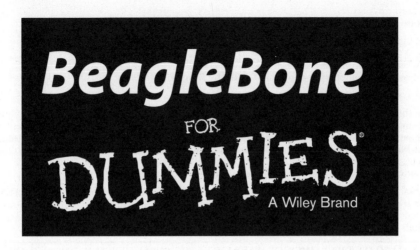

BeagleBone

FOR

DUMMIES®

A Wiley Brand

by Rui Santos and Luís Perestrelo

FOR

DUMMIES®

A Wiley Brand

BeagleBone For Dummies®

Published by: **John Wiley & Sons, Inc.,** 111 River Street, Hoboken, NJ 07030-5774, www.wiley.com

Copyright © 2015 by John Wiley & Sons, Inc., Hoboken, New Jersey

Media and software compilation copyright © 2015 by John Wiley & Sons, Inc. All rights reserved.

Published simultaneously in Canada

For general information on our other products and services, please contact our Customer Care Department within the U.S. at 877-762-2974, outside the U.S. at 317-572-3993, or fax 317-572-4002. For technical support, please visit www.wiley.com/techsupport.

Wiley publishes in a variety of print and electronic formats and by print-on-demand. Some material included with standard print versions of this book may not be included in e-books or in print-on-demand. If this book refers to media such as a CD or DVD that is not included in the version you purchased, you may download this material at http://booksupport.wiley.com. For more information about Wiley products, visit www.wiley.com.

Library of Congress Control Number: 2014954656

ISBN: 978-1-118-99291-3 (pbk); ISBN 978-1-118-99292-0 (ebk); ISBN 978-1-118-99305-7 (ebk)

Manufactured in the United States of America

10 9 8 7 6 5 4 3 2 1

Contents at a Glance

Table of Contents

Introduction

In recent years, there has been a trend to make programming and electronics not only more powerful, but also more accessible. These sciences used to be within the reach of only those who had dedicated plenty of years to them. Today, there's a different paradigm on the horizon: easy to learn, hard to master. Development boards such as the BeagleBone have introduced the possibility of easily being launched into the world of electronics and programming, resulting in an outpouring of creativity all over the world. Previously, there was an enormous gap between having an idea for a project and going through with it. Now hobbyists and enthusiasts can use the boards to get started with electronics and programming, but these boards also have the computational power that enables advanced users to create the most daunting projects.

How the BeagleBone manages to be a board that's at the same time easy to use and extremely powerful is truly a marvel. This book's purpose is to give you the joy of experiencing that marvel personally.

About This Book

The BeagleBone is a powerful and versatile development board. Using it is easy and intuitive. This book's intention is to walk you through the world of digital electronics and programming using the BeagleBone.

We believe that the best way to discover new concepts is through practice. In this book, you get to know all the important concepts by building circuits and programming them with the BeagleBone. Blinking an LED is a classic place to start, and you'll be doing it in no time. From there, you find out how to control motors and read from sensors. Ultimately, you gather all the basic concepts in the book and take a dive into web-based projects and home automation.

BeagleBone For Dummies tries to strike a balance between the technical and important details while striving to be a lightweight read. If you don't have fun while trying out the projects provided throughout this book, we've failed.

Foolish Assumptions

Regarding your expertise with electronics, programming, and embedded platforms in general, we assume nothing. This book has the necessary information to get you started from absolutely nothing. We have to assume two things, though:

- ✔ You have a personal computer, and you know how to use it to do basic things such as navigate a web browser, create folders and files, and write emails.
- ✔ You have a router with an Internet connection and an Ethernet cable you can use to connect it to the BeagleBone.

Because Linux is an operating system that isn't as widely used as Mac OS X and Windows, this book provides the necessary information in case you're using Linux for the first time. If you've previously worked with Linux, you can skip the parts of the book that refer to that topic and just visit them when you need a refresher on a particular subject.

Icons Used in This Book

For Dummies books use icons to highlight pieces of information that are worthy of special attention. This book uses the following icons:

Information following this icon provides shortcuts or small details that may make your life a little bit simpler — or a lot simpler! Paying attention to Tips is a great way not only to see how to do things in the most efficient way, but also to discover some extra information that may be helpful.

This book deals with a lot of electronics, which is a world of tiny and fragile things. Also, the BeagleBone is a computer, and everyone has a story of something bad that a computer may have done. In most cases, though, it isn't the computer's fault that an important file was deleted, that it crashed at a crucial moment, or that it discarded the lengthy changes you made in a document. You have to use care with a computer. This icon highlights common, harmful mistakes that you might make to ensure that you don't.

This icon is used for concepts that are used a lot throughout a chapter, a part, or even the entire book. Saving Remember items in the long-term-memory drive of your brain is probably a good idea!

The science behind computers and electronics is quite vast and complex. For the most part, we put technical details in sections highlighted by this icon. It's not obligatory to read them to proceed through the book. These items provide some cool little facts, though. More important, they provide insight into how things are working from a scientific point of view, which may make it easier to understand some concepts.

Beyond the Book

A useful resource at your disposal is the book's dedicated website — www. dummies.com/go/beaglebone — where you can download several files and all the code that is used throughout the book. You can also read the eCheat Sheet, which provides a simple way for you to quickly see how to power your BeagleBone, install your BeagleBone's drivers, and access your BeagleBone through your browser.

Additionally, there are several web articles with insightful and helpful information about some extra topics related to the BeagleBone, programming, and digital electronics. For example, you can find out how to use a multimeter to troubleshoot your circuits, discover ten software packages to install in your BeagleBone, and be introduced to the keyboard shortcuts you can use in the Cloud9 IDE (Integrated Development Environment). You can find these articles at www.dummies.com/go/beaglebone/webextras.

Rui maintains a personal website, which contains additional information and interesting projects for the BeagleBone and other development boards. Feel free to check it out at http://RandomNerdTutorials.com.

Where to Go from Here

Now is the time to initiate the launch sequence. You don't have to start with Chapter 1, but it's a good place to begin to get acquainted with the BeagleBone and all the possibilities it offers you.

Your second destination, however, depends on your experience with electronics and programming. If that experience is nonexistent, that's totally fine! This book has been written so that going through it sequentially makes the most sense. But playing around with an embedded platform such as the BeagleBone involves many different types of knowledge, and we don't want you to go through something that you're already familiar with. We strived to create a book that is appealing for both beginners and experienced users.

If you've dabbled in circuit design before, Chapters 5 and the beginning of Chapter 6 may not contribute much to your knowledge. If you're already a Linux user, you may want to skip Chapter 4, because it doesn't tell you much that you don't already know.

We suggest that whenever you decide to skip a chapter, you at least skim the titles of each section to make sure that no concepts that are new to you are left out.

Parts III, IV, and V are somewhat independent and can be read in whatever order you prefer. If Parts III and IV get you all excited about taking on the advanced electronic projects at the end of this book, maybe leaving Part V for later is a good choice. Conversely, if you want to use the BeagleBone as a desktop computer as fast as possible, you can go straight to Part V right after Part I.

After spending some time with this book, you should be more than ready to take on projects of your own. There's no limit to your creativity with the BeagleBone. Strap yourself in!

Part I
Getting Started with the BeagleBone

Visit www.dummies.com/go/beaglebone for additional *For Dummies* content and resources.

In this part . . .

- ✔ Getting to know the BeagleBone and all its features
- ✔ Discovering other components that you may need
- ✔ Preparing your BeagleBone with the latest operating system
- ✔ Booting your BeagleBone for the first time
- ✔ Getting started in digital electronics by blinking an LED

Chapter 1

Introducing the BeagleBone

*W*elcome to the world of BeagleBone, the low-cost embedded Linux computer for hobbyists and developers used by hundreds of thousands of people all around the world

The BeagleBone is a tiny board, but don't be fooled by its size: Its potential is huge. That board has a brain — the processor — that's almost as smart as the latest popular smartphones, yet you can buy the BeagleBone at a fraction of the cost. Use it to control your home remotely, host your own server, or build a robot. You're limited only by your imagination.

Actually, there's no right or wrong way to use this small computer. Some people want to use it for programming; others want to use it find out about electronics. Still other people (such as the authors of this book) prefer to mix the two worlds to produce some awesome projects.

The day this tiny board hit the market, the price for entrée into the world of programming and electronics was significantly lowered — both in terms of actual money and in terms of ease of understanding. With the BeagleBone's easy-to-use libraries and project examples, a novice can start creating a project in no time.

 If you're already familiar with these concepts — in the sense that you've worked with a microcontroller before, such as an Arduino — you'll find that the BeagleBone can help you "one-up" your projects because it offers a lot more computational power and, consequently, a lot more capabilities than the Arduino and similar microcontrollers. With the BeagleBone, there are very few hardware limitations or software constraints, so you are able to tackle the most ambitious projects.

With an ever-growing community of makers, designers, and programmers around the world sharing their projects on the Internet, the BeagleBone is hands down one of the best ways to express your enthusiasm for technology. We highly encourage that you share your knowledge with others when you get to that point.

Touring the Original BeagleBone and the BeagleBone Black

When you first get your BeagleBone, you'll find the board and a Mini USB cable inside the box. If you purchased an Original BeagleBone, you also get a 4GB microSD card. That's everything you need to get started, along with your computer.

There are two distinct versions of the BeagleBone: the Original BeagleBone and the BeagleBone Black. The two boards are similar except for a few small details, which we explain in the next two sections of this chapter.

The contents of this book will generally make sense whether you're using the Original BeagleBone or the BeagleBone Black. Whenever there's a need to differentiate the two, we do so appropriately.

Another familiar, common designation on the web for the BeagleBone Black is BBB. We don't use that designation throughout this book, but you may find it often if you do online research about matters related to the BeagleBone Black.

Whenever we simply use the term *BeagleBone,* there's no difference between the two versions with regard to the concept we're exploring.

At a first glance, you may feel intimidated about grabbing such bare boards (see Figure 1-1 and Figure 1-2). They are so tiny and seemingly fragile, yet so powerful. Certainly, you're curious to understand all the tiny components sitting on top of your BeagleBone.

Following are the components featured in both the Original BeagleBone and the BeagleBone Black:

- ✔ **Processor:** You can call the processor the "brains" of your BeagleBone. Both boards feature an ARM Cortex-A8 operating at a maximum speed of 720MHz for the Original BeagleBone and 1GHz for the BeagleBone Black. This means that the latter makes a decision/calculation every 0.000000001 second!

- ✔ **RAM:** The Original BeagleBone has 256MB of DDR2 (Double Data Rate 2), whereas the BeagleBone Black has 512MB of DDR3.

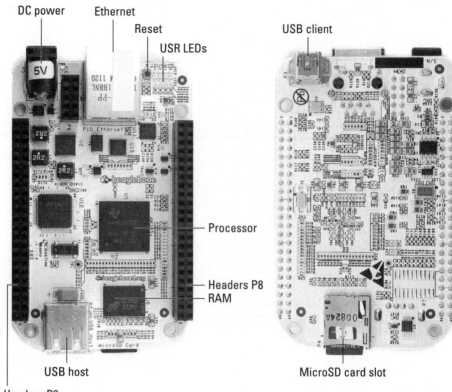

DC power   Ethernet

Reset

USR LEDs

USB client

Processor

Headers P8

RAM

Figure 1-1:
The Original
BeagleBone.

USB host

MicroSD card slot

Headers P9

Photo courtesy of Adafruit Industries

✓ **microSD card slot:** The Original BeagleBone doesn't have any built-in memory, so it always needs to have a microSD card inside to be able to work. By default, it comes with a 4GB microSD card. The BeagleBone Black doesn't come with a microSD card because it has built-in memory. Regardless, you can still insert a microSD card into it to install or update your operating system or because you want to have more available memory to play around with.

✓ **DC power connector:** Your BeagleBone needs 5 volts (V) and 500 milli-amps (mA) of direct current to power up.

Connecting the BeagleBone to your computer with a USB cable also provides the necessary power for the board to power up.

If you have a connector that fits into your BeagleBone connector, that doesn't necessarily mean that it's the right power adapter! Not all power adapters provide exactly 5V; some of them actually provide 12V. You also need to check for the connector's polarity; the center ring has to provide the 5V and the outer ring has to provide Ground (GND). You need to be careful. Even though the board has a voltage regulator, feeding it excess power or wrong polarity could permanently damage it!

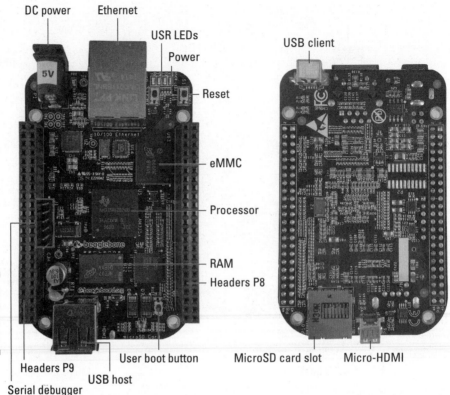

Figure 1-2: The BeagleBone Black.

✔ **USB client:** Both boards offer an USB client for powering up, communications, and debugging.

✔ **USB host:** Both boards include one USB port. This port enables you to connect peripherals such as a keyboard or a USB stick.

✔ **Ethernet:** Both boards feature a standard RJ45 Ethernet port. By plugging an Ethernet cable in it and connecting the BeagleBone directly to a router or by sharing the Wi-Fi connection of your computer, you can easily manage software on your BeagleBone, as well as build projects that require an Internet connection.

✔ **Headers:** The BeagleBone headers, labeled P8 and P9, can be used in many ways. You can use them to insert capes or supply power, for example, and you can program them to establish communications with other devices or act as inputs or outputs.

✔ **USR LEDs:** The USR LEDs indicate the status of your board:

- *USR0:* Blinks for as long as the system is running

- *USR1:* Blinks whenever the microSD card is being accessed

- *USR2:* Blinks to indicate that the central processing unit (CPU) is active

- *USR3:* For the BeagleBone Black, this LED blinks when the eMMC (embedded MultiMediaCard) memory is being accessed

✔ **Reset button:** This button resets your board when you press it. Keep in mind, though, that your BeagleBone is just like a regular computer; you should reboot it this way only when it crashes.

Besides the previously mentioned components, the BeagleBone Black has a few additional components (refer to Figure 1-2). These are:

✔ **eMMC:** The eMMC memory is the built-in memory on your BeagleBone Black. The amount you have depends on your BeagleBone Black's revisions (Rev):

- *BeagleBone Black Rev A and B:* 2GB of eMMC memory

- *BeagleBone Black Rev C:* 4GB of eMMC memory

✔ **Micro HDMI:** This port is used to connect your BeagleBone Black to a computer display or a television set.

✔ **Serial header:** The BeagleBone Black has a separate header for one of its serial ports, enabling you to easily connect a USB-to-TTL serial cable (read Chapter 3 for more on this topic).

✔ **Power button:** If you press the power button, the board shuts down after a few seconds. You can turn it ON once more by pressing the power button again. You can also do a full power cycle by pressing the board for about 10 seconds; the board turns OFF and then comes back ON. You should avoid this, though, as it may corrupt the eMMC or SD card. Use it only if your board is not responding to your commands.

✔ **User boot button:** By default, your BeagleBone Black boots from onboard memory with the operating system (OS) installed there. By holding down this button when you power the board, you indicate that you want it to boot from the microSD card. You also use this button to install an operating system on the eMMC.

If you're buying a BeagleBone now, it's very unlikely that you'll find an Original BeagleBone.

You can find all the boards available if you visit `http://beagleboard.org/boards`. At the bottom of the page, you also see a table that compares the features of the boards. Additionally, at that same link you can find distributors all around the world that have the BeagleBone Black (and perhaps the other boards) available for purchase.

Original BeagleBone and BeagleBone Black interfaces

If you're an advanced user, knowing the supported interfaces is often quite important, so they're listed here. If the following list makes no sense to you, don't worry; the book covers some of these concepts. For now, the important thing to know is that both the Original BeagleBone and the BeagleBone Black support a huge number of different interfaces, enabling you to connect with most devices and components.

The following list includes interfaces featured on both boards:

✔ 4x UART

✔ 8x PWM

✔ LCD

✔ GPMC

✔ MMC1

✔ 2x SPI

✔ 2x I2C

✔ A/D converter

✔ 2x CAN

✔ Bus

✔ 4 timers

Additionally, the Original BeagleBone features two other interfaces:

✔ FTDI USB to serial

✔ JTAG via USB

Discovering the BeagleBoard and BeagleBoard-xM

The BeagleBoard appeared on the scene in 2008. The BeagleBoard xM showed up two years later. These two boards differ somewhat from the BeagleBone Black and the Original BeagleBoard, so this book wasn't written with support for these platforms in mind.

Despite being older, these boards still offer a lot of capabilities and may even be advantageous for some very specific, high-end projects. For hobbyists, however, the BeagleBone Black is hands down the best option due to its reduced cost and great versatility. Also, it's a much better tool to use to get initiated in electronics and computation.

Exploring Uses for the BeagleBone

The BeagleBone is one of the best tools to use to discover programming and electronics. It's also a good way to see and understand more closely how a computer works. Throughout this book, you explore some of the many capabilities that this board offers.

You can create electronics projects, for example, by using BoneScript (see Chapters 7 and 8) and Python (see Chapters 9 and 10). You can use the BeagleBone to build a web page (see Chapter 13) and to run a home automation webserver (see Chapter 15). You can build projects to automatically access your email, notify you when a new one arrives and display it on an external screen (see Chapter 14).

You can control your BeagleBone remotely with the Linux terminal (see Chapter 4) and even set up the BeagleBone Black as a desktop computer (see Chapter 12). For such a low-cost device, the variety of uses for the BeagleBone is nothing short of amazing. And all these ideas are just scratching the surface. Just as a beagle is often a person's best friend, so is your imagination when it comes to playing around with the BeagleBone.

Accessorizing Your BeagleBone

Digital Electronics can quickly become an expensive hobby, but to get started, you need to spend only a few bucks on a BeagleBone Black. With a BeagleBone Black and a Mini USB cable, you have everything you need to create your first project: making the onboard LEDs blink. Don't feel overwhelmed by all the accessories listed in this section, because you don't need all of them right out of the gate. You may find that you already have most of these accessories on hand, so you may need to purchase only some of the accessories to complete our projects.

Here's a list of all the accessories you may need for the projects covered in this book:

- **USB A–to–Mini B cable:** The BeagleBone comes with one Mini USB cable. This cable not only powers up your BeagleBone, but also enables you to connect your BeagleBone to your computer. (Read more about this topic in Chapter 3.)

- **microSD card:** The Original BeagleBone doesn't have any kind of internal memory, so you need a microSD card to install and run the operating system; the Original BeagleBone already comes with a microSD card. On the other hand, the BeagleBone Black Rev A and B have 2GB of built-in memory, and Rev C has 4GB. The operating system can be run on the built-in memory and so these boards don't include a microSD card in their standard package

You must have a microSD card to install a new operating system or to update the existing one, however. We recommend that you get a branded microSD card with at least 4GB of storage for your BeagleBone Black.

✔ **microSD card adapter and writer:** Most computers have a slot for SD cards, so you can insert your microSD card into a microSD card adapter (see Figure 1-3) and connect it to your computer. If your computer doesn't have an SD card slot, you might consider buying an SD card writer.

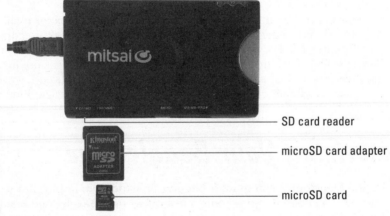

Figure 1-3:
A microSD
card,
microSD
card
adapter, and
external SD
card writer.

SD card reader

microSD card adapter

microSD card

There are many different types of microSD cards and SD card writers. Generally, their prices are based on the speed at which data is written on them. We recommend that you go for branded versions of both the writer and the card, and that you get at least a class 4 microSD card.

✔ **Ethernet cable:** Connecting your BeagleBone to your router with an Ethernet cable enables you to install and update software; additionally, the BeagleBone is a great platform to create Internet-related projects. It also provides you an extra way to control your BeagleBone remotely. (Read more about this topic in Chapter 3.)

✔ **5V DC power supply:** The BeagleBone can be powered up with a Mini USB cable by just being connected to your computer, but if you want to use your BeagleBone at maximum performance, capability, and featuring lots of USB peripherals — and/or for portable applications — we recommend that you use the 5V barrel connector. The power adapter that's required needs to provide 5V over a 5.5mm outer diameter and 2.1mm inner diameter. It must supply a minimum of 500 mA to power up your BeagleBone.

A USB connection provides either 500 mA or 900 mA of current (depending on whether it is USB 2.0 or USB 3.0). This is generally enough to have a BeagleBone connected through Ethernet and powering several electrical components. However, if you connect many USB peripherals, you are advised to go for an external 1.2A to 2A power supply.

✔ **Display:** Most displays with an HDMI output work with the BeagleBone Black. You can also buy an LCD cape that's specially designed to act as a display (see Chapter 6).

Not all displays are compatible with the BeagleBone Black. Make sure that you carefully read the sidebar at the end of this chapter to find out more about compatible accessories.

The Original BeagleBone doesn't have a built-in Micro HDMI port. Worry not, though: You can still output image and sound with an LCD cape.

✔ **HDMI–to–Micro HDMI cable:** If you have a BeagleBone Black with an HDMI–to–Micro HDMI cable, you can output video and sound to a display (see Figure 1-4).

✔ **USB keyboard and mouse:** Most standard USB keyboards and mice are compatible with the BeagleBone. Keep in mind, though, that the board has only a single USB host port, so you have to connect a USB hub if you want to add more than one peripheral (see Figure 1-4).

Figure 1-4:
BeagleBone
Black as
a desktop
computer,
connected
to a display,
a mouse,
and a
keyboard.

✔ **USB hub:** The USB hub enables you to expand the number of USB ports on your BeagleBone. This accessory is essential if you want to have multiple peripherals connected at the same time (see Figure 1-4).

✔ **USB-to-TTL serial cable:** If you have a BeagleBone Black, this cable could be useful to debug your BeagleBone Black during the booting process.

The Original BeagleBone has this feature built in, so you don't need the extra cable.

✔ **Other cables:** If your display doesn't have an HDMI output, you may be able to use a Micro HDMI-to-VGA or Micro HDMI-to-DVI converter. That way, you can repurpose your old desktop display.

Using converters for the Micro HDMI adds a whole other layer of incompatibilities. We recommend that you check our sidebar at the end of this chapter.

✔ **Case:** The BeagleBone arrives without a case, and some people actually prefer that look and feel, but it's important that your board stay away from static electricity, conductive metal, and liquids. It's a piece of electronics, after all. The best way to protect your BeagleBone is with a case.

✔ **Breadboard:** Using a solderless breadboard is the best way to prototype. It's really easy to use, as it doesn't require any soldering. That means that you don't make any permanent connections and can easily modify your circuit at any time.

✔ **Multimeter:** A multimeter is a useful device that measures many things related to electricity.

✔ **Soldering iron:** Solder is a metal that liquefies easily when heat is applied to it and quickly goes solid again the moment it's exposed to air temperature. A soldering iron is used to melt solder to establish permanent metallic connections.

✔ **Other components:** Some projects in this book use extra components such as LEDs, servos, motion sensors, and electrical wires. You don't need to get anything right away; we tell you when the time is right.

Compatible accessories for the BeagleBone Black

If you're looking for additional information regarding compatible accessories for your BeagleBone Black, visit http://elinux. org/Beagleboard:BeagleBone_ Black_Accessories.

Note: The accessories listed on that web page aren't the only compatible accessories that exist, but the ones that are listed have been verified to work with the BeagleBone Black. If your accessory is not working properly, but you find its name on that list, then you can be sure that the problem is not an incompatibility, and you can continue to troubleshoot.

Chapter 2

Installing the Operating System

● ●

In This Chapter

▶ Getting to know Linux

▶ Obtaining your Linux distribution

▶ Preparing your microSD card

▶ Preparing the onboard eMMC

● ●

*T*he BeagleBone is a tiny computer with all the features of today's computers, which ultimately means that it also needs an operating system (OS). Because BeagleBone is an open-hardware project, it runs on Linux — an open-source OS. Using free software makes using the board less expensive and creates the perfect tool to use to learn programming.

As with any other computer, you can use a BeagleBone to store files, surf the web, install applications, and do pretty much all the everyday stuff that you're used to doing. The real advantage of your BeagleBone over a typical computer, however, is that the BeagleBone has input and output pins that bridge the gap between the realms of computing and electronics. With a BeagleBone, you can create and control interesting electronic projects with a very high degree of complexity. After all, the foundation of your project is a computer. Also, because the BeagleBone is a low-cost device, it doesn't cost a fortune to replace it if you somehow break it!

This chapter explains which distribution of Linux to use, as well as where you can download it and how to install it. In Chapter 4 and Chapter 12, you dive deeper and see how to use the Linux shell and its desktop environment.

If your BeagleBone has just arrived, and you haven't done anything with it yet, your board already has a fresh OS installed. To prevent unexpected issues, however, you should be running the latest version of the same OS shown in this book, so we recommend that you follow the instructions in this chapter to ensure that everything throughout the book works for you.

The BeagleBoard Black comes from the factory with an empty microSD card slot. We highly recommend that you buy a microSD card with at least 4GB of storage to install the new Linux distribution as described in this chapter. If you have a 2GB card handy, however, you can use it to get started. Keep in mind, though, that there'll be very little space left on the card after you install Linux. You'll be able to use it to work through the procedures in the following chapters, but eventually, you'll need more memory.

Introducing Linux

Linux was created as a free OS for personal computers. Because of its many advantages, it quickly made its way into a plethora of applications. Nowadays, Linux is used on a wide range of hardware platforms, such as mobile phones, tablets, embedded systems, servers, and routers.

Linux is a good example of the strength of an open-source community. No company developed this OS. Instead, thousands of people all around the world contributed their knowledge to create and improve this software — at no cost at all.

Linux is hands-down the most popular software around for programmers and developers, mainly because anyone can have full access to the code, modify it, study it, and distribute it. Read Chapter 4 for a more detailed description of Linux, including its advantages and proper use.

The Linux kernel is the core of your computer's software. It's the lowest level of software that interfaces with the hardware; it's the code that controls everything, translating whatever you do on your computer into a language that the hardware can understand.

Selecting a Distribution

A *distribution* is a complete Linux package that contains the Linux kernel and a couple of other pieces of open-source software that provide a wide variety of functionalities.

Knowing the factory defaults on your BeagleBone

We recommend that you follow the instructions in this chapter to install the latest Debian distribution, which is used throughout this book. Every new BeagleBone is configured to work out of the box by default, however. The original configuration depends on your board:

- ✔ The Original BeagleBone includes a microSD card that has the Ångström distribution installed.
- ✔ BeagleBone Black ships from the factory with Linux installed on the board's eMMC memory and with an empty microSD card slot, which we recommend that you use to install Debian.

The Linux distribution depends on the board version:

- ✔ BeagleBone Black Rev A and Rev B have Ångström installed in the built-in memory.
- ✔ BeagleBone Black Rev C comes with Debian preinstalled.

We opted to use the Debian distribution for this book because Debian currently is the most-supported distribution in this embedded platform. The next sections of this chapter walk you through the procedure for installing Debian.

If you want to see a list of all OSes that are fully compatible with BeagleBone, visit `http://elinux.org/Beagleboard:BeagleBoneBlack#Software_Resources`.

Even though there are plenty of similarities between one Linux distribution and the next, there are also a few differences. The commands presented through this book assume that you're using Debian, which means that some of the commands that we present won't work in other distributions.

Downloading your Linux distribution

You need to use a computer to download the distribution from the Internet and flash your microSD card. (Flashing is the process used when you completely rewrite a data storage device rather than simply saving files on it.) You can use a Windows, Mac OS X, or Linux computer; we illustrate how to prepare your microSD card on all three systems. You can find the official distributions available for download at `http://beagleboard.org/latest-images`.

The distribution you need to work with on this book depends on how you intend to run Linux and is subject to change with future releases. Regardless, the process of downloading the newest image should be very similar, as should the respective filenames. You have two alternatives:

- ✔ If you're booting Linux from a microSD card on a BeagleBone Black or an Original BeagleBone, download Debian using the file labeled as Debian (BeagleBone, BeagleBone Black – 2GB SD) 2014-05-14.
- ✔ If you're booting Linux from your BeagleBone Black's eMMC memory, download Debian eMMC flasher using the file labeled as Debian (BeagleBone, BeagleBone Black – 2GB eMMC) 2014-09-04.

If you have a BeagleBone Black and, thus, the chance to flash the eMMC memory, we recommend that you use the second option, which not only increases system performance, but is also much more practical. You won't need to have the microSD card with you at all times.

If you don't want to reflash the eMMC memory on the BeagleBone Black — in other words, if you want to keep the factory default OS — you can choose the standard Debian image and boot the OS directly from the microSD card.

You can download the distribution in two ways. The first way is much simpler but may take some more time than the second way. Here are your options:

✔ **Web browser:** You can download the distribution directly from your web browser by clicking the distribution name. When you click the name of the distribution, a new web page opens. After about 3 seconds, your file should start downloading.

✔ **BitTorrent:** BitTorrent enables you to download larger files faster. It gathers all the small pieces of the file you want and starts downloading your file from people who already have them, maximizing the transfer speed. To use this method, you must have a BitTorrent application on your computer. When you open the BitTorrent link, a torrent file that's compatible with the BitTorrent application is downloaded to your computer.

You can find a free BitTorrent application that works in all three OSes at www. utorrent.com.

Decompressing your Linux distribution

The Linux distribution you download is compressed in an .xz file. You have to decompress the .xz file so that you can access the .img file contained inside. The procedure you use to decompress the file depends on your computer's OS.

Windows

If you're using a Windows PC to decompress your Linux distribution, you need to install the application 7-Zip. Follow these steps:

1. **Go to www.7-zip.org/download.html.**

2. **Download the .exe file.**

3. **Run the .exe file to install 7-Zip.**

With 7-Zip installed, you're ready to decompress your .xz file. Follow these steps:

1. **Open the 7-Zip application.**

2. **Click the Extract icon.**

   The Extract dialog box opens (see Figure 2-1).

Extract icon

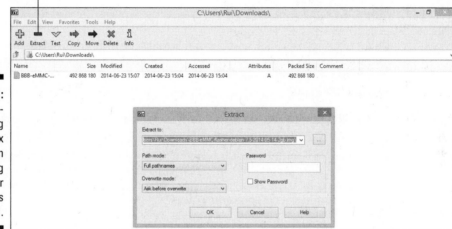

Figure 2-1:
Decom-
pressing
your Linux
distribution
by using
7-Zip for
Windows
8.1.

3. **Navigate to the folder where you saved your Linux distribution.**

4. **Save the file in your preferred folder, and click OK.**

   Your .img file is extracted.

Mac OS X

If you're using a Mac to decompress your Linux distribution, follow these steps:

1. **Go to the App Store.**

2. **Search for and install the free application The Unarchiver.**

3. **Navigate to your Downloads folder.**

4. **Double-click your .xz file.**

   The decompressing process starts immediately.

Linux

If you're using Linux, you don't need to install a new decompression application because Linux already has built-in software that can decompress .xz files. You see how to extract the .img file in Linux later in section "Flashing a microSD Card in Linux."

Flashing and Inserting Your microSD Card

Chapter 1 suggests that you buy a microSD card for your BeagleBone. If you followed that recommendation, you should have a 4GB microSD card of at least Class 4 with an adapter. You have two options for writing the .img file to a microSD card:

- ✔ If your computer has an SD card slot, insert your microSD card into a microSD card adapter (see Figure 2-2) and connect it to your computer.

- ✔ If your computer doesn't have an SD card slot, you need an external SD card writer. Insert your microSD card into a microSD card adapter (see Figure 2-2); then insert your SD card into your external SD card writer and connect it to your computer.

Figure 2-2:
A microSD card, microSD card adapter, and external SD card writer.

SD card reader

microSD card adapter

microSD card

Flashing an image file to your microSD card isn't like copying a photograph or document to your common flash drive. You need to use a special program that converts the Linux distribution to a couple of files that your BeagleBone is able to read. The following sections explain how to properly use programs to flash data storage devices.

You have to be really careful while flashing your microSD card. Before pressing Enter or Return, you need to be completely sure you are selecting the right device name. Selecting the wrong device name results in irreversible data loss, such as erasing your computer's hard disk.

Flashing your microSD card completely erases it. Make sure that you've copies of any files on the microSD card that you may need later.

Flashing a microSD card in Windows

Flashing a microSD card in Windows requires an application called Win32 Disk Imager (see Figure 2-3), which is available for free download.

Figure 2-3:
Flashing a microSD card on Windows by using Win32 Disk Imager.

Follow these steps to install it:

1. **Go to the Win32 Disk Imager download page at** `http://sourceforge.net/projects/win32diskimager`.

2. **Click the Download button to retrieve the installer.**

3. **Run the Win32 Image Writer application installer.**

With Win32 Disk Imager installed, you're ready to write the `.img` file to your microSD card. Follow these steps:

1. **Connect your microSD card to your computer.**

2. **Open Win32 Disk Imager.**

3. **Select your Linux-distribution** `.img` **file.**

4. **Select your microSD card as the device.**

This process erases and overwrites the selected device. Be certain that you've selected the microSD card, and be certain that you have copies of any files that you need from the card. We can't stress this enough: Be certain that the microSD card is the device you chose!

5. **Click Write to start writing the image to the microSD card.**

   This process takes between 10 and 20 minutes, depending on your microSD card class number and your SD card writer's transfer speed.

Flashing a microSD card in Mac OS X

On a Mac, you can use the Terminal application to copy the image to your microSD card, as shown in Figure 2-4.

Figure 2-4:
Flashing a
microSD
card on
a Mac
by using
Terminal.

```
                                    ⬆ rui — bash — 107×25
Last login: Sun Jul 13 16:16:18 on ttys000
rui:~ rui$ df -h
Filesystem      Size   Used  Avail Capacity  iused    ifree %iused  Mounted on
/dev/disk0s2    465Gi   96Gi  369Gi    21% 25260096 96626646   21%   /
devfs           190Ki  190Ki   0Bi   100%      658        0  100%   /dev
map -hosts        0Bi    0Bi   0Bi   100%        0        0  100%   /net
map auto_home     0Bi    0Bi   0Bi   100%        0        0  100%   /home
/dev/disk1       96Mi   74Mi   22Mi    77%      512        0  100%   /Volumes/boot
/dev/disk2s1    7.3Gi  2.8Mi  7.3Gi     1%        0        0  100%   /Volumes/MICROSDCARD
rui:~ rui$ sudo diskutil umount /dev/disk2s1
rui:~ rui$ sudo dd if=~/Downloads/BBB-eMMC-flasher-debian-7.5-2014-05-14-2gb-1.img of=/dev/disk2 bs=1m
1700+0 records in
1700+0 records out
1782579200 bytes transferred in 1011.784529 secs (1761817 bytes/sec)
rui:~ rui$
```

Follow these steps:

1. **Navigate to /Applications/Utilities.**

2. **Double-click Terminal to open a new Terminal window.**

3. **Connect your microSD card to your computer.**

4. **Type df –h to get a listing of the devices connected to your computer.**

5. **Find out which device is your microSD card.**

   It will be something similar to /dev/sdisk2s1.

   Be very careful that you choose the right /dev device. Using an incorrect device name results in permanent data loss from the device you choose. You can even overwrite the disk that contains your computer's OS. We can't stress this enough: Be certain that the microSD card is the device you choose!

6. **Type sudo diskutil umount /dev/disk2s1 to unmount your micro SD card.**

   The command is umount even though you say "unmount."

For the next command, you have to ignore the device number. For this example, /dev/disk2s1 becomes /dev/disk2.

7. **Run** sudo dd if=~/<downloads folder>/<filename>.img of=/dev/disk2 bs=1m.

This process takes between 10 and 20 minutes, depending on your microSD card and your SD card writer's transfer speed.

Flashing a microSD card in Linux

With Linux, you don't have to install extra applications; the OS already has everything you need to decompress the .xz file and flash your microSD card with the latest OS (see Figure 2-5).

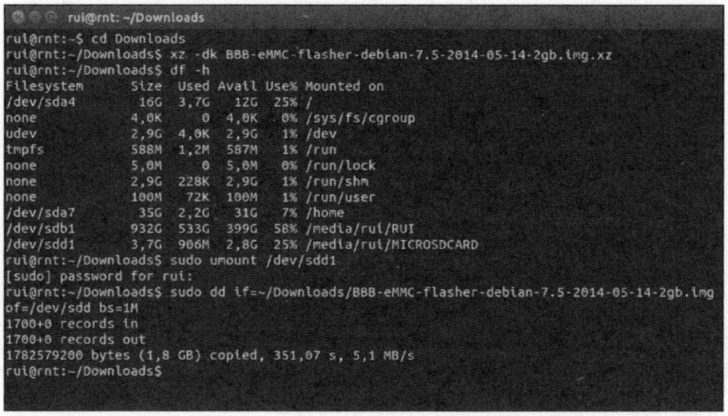

Figure 2-5:
Flashing a
microSD
card on
Linux by
using the
terminal in
Ubuntu.

To flash a microSD card in Linux, follow these steps:

1. **Press Ctrl+Alt+T to open the terminal window.**
2. **Connect your microSD card to your computer.**
3. **Type** cd **to navigate to your Downloads folder (**cd /Downloads**).**
4. **Type** xz -dk <filename>.img.xz **to decompress your** .xz **file.**
5. **Type** df –h **to get a list of the devices connected to your computer.**
6. **Find out which device is your microSD card.**

It will be something similar to /dev/sdb1.

Be very careful that you choose the right /dev device. Using an incorrect device name results in permanent data loss from the device you choose. You can even overwrite the disk that contains your OS. We can't stress this enough: Be certain that the microSD card is the device you choose!

7. **Type** sudo umount /dev/sdb1 **to unmount your micro SD card.**

   The command is umount even though we say "unmount."

   For the next command, you have to ignore the device number. For this example, /dev/sdb1 becomes /dev/sdb.

8. **Run** sudo dd if=~/<downloads folder>/<filename>.img of=/dev/sdb bs=1m.

   This process takes between 10 and 20 minutes, depending on your microSD card and your SD card writer's transfer speed.

Inserting your microSD card

When your microSD card is all set, you need to insert it into your BeagleBone. The card slot is on the back of your board, right next to the MicroHDMI port, as shown in Figure 2-6. Just press the card gently into the slot until you feel a click. Done! Your BeagleBone now happily boots with the freshly installed Debian distribution.

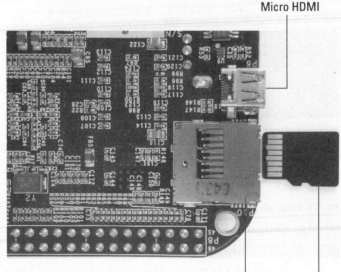

Micro HDMI

Figure 2-6:
Inserting
a microSD
card into a
BeagleBone
Black.

MicroSD card slot   MicroSD card

If you're going to boot Linux directly from a microSD card with your BeagleBone Black, you need to hold the user boot button down (see Figure 2-7) for about 5 to 7 seconds every time you power on your BeagleBone Black. Otherwise, the BeagleBone Black boots from the preinstalled OS on the onboard eMMC memory.

User boot button

Flashing the Onboard eMMC

If you're using a BeagleBone Black and want to flash your onboard eMMC memory, you need to do one more thing.

If you're going to boot Linux directly from a microSD card or you are using an Original BeagleBone, you can skip this section and go straight to Chapter 3.

The amount of built-in storage of your BeagleBone Black depends on the board revision:

✔ BeagleBone Black Rev A and Rev B have 2GB.

✔ BeagleBone Black Rev C comes with 4GB.

When we talk about using built-in storage, we mean something slightly different from running your OS on your microSD card. You don't need to worry about the fact that BeagleBone Black Rev A and Rev B have only 2GB of onboard eMMC memory.

To flash your BeagleBone Black's eMMC memory, follow these steps:

1. **While your BeagleBone Black is powered off, insert your microSD card into the microSD slot (refer to Figure 2-6).**

2. **Hold down the user boot button of the BeagleBone (refer to Figure 2-7).**

3. **While holding the user boot button, press the power button on your board. When the board is powered up, you should continue to hold the user boot button for 5 to 7 seconds and then release it.**

   The USR LEDs blink during this process.

   Flashing can take about 30 to 40 minutes. When this process is finished, all four USR LEDs will be off.

4. **Unplug your board.**

5. **Remove the microSD card.**

   If you don't remove the microSD card the next time you boot your BeagleBone Black, or if you remove the microSD card while the flashing process is occurring, your eMMC memory can get corrupted and your BeagleBone Black won't boot. If the card does become corrupt, you have to repeat this section again to flash your BeagleBone's eMMC memory properly.

You're done! The next time you plug in your board, it boots with the new OS.

Chapter 3

Connecting Your BeagleBone

In This Chapter

▶ Connecting your BeagleBone via USB and installing drivers

▶ Blinking the onboard LEDs

▶ Controlling your BeagleBone remotely via SSH and serial

*T*he BeagleBone was designed in such a way to be both easy and inexpensive to set up. With just a computer and a Mini USB cable, you can start programming your BeagleBone right off the bat.

This chapter presents multiple ways to accomplish something that we've found to be quite useful: controlling your BeagleBone remotely. We prefer to program the BeagleBone by connecting a USB cable to a computer or having an Ethernet cable connected to a router.

Connecting your BeagleBone to a terminal enables you to do things such as run scripts, install software, and manage files.

Connecting via USB

If your BeagleBone is running the OS through the microSD card, insert it before powering up your BeagleBone. Then follow these steps to set up your BeagleBone:

1. **Using the Mini USB cable that came with your board, connect your BeagleBone to your computer.**

   After a few seconds, a drive called BeagleBone Getting Started should appear in your computer's file system. Your BeagleBone comes with everything you need to get started: the drivers for its setup, as well as documentation and project examples.

2. **Go to your file system, and double-click the BeagleBone Getting Started disk.**

3. **Open the file called START.htm in your default web browser (see Figure 3-1).**

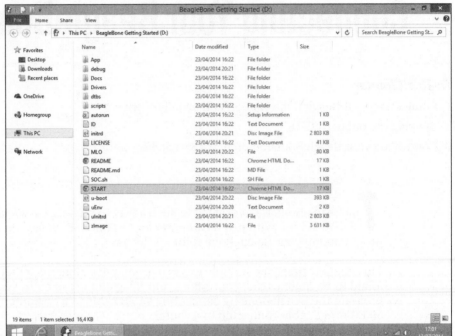

Installing drivers

With the file you just opened on your web browser, click Step 2: Install Drivers in the menu on the left side of the web page (see Figure 3-2). Use the appropriate installation method based on your OS (Windows or Mac OS X).

If you're using Linux, it isn't necessary to install the drivers.

- ✔ **Windows:** If you're using Windows, we recommend that you try to install the drivers for the 64-bit version. If that installation fails, you're running a 32-bit version, so install the 32-bit drivers. Doing things this way guarantees that you won't install 32-bit drivers on a 64-bit machine.

- ✔ **Macintosh:** In Mac OS X, you have to install the network and serial drivers. This process is very straightforward. After you open each driver file, you click the Next button until the installation is finished.

Click to install drivers

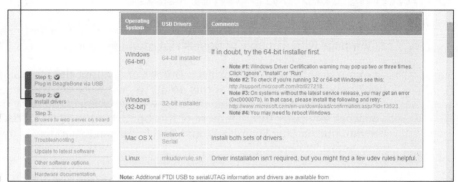

Figure 3-2:
Installing
the drivers.

Browsing to your BeagleBone

After your drivers are installed, you need to open an URL on your web
browser. Enter **192.168.7.2** in the address bar.

We recommend that you use only Google Chrome or Mozilla Firefox, because
other web browsers don't offer some JavaScript functionalities that the
BeagleBone requires. Both web browsers are free to download at their official
websites: `https://www.google.com/chrome/browser` and `https://
www.mozilla.org`.

If everything is working properly, you should see a green box at the top of the
screen that says `Your board is connected!` (see Figure 3-3).

BoneScript option

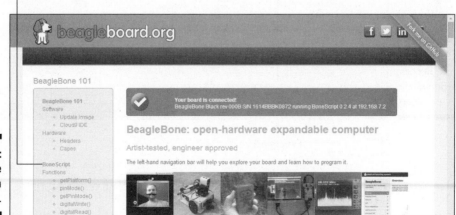

Figure 3-3:
A web page
hosted by a
BeagleBone.

Blinking the onboard LEDs

On the leftmost menu of the web page, click BoneScript (refer to Figure 3-3). A new page with a couple of BoneScript examples opens.

Try your first blink-an-LED project. Don't worry about the programming; you don't need to understand it at this point. We just want to give you a glimpse of what you should be capable of doing with your BeagleBone by the time you work your way through more of this book. For now, just sit back, click the Run button (see Figure 3-4), and watch the magic happen — by looking at your board, of course.

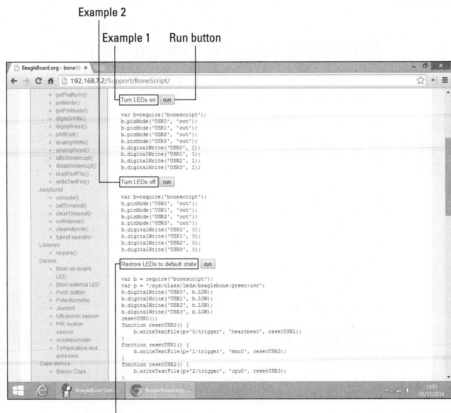

Example 2

Example 1   Run button

Example 3

Figure 3-4:
Running
BoneScript
examples.

The first example (refer to Figure 3-4) turns ON all four USR LEDs. Take a look at Figure 3-5 to see where they're located.

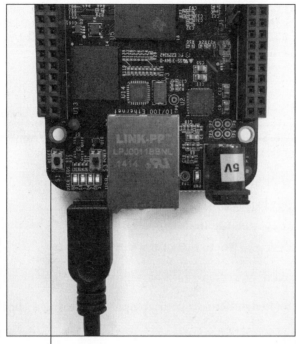

Figure 3-5:
BeagleBone
Black's four
USR LEDs
turned on.

LEDs

The second example (refer to Figure 3-4) should turn all four USR LEDs off, and the last example (also shown in Figure 3-4) returns the LEDs to their default state. They blink in the way they normally do from the moment you power up the BeagleBone.

If nothing occurs when you click the Run button in all three examples, something must be wrong! Make sure that your BeagleBone is connected to your computer. If it still doesn't work, it may be because the browser you're using doesn't support these features. In that case, use Chrome or Firefox as recommended earlier.

Connecting via SSH over USB

SSH (which stands for *secure shell)* is a method of establishing a communication with another computer securely. All data sent via SSH is encrypted. SSH is based on a Unix shell, so it allows you to access your BeagleBone files from a remote machine by using terminal commands. It has grown to be one of the most popular methods for communication between different devices.

Unix was an operating system that originated in the mid-1960s, with a few characteristics that made it quite appealing: portability, multitasking, and multiuser capability, and a few more advanced concepts. Today, many OSes are based on Unix; the most prominent are Linux and Mac OS X.

Windows

If you use Windows, you need to download and install a free application called PuTTY. Here's how to install it:

1. **Open your web browser.**

2. **Go to** www.putty.org.

3. **Click the** putty.exe **file to download it.**

4. **Run the** putty.exe **file to install the software.**

With PuTTY installed, power up your BeagleBone and follow these steps:

1. **Connect your BeagleBone to your computer by using a Mini USB cable.**

2. **Open PuTTY.**

3. **In the PuTTY Configuration dialog box, select SSH.**

4. **Type** 192.168.7.2 **as the host.**

   The port needs to remain at the default number, which is 22. The dialog box should have the settings shown in Figure 3-6.

5. **Click Open.**

6. **When you're asked to log in, type** root **and press Enter.**

7. **When you're asked to type a password, press Enter.**

   By default, no password is set.

When you connect your computer to your BeagleBone for the first time, you're prompted by a message warning you that you're attempting to establish a connection with an unknown host. This message just means that your computer and the BeagleBone aren't friends yet. Simply click OK to proceed.

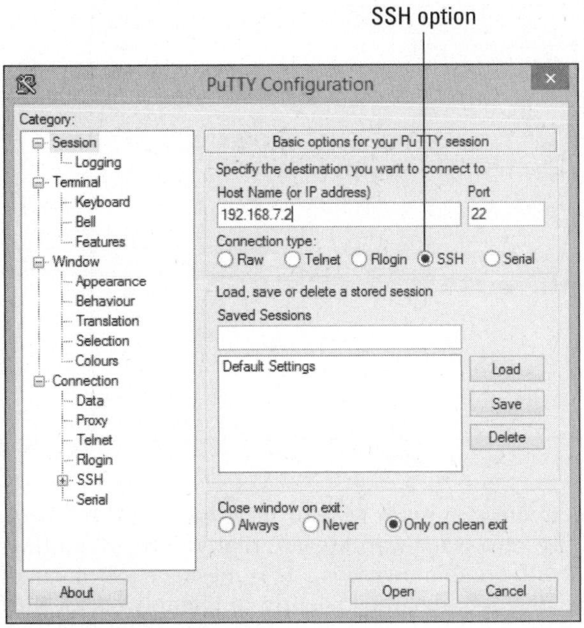

SSH option

Figure 3-6:
PuTTY settings for establishing an SSH communication over USB.

Mac OS X and Linux

In Mac OS X and Linux, you can use the default terminal window to establish an SSH communication, because SSH comes in all Unix-based OSes. Follow these steps:

1. **Connect your BeagleBone to your computer by using a Mini USB cable.**

2. **Open a new window, as follows:**

   • On a Mac, navigate to /Applications/Utilities and double-click Terminal to open a new terminal window.

   • In Linux, press Ctrl+Alt+T to open a new terminal window.

3. **Type** sudo ssh root@192.168.7.2.

4. **Enter your computer password, and type** yes.

5. **When you're asked to type a password, press Enter or Return.**

   By default, no password is set.

   Your terminal window should look like Figure 3-7.

Figure 3-7:
Connecting a
BeagleBone
via SSH
over USB
by using
the Mac
Terminal
application.

When you connect your computer to your BeagleBone for the very first time, you're prompted by a message warning you that you're attempting to establish a connection with an unknown host. This message just means that your computer and the BeagleBone aren't friends yet. Simply click OK to proceed.

Connecting via SSH over Ethernet

Having an Ethernet cable connected to your BeagleBone ensures that you have access to the Internet. This access is really handy, as you may need to install or update an application or work on Internet-related projects.

Establishing this type of communication also enables you to access your BeagleBone from any other devices as long as you remain connected to the same network.

Simply open your terminal window or PuTTY, and you can establish an SSH connection in a similar fashion to the method you use to connect via USB, as described in the following sections.

Windows

If you haven't downloaded it yet, you need a free application called PuTTY to establish an SSH connection using a Windows PC. Refer to the instructions earlier in this chapter in the "Connecting via SSH over USB" section

With PuTTY installed, you need to power up your BeagleBone and follow these steps:

1. **Power up your BeagleBone with a Mini USB cable or with a 5V DC power supply.**

   Any time that it is possible, it's recommended that you power your BeagleBone with a DC power supply so that you are guaranteed to not have any issues with power. Make sure that the outer ring of the plug is ground and the center is 5V. You can find more information about this in Chapter 1.

2. **Connect an Ethernet cable from your router to your BeagleBone.**

3. **Open PuTTY.**

4. **In the PuTTY Configuration dialog box, select SSH.**

5. **Type** beaglebone **as the host.**

   The port needs to remain at the default number, which is 22.

   Your dialog box should have the settings shown in Figure 3-8.

6. **Click Open.**

7. **When you're asked to log in, type** root **and press Enter.**

8. **When you're asked to type a password, press Enter.**

   By default, no password is set.

When you connect your computer to your BeagleBone for the very first time, you're prompted by a message warning you that you're attempting to establish a connection with an unknown host. This message just means that your computer and the BeagleBone aren't friends yet. Simply click OK to proceed.

SSH option

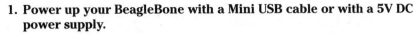

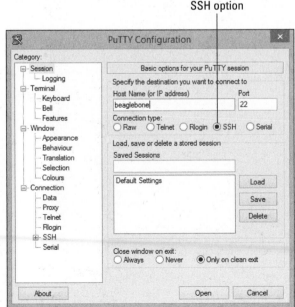

Figure 3-8: PuTTY settings for establishing an SSH communication over Ethernet.

Mac OS X and Linux

In Mac OS X and Linux, you can use the default terminal window to establish an SSH communication, because SSH comes in all Unix-based OSes. Follow these steps:

1. **Power up your BeagleBone with a Mini USB cable or with a 5V DC power supply.**

   Any time that it is possible, it's recommended that you power your BeagleBone with a DC power supply so that you are guaranteed to not have any issues with power. Make sure that the outer ring of the plug is ground and the center is 5V. You can find more information about this in Chapter 1.

2. **Connect an Ethernet cable from your router to your BeagleBone.**

3. **Open a new window, as follows:**

   • On a Mac, navigate to /Applications/Utilities and double-click Terminal to open a new Terminal window.

   • In Linux, press Ctrl+Alt+T to open a new terminal window.

4. **Type** sudo ssh root@beaglebone.local.

5. **Enter your computer password, and type** yes.

6. **When you're asked to type a password, press Enter or Return.**

   By default, no password is set.

   The window should look like Figure 3-9.

```
       rui@rnt: ~
rui@rnt:~$ sudo ssh root@beaglebone.local
[sudo] password for rui:
The authenticity of host 'beaglebone.local (192.168.7.2)' can't be established.
ECDSA key fingerprint is c0:81:1a:f4:58:b9:51:15:00:df:ee:71:c4:d9:fd:54.
Are you sure you want to continue connecting (yes/no)? yes
Warning: Permanently added 'beaglebone.local,192.168.7.2' (ECDSA) to the list of
 known hosts.
Debian GNU/Linux 7

BeagleBoard.org BeagleBone Debian Image 2014-04-23

Support/FAQ: http://elinux.org/Beagleboard:BeagleBoneBlack_Debian
Last login: Sun Jul 13 16:19:59 2014
root@beaglebone:~#
```

Figure 3-9: Connecting a BeagleBone via SSH over Ethernet by using the Linux terminal in Ubuntu.

When you connect your computer to your BeagleBone for the very first time, you're prompted by a message warning you that you're attempting to establish a connection with an unknown host. This message just means that your computer and the BeagleBone aren't friends yet. Simply click OK to proceed.

Connecting the Original BeagleBone via Serial over USB

Note: If you're working with a BeagleBone Black, skip to the next section, as the following instructions are specific to the Original BeagleBone.

The serial port is a way to send data between your Original BeagleBone and another device. Establishing a serial communication between your computer and your Original BeagleBone requires a Mini USB cable, which comes with the board.

For most applications, we think that connecting the Original BeagleBone via SSH over USB is the way to go. Still, it's useful to know about this connection technique because it enables you to send data to and from many devices other than PCs, which may be useful if you're experiencing booting problems or networking issues. You can see what's happening to your board right after plugging in the power with a serial debugger.

At this point, you should have the Original BeagleBone drivers installed. Go back to section "Installing drivers" at the beginning of this chapter if that isn't the case.

Windows

Before you power up your board, you need to download and install a free application called PuTTY on your computer. Refer to the instructions in the "Connecting via SSH over USB" section earlier in this chapter.

With PuTTY installed, you can establish a serial communication with your Original BeagleBone. Follow these steps:

1. **Connect your Original BeagleBone to your computer with a Mini USB cable.**

2. **Open PuTTY.**

3. **In the PuTTY Configuration dialog box, select Serial.**

4. **Type the name of your Original BeagleBone's serial port.**

   Open Device Manager to see the serial port's name. Press Windows+R, type **devmgmt.msc**, and press Enter. The name of your BeagleBone's serial port is listed below Ports.

5. **Type** 115200 **in the Speed field.**

   At this point, the dialog box should look similar to Figure 3-10.

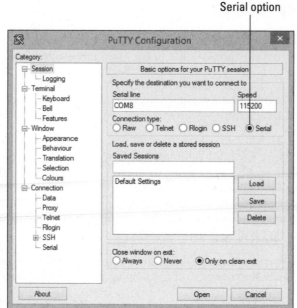

Figure 3-10: PuTTY settings for establishing a serial communication over USB.

6. **Click Open.**

7. **Press Enter.**

   If you don't press Enter, you're left with a blank screen and a blinking cursor.

8. **When you're asked to log in, type** root **and press Enter.**

9. **When you're asked to type a password, press Enter.**

   By default, no password is set.

Mac OS X and Linux

In Mac OS X and Linux, you can use the default terminal window to establish a serial communication. Follow these steps:

1. **Connect your Original BeagleBone to your computer with a Mini USB cable.**

2. **Open a new window, as follows:**

    - On a Mac, navigate to /Applications/Utilities and double-click Terminal to open a new Terminal window.

    - In Linux, press Ctrl+Alt+T to open a new terminal window.

3. **Type** sudo screen /dev/tty.usbserial-*B 115200.

4. **Type your computer password, and press Enter or Return.**

5. **Press Enter or Return again.**

    If you don't press Enter or Return, you'll be left with a blank screen and a blinking cursor.

6. **When you're asked to log in, type** root **and press Enter or Return.**

7. **When you're asked to type a password, press Enter or Return.**

    By default, no password is set (see Figure 3-11).

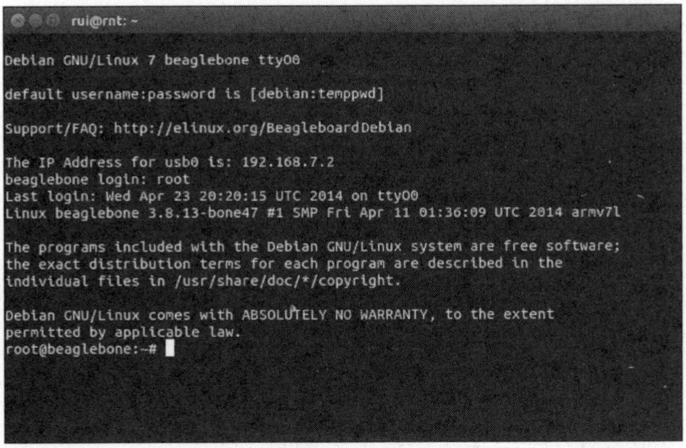

Figure 3-11: Linux terminal with a serial communication established with an Original BeagleBone.

Connecting the BeagleBone Black via Serial over USB

The serial port is a way to send data between the BeagleBone Black and another device. Establishing a serial communication between your computer and your BeagleBone Black requires a USB-to-TTL Serial cable (see Figure 3-12).

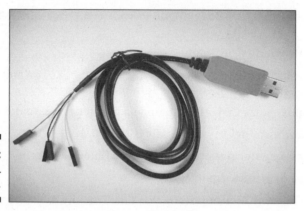

Figure 3-12: USB-to-TTL Serial cable.

For most applications, we think that connecting the BeagleBone Black via SSH over USB is the way to go. This connection technique allows you to send data to and from many devices other than PCs, which may be useful if you're experiencing booting problems or networking issues. You can see what's happening to your board right after plugging in the power with a serial debugger.

Windows

Before you power up your board, you need to make a few connections and install PuTTY. For instructions on installing PuTTY, see the "Connecting via SSH over USB" section earlier in this chapter.

1. **Connect the USB side of the TTL cable to your computer.**

2. **Connect the wires to the J1 headers on your BeagleBone Black as shown in Figure 3-13:**

    • Black wire to Pin 1

    • Green wire to Pin 4

    • White wire to Pin 5

With PuTTY installed, you can establish a serial communication with your BeagleBone Black. Follow these steps:

1. **Open PuTTY.**

2. **In the PuTTY Configuration dialog box, select Serial.**

3. **Type the name of your BeagleBone Black's serial port.**

    Open Device Manager to see the serial port's name. Press Windows+R, type **devmgmt.msc**, and press Enter. The name of your BeagleBone's serial port is listed below Ports.

4. **Type** 115200 **in the Speed field.**

5. **Click Open.**

6. **Power on your BeagleBone Black with a Mini USB cable.**

    You see all sorts of information about the booting process (see Figure 3-14).

7. **When you're asked to log in, type** root **and press Enter.**

8. **When you're asked to type a password, press Enter.**

    By default, no password is set.

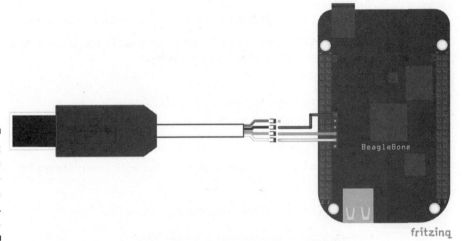

Figure 3-13:
BeagleBone
Black con-
nected to a
USB-to-TTL
Serial cable.

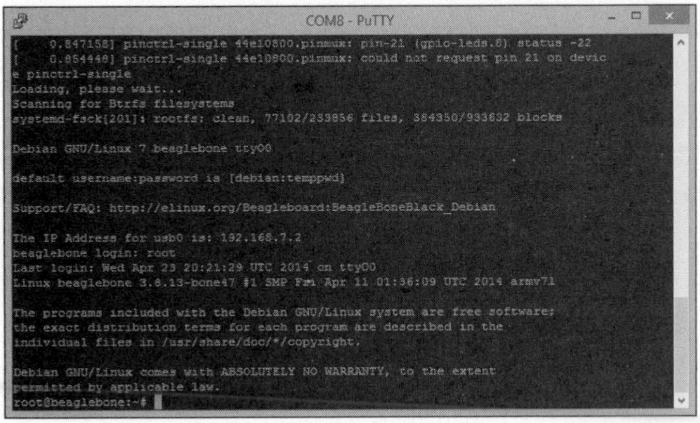

Figure 3-14:
Establishing
serial com-
munication
over USB.

Mac OS X and Linux

In Mac OS X and Linux, you can use the default terminal window to establish a serial communication. With your BeagleBone Black unplugged, follow these steps:

1. **Open a new window, as follows:**

   • On a Mac, navigate to /Applications/Utilities and double-click Terminal to open a new Terminal window.

   • In Linux, press Ctrl+Alt+T to open a new terminal window.

2. **Type** ls /dev/tty*.

3. **Connect the USB side of the TTL cable to your computer.**

4. **Connect the wires to J1 headers on your BeagleBone Black as shown in Figure 3-13, earlier in this chapter:**

   • Black wire to Pin 1

   • Green wire to Pin 4

   • White wire to Pin 5

5. **Type** ls /dev/tty*.

   Now you can see a new device connected to your computer — in Figure 3-15, ttyUSB0.

To establish the serial communication, follow these steps:

1. **Type** sudo screen /dev/ttyUSB0 115200.

2. **Power on your BeagleBone Black with a Mini USB cable.**

   You see all sorts of information about the booting process (see Figure 3-16).

3. **Enter your computer password, and press Enter or Return.**

4. **When you're asked to log in, type** root **and press Enter or Return.**

5. **When you're asked to type a password, press Enter or Return.**

   By default, no password is set.

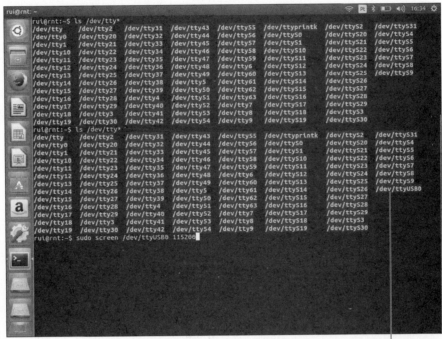

Figure 3-15:
Detecting a
new device
connected
on Linux
terminal.

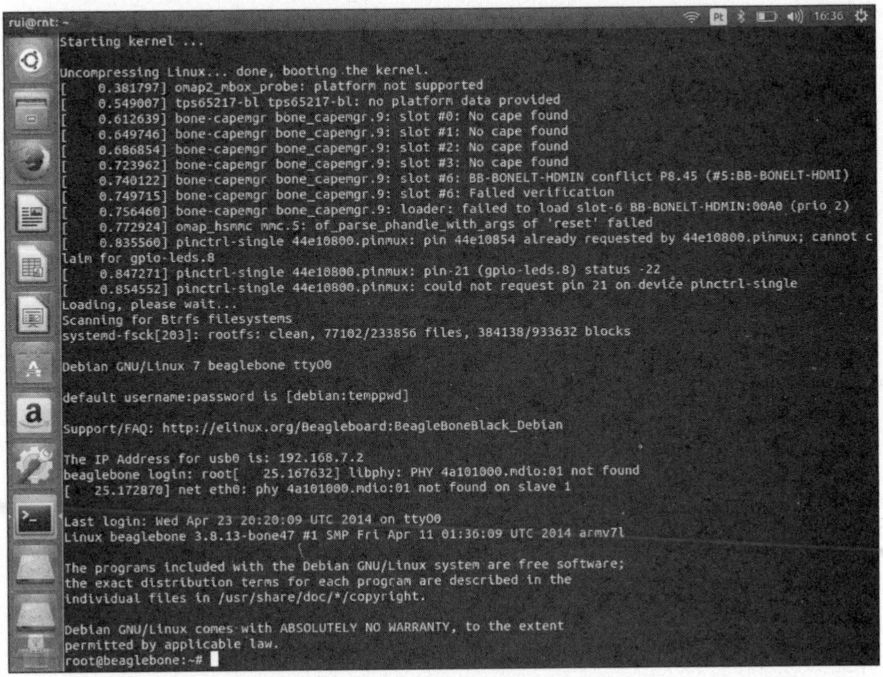

The new device

Figure 3-16:
Linux ter-
minal with
a serial
communica-
tion with a
BeagleBone
Black.

Part II
Covering the Basics

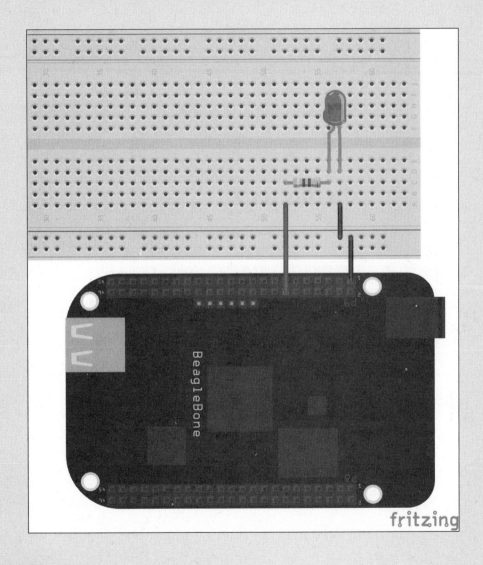

In this part . . .

- ✔ Exploring the Linux world and getting acquainted with the Linux Shell
- ✔ Discovering electricity: the equations, circuit diagrams, and various components
- ✔ Taking a closer look at your BeagleBone and expanding its functionalities

Chapter 4

Introducing the Linux Shell

. . . .

. . . .

A t a first glance, the Linux operating system (OS) may look like a weirder, more complex, and less pretty way to do the things that the beloved Windows and Mac OS X are capable of. Often, it's said that Linux isn't a user-friendly OS, which explains why a typical computer user who simply wants to browse the web, for example, prefers to use Windows or Mac OS X.

The added complexity of Linux, however, paves the way for heavy customization and versatility, as well as user efficiency. These perks, along with the fact that Linux is free, has led to the existence of a huge community of users who are keen on constantly improving the system. Ultimately, Linux has become the best option for embedded systems such as the BeagleBone.

This chapter shows you how you can use the command prompt to get around a computer in a way that you're probably not used to: using only text. You can forget about using a graphical user interface (GUI) for a while. Although using the command line may seem odd at first, this approach has plenty of advantages, as you see in this chapter.

Examining the Prompt

To open the command-line prompt, start by connecting to your BeagleBone via SSH. You can do that by either connecting the BeagleBone to your computer via USB or by connecting the BeagleBone to your router using an Ethernet cable. If you have previously worked through Chapter 3, the steps presented here are similar to the steps in that chapter except that this time you are logged in as `debian` instead of `root`.

If you connected by USB, do one of the following:

✔ *Windows:* In Windows, while using PuTTY, choose SSH and type **192.168.7.2** at the Host Name (or IP address) dialog box. A login prompt should appear a few seconds later: Type **debian** as the username and **temppwd** as the password.

✔ *Linux or Mac OS X:* If you're using Linux or Mac OS X, simply type **sudo ssh debian@192.168.7.2** in the terminal window and then type **temppwd** as your password.

If you connected by Ethernet, do one of the following:

✔ *Windows:* In Windows, while using PuTTY, choose SSH and type **beagle-bone** at the Host Name (or IP address) dialog box. A login prompt should appear a few seconds later: Type **debian** as the username and the password **temppwd**.

✔ *Linux or Mac OS X:* If you're using Linux or Mac OS X, simply type **sudo ssh debian@beaglebone.local** in the terminal window and then type **temppwd** as your password.

You run the show from the terminal window. This is where you type commands to accomplish various tasks, from organizing your files and directories (by creating, removing, copying, or moving them) to compiling and running programs you've written.

Your BeagleBone's prompt should look like Figure 4-1.

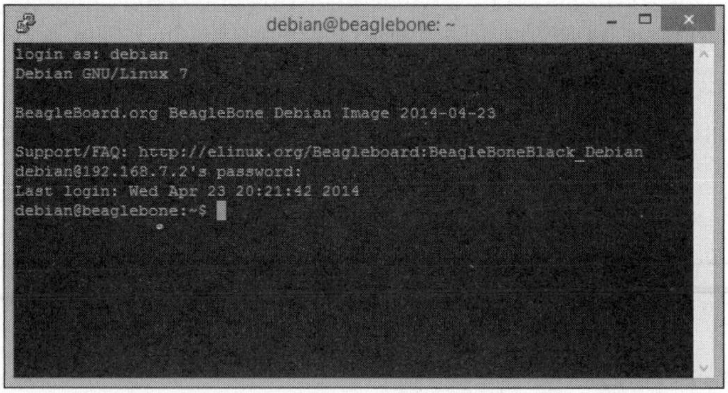

Figure 4-1:
Logging in
as Debian.

The last line on the screen shown in Figure 4-1 reads `debian@beaglebone:~$`. You need to understand a few things from that single line:

✔ The first part, `debian`, is the user you're logged in as. Under other circumstances, that name could be `Richard` or `OfficePC-4`.

✔ The next part, `beaglebone`, is the hostname. If you're connected in a network, that name is the name your BeagleBone displays to other computers. You find out how to alter that name in the "Changing the Hostname and Password" section later in this chapter.

✔ After the colon is the current *working directory* — the folder that you're currently inside — so all commands that you type, unless you specify otherwise, refer to files inside that directory. In this case, you see a tilde (~) because that's shorthand for the logged-in user's home directory. When you're logged in as `debian`, the home directory is `/home/debian`. Another very important user, called `root`, is the administrator of the system and is known as *superuser* in the Linux OS. We talk more about the `root` account throughout this chapter.

✔ The last part is the prompt for input, which is $ in this example because you're logged in as a regular user. When you're logged in as `root`, the prompt is #.

Introducing the root superuser

In the Linux community the administrator of the system is called the *superuser*. This section introduces you to the superuser.

In Chapter 3, you log in as `root`, which is the superuser of most Linux systems. `root` is used for privileged tasks, such as installing and updating software, messing around directories with restricted access, and controlling the BeagleBone's input and output pins.

In this chapter, you don't need to log in as `root`, but the root user shows up throughout this chapter and the remainder of this book. Actually, even when you're not logged in as `root`, you run programming scripts and commands with root permission. As such it's important that you know about what the root superuser is capable of.

To log in as a superuser, type the following command:

```
debian@beaglebone:~$ sudo su
root@beaglebone:/home/debian#
```

By default, no password is required to log in as `root`, but if you've defined one, you're prompted to type it.

As superuser, you have the power to do practically whatever you want. Cool. But that also means the system won't protect you from yourself: If you're careless, you may make changes on your board that will be difficult to rectify! For that reason, it's often considered to be hazardous to work as root. Generally, you should only log in as `root` when absolutely necessary.

As previously mentioned, for the remainder of this chapter you don't need to be logged in as root — although some sections prompt you to execute commands with *root access* (read more on this later in the "Managing Software on Your BeagleBone" section). You should only exercise the superuser's powers when whatever it is that you tried to do as a regular user didn't work.

The default username and password are debian and temppwd, respectively. You find out how to change the username and password in the "Changing the Hostname and Password" section later in this chapter. Log in as a regular user by entering the following command:

```
root@beaglebone:~# login debian
Password:
Last login: Wed Apr 23 20:21:20 UTC 2014 on pts/0
Linux beaglebone 3.8.13-bone47 #1 SMP Fri Apr 11 01:36:09 UTC 2014 armv7l

The programs included with the Debian GNU/Linux system are free software;
the exact distribution terms for each program are described in the
individual files in /usr/share/doc/*/copyright.

Debian GNU/Linux comes with ABSOLUTELY NO WARRANTY, to the extent
permitted by applicable law.
debian@beaglebone:~$
```

The password text isn't visible while you're typing (someone may be looking!) so simply press Enter or Return when you're done typing.

Exploring the Linux File System

It's time to play around with the command line. For starters, type **pwd,** (which means *print working directory*):

```
debian@beaglebone:~$ pwd
/home/debian
```

The output is /home/debian. The first forward slash (/) is the root of the file system (which is not the same as the root user!). Forward slashes are always used to indicate folders and files within other folders. In this case, the current working directory is debian, which is inside home, which is inside the root of the file system. Here, debian is the username with which you are logged in.

Even though the directory home is one level above the directory debian, the so-called "home directory" represented by the tilde (~) is actually /home/debian.

The commands in Linux are case-sensitive, which means that PWD, PwD, pWd, and any other variations are completely different from pwd. The same holds true for all other commands and for any code written in the programming languages addressed in this book.

Listing files and directories

If you type the command **ls**, a list of the files and directories within your working directory is printed. Right now, you should be inside your home directory, which should have the directories Desktop and bin:

```
debian@beaglebone:~$ ls
bin Desktop
```

This directory is the same as the desktop on your general-use computer; it holds the files that appear on the desktop when you use the GUI. We cover this topic in more detail in Chapter 12.

In reality, the complete syntax for the ls command (and for a great many other commands) is

```
ls [OPTIONS] <filename>
```

Don't be confused by the fact that we use <filename> when <directoryname> would make more sense. We use <filename> for two reasons:

- ✔ The Linux OS interprets everything that exists on your computer as a file, from your hard drive to a photograph you just uploaded to your hard drive to your keyboard. In this case, a container of files, also known as a directory, is itself considered to be a file.
- ✔ <filename> That is the general syntax for many commands that deal with files in general.

When typing commands, you can also use ~ as shorthand for /home/root. Also keep in mind that the first forward slash that appears when you type **pwd** (that is, the root of the file system) is, for all practical purposes, a folder like any other; thus, it can be accessed by its name just like any other folder.

By default, ls with no options and no directory specified prints a list of the files and directories of your current working directory. You can specify exactly which directory you want to be listed, such as Desktop (which doesn't have anything in it at the moment) or the root of the file system:

```
debian@beaglebone:~$ ls Desktop
```

Here is the root:

```
debian@beaglebone:~$ ls /
bin  dev home lost+found mnt proc root selinux sys usr
boot etc lib  media      opt root sbin srv      tmp var
```

Many options are available for the `ls` command. A rundown of all of them isn't necessary to get through the remainder of this book, but you should know about one useful option: `-l`, which makes the `ls` command print its list in a long format. Here's an example:

```
debian@beaglebone:~$ ls -l
total 8
drwxr-xr-x 2 debian debian 4096 Apr 23 20:27 bin
drwxr-xr-x 2 debian debian 4096 Apr 23 20:21 Desktop

debian@beaglebone:~$ ls -l /
total 76
drwxr-xr-x 2 root root 4096 Apr 23 20:35 bin
drwxr-xr-x 3 root root 4096 Apr 23 20:36 boot
drwxr-xr-x 14 root root 3600 Apr 23 20:20 dev
drwxr-xr-x 103 root root 4096 Jun 30 22:31 etc
drwxr-xr-x 3 root root 4096 Apr 23 20:57 home
drwxr-xr-x 15 root root 4096 Apr 11 01:41 lib
drwx------ 2 root root 16384 Apr 23 20:21 lost+found
drwxr-xr-x 2 root root 4096 Apr 23 20:20 media
drwxr-xr-x 2 root root 4096 Feb 3 10:24 mnt
drwxr-xr-x 5 root root 4096 Apr 23 20:36 opt
dr-xr-xr-x 117 root root 0 Jan 1 1970 proc
drwx------ 3 root root 4096 Apr 23 21:02 root
drwxr-xr-x 23 root root 740 Apr 23 20:20 run
drwxr-xr-x 2 root root 4096 Apr 23 20:40 sbin
drwxr-xr-x 2 root root 4096 Jun 10 2012 selinux
drwxr-xr-x 2 root root 4096 Apr 23 20:14 srv
dr-xr-xr-x 12 root root 0 Jan 1 2000 sys
drwxrwxrwt 8 root root 4096 Jun 30 22:17 tmp
drwxr-xr-x 10 root root 4096 Feb 21 04:24 usr
drwxr-xr-x 12 root root 4096 Apr 23 20:34 var
```

Note that because these options are optional, they're always preceded by a dash (as in `-l`) so that the command knows that `l` is an option, not a file.

For now, you don't need to get too caught up on all the information that this so-called *long listing* provides. It's covered in more detail later in this chapter, in the "Using long-listing format and permissions" section.

Understanding the directory tree

When talking about how the file system is organized within a computer, the analogy of a tree makes complete sense: Just as a tree has a trunk from which branches sprout, and other branches in turn sprout from those branches, the Linux file system is a root directory (the trunk) that holds a bunch of directories that include other directories, which hold files.

Figure 4-2 illustrates the directory tree on your BeagleBone (and generally in any Linux OS). *Note:* The directory tree isn't complete because it doesn't include all the directories that branch off root; neither does it include their subdirectories or files. You can see, however, where home is relative to the other directories, as well as how you can get to Desktop.

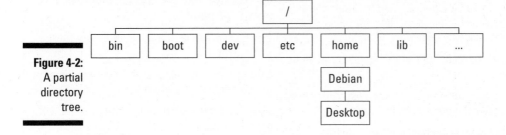

Figure 4-2:
A partial directory tree.

Changing directories

In many situations, you want to change the working directory of your system. You accomplish this task with the cd command. Generally, you type **cd** [*name of the directory you want to go to*]. You can use a couple of variations, or shortcuts, with the command.

Using the general case

The general case is cd [*directory*], as shown here:

```
debian@beaglebone:~$ cd Desktop
debian@beaglebone:~/Desktop$
```

By using pwd, you can verify that you're now inside Desktop:

```
debian@beaglebone:~/Desktop$ pwd
/home/debian/Desktop
```

Discovering the root directory

The directories that are inside the root make up the core of your BeagleBone, as they contain everything that's necessary for it to run — from all the regular programs and files on your computer to various configuration files and files that represent the devices on the system (such as a mouse or a disk). Most likely, you won't find yourself working inside any of them very often, if ever. In case you're curious, though, here's a brief description of most of them:

bin: Short for *binaries;* contains programs and commands for the user. (The program ls is contained inside this directory, for example.)

boot: Contains the files necessary at boot time.

dev: Short for *devices;* stores a list of files that represent the devices on the system.

etc: Contains various configuration files.

home: Contains a directory for each user.

lib: Contains system libraries and drivers that are used by different programs of the OS.

lost+found: Contains files that were saved during system failures.

media: Stores the details of removable storage devices such as USB flash drives and microSD cards.

mnt: Represents the mount point for external systems. If you plug in your cellphone by using a Micro USB cable, for example, you'll find the phone's data in this directory.

opt: Normally contains third-party software and/or extra software.

proc: Contains files that represent information about the system, providing insight into matters such as the CPU (central processing unit) and the memory. This information, however, isn't trivial to interpret.

root: Represents the home directory for the root user.

sbin: Contains programs that usually are usable only by the root user.

sys: Contains files directly related to the OS itself.

tmp: Stores temporary files; whatever's in here is removed upon reboot.

usr: Contains programs and files accessible by all users.

var: Contains files whose size vary, such as databases and system log files.

To go back to /home/debian, you use a similar approach:

```
debian@beaglebone:~/Desktop$ cd ~
debian@beaglebone:~$
```

Moving up one directory

The command cd .. places you inside the current directory's parent, as shown here:

```
debian@beaglebone:~$ pwd
/home/debian
debian@beaglebone:~$ cd ..
debian@beaglebone:/home$ cd ..
debian@beaglebone:/$
```

Moving to the previous directory

When you type **cd -**, you move to the directory you were previously in. Unlike other shortcuts, cd - also prints on the terminal the folder that you jumped to:

```
debian@beaglebone:/$ cd ~
debian@beaglebone:~$ cd Desktop
debian@beaglebone:~/Desktop$ pwd
/home/debian/Desktop
debian@beaglebone:~/Desktop$ cd -
/home/debian
debian@beaglebone:~$
```

Returning to the home directory

When you use cd by itself, you return to the home directory. This command is the same as cd ~:

```
debian@beaglebone:~$ pwd
/home/debian
debian@beaglebone:~$ cd /
debian@beaglebone:/$ pwd
/
debian@beaglebone:/$ cd
debian@beaglebone:~$ pwd
/home/debian
debian@beaglebone:~$
```

Understanding relative and absolute paths

So far in this chapter, we've talked about how you can go inside directories that are directly above or below one another in the directory tree, similar to the way you usually navigate a computer with a GUI, clicking your way through directories until you arrive at your destination. Clickable interfaces are intuitive and easy to use, which is why they're considered to be user-friendly.

Imagine, however, that you want to access one folder that's buried deep in the darkest recesses of your directory tree. Even with a GUI, you may consider it to be quite bothersome to navigate that far through the file system. Now imagine doing it with the command prompt and having to type the cd command so many times!

Understanding command line, prompt, and shell

The terms *command line, prompt,* and *shell* are often used interchangeably. *Command line* and *prompt* mean pretty much the same thing, but there's a slight difference between them and *shell.* The command line or prompt is where you type the commands that the shell carries out. The shell is the brains of the operation, whereas the command line or prompt is simply where you tell the shell what task you want it to perform.

Fortunately, the Linux shell offers a solution through relative and absolute paths. So even though the command prompt might seem confusing and not as intuitive as a GUI, it provides tools that enable you to do work much faster than you can with a GUI.

The best way to understand absolute and relative paths is to view an analogy:

- **Relative paths:** Imagine that you're following the directions someone gave you to arrive at your destination — a directory or a file. In that sense, the destination is *relative* to where you are right now: your current working directory.

- **Absolute paths:** Imagine that you don't need to follow someone's directions to get to a destination because you have the specific address; you put this address in your GPS system and get there directly. The absolute path is the exact, complete address of the file you want to access.

Absolute paths are always measured from the root, so they always start with /, followed by the complete list of directories you have to go through to arrive at your destination. (You used absolute paths in the preceding section with the commands cd / and cd ~.) Here's an example:

```
debian@beaglebone:~$ cd /home/debian/Desktop
debian@beaglebone:~/Desktop$
```

The tilde (~) is short for /home/debian, so in the preceding example, you could also use cd ~/Desktop to achieve the same results. This command *always* gets you to Desktop, regardless of your current working directory. That's what differentiates it from using a relative path. The computer knows that you're using a relative path from the fact that you never start with / when writing one.

To go to a subdirectory somewhere below your current directory, list the path through the subdirectories you have to go through, separated with slashes(/):

```
debian@beaglebone:~/Desktop$ cd ..
debian@beaglebone:~$ cd ..
debian@beaglebone:/home$ cd debian/Desktop
debian@beaglebone:~/Desktop$
```

If you ever get confused while using relative paths, think about the analogy of following directions to a destination. Imagine that you're in the boot folder and want to go to Desktop (refer to Figure 4-2). The directions would be "You have to go up one directory, then down to home, down again to Debian, and then down again to Desktop." The following example shows you how those directions are written as commands. You start by getting inside the boot folder by using an *absolute* path and then get to Desktop by using a *relative* path:

```
debian@beaglebone:~/Desktop$ cd /boot
debian@beaglebone:/boot$ cd ../home/debian/Desktop
debian@beaglebone:~/Desktop$
```

Always use cd .. to go "up" and the directory name to go "down." Here's one last example:

```
debian@beaglebone:~/Desktop$ cd ../../../etc
debian@beaglebone:/etc$
```

You use a relative or absolute path based on which is more convenient at the moment. Normally, you should use an absolute path if the folder you're currently in is very far away from the one you want to access. In the preceding example, it probably would have made more sense to use an absolute path, because the command could have been shortened to cd /etc. Otherwise, using a relative path may be more convenient.

Paths are extremely helpful and convenient, because with paths, you can do anything from anywhere. You can use them with any command to accomplish tasks in different locations from your current working directory, such as when you want to list the contents of debian while you're at the root:

```
debian@beaglebone:/$ ls home/debian
bin Desktop
```

The preceding example uses a relative path, but the absolute path /home/debian renders the same result. After all, the root is the starting point of everything.

Checking file types

The file command followed by a filename gives you a brief description of the file you requested; how detailed the information is depends on each file, but the file type (directory, special file, and so on) is always shown. Because there aren't many files on your BeagleBone yet, the example in this section uses the files in the directory /dev. The following succession of commands starts by changing to the /dev directory, listing it, and using the file command on those files:

```
debian@beaglebone:~$ cd /dev
debian@beaglebone:/dev$ ls
alarm           loop0           ram12       tty16   tty43
          ttyS2
ashmem          loop1           ram13       tty17   tty44
          ttyS3
audio           loop2           ram14       tty18   tty45
          ubi_ctrl
autofs          loop3           ram15       tty19   tty46
          uinput
binder          loop4           ram2        tty2    tty47
          urandom
block           loop5           ram3        tty20   tty48
          usbmon0  (...)
debian@beaglebone:/dev$ file alarm block log
alarm: character special
block: directory
log:   socket
```

The previous example demonstrates that you can use a command with more than one file. The command is carried out for all the files you type in.

Some of the files within the directories of the root directories are very important for the system to run; therefore, you rarely find yourself doing anything inside them. Not working as a superuser guarantees safety, however, so nosing as described with the preceding code is perfectly safe.

These files don't have many details to show you. If you had an image on your BeagleBone, using file on it would output details such as the format and resolution:

```
debian@beaglebone:~$ file firstView.png
firstView.png: PNG image data, 1920 x 1080, 16-bit/color
          RGB, non-interlaced
```

Creating directories

You've probably felt the need to create directories (or folders) when working on your standard computer. In Linux, you can create directories by using the mkdir command followed by the name you want to give the directory, like so:

```
debian@beaglebone:~$ mkdir project
```

Then you can use the `ls` command to verify that a new folder has been created:

```
debian@beaglebone:~$ ls
bin Desktop project
```

You can get inside this new directory with the `cd` command. Also, you can create several folders in a single use of `mkdir`, as shown here:

```
debian@beaglebone:~$ cd project
debian@beaglebone:~/project$ mkdir ListOfMaterials
        theoretical_stuff circuitSchematic Code_for_
        the_project
debian@beaglebone:~/project$ ls
circuitSchematic   Code_for_the_project   ListOfMaterials
        theoretical_stuff
```

We recommend that you avoid using spaces between words whenever possible. The preceding command is a good example of the wisdom of that guideline: If you'd typed **mkdir List of materials**, you would have created three folders — `List`, `of`, and `materials` — rather than one. If absolutely necessary, you can say "Hey Shell, the name of the file I want to access starts and ends here, not at the space" by wrapping the file in quotation marks. When you type **mkdir "List of Materials"**, you create a folder named `List of Materials`.

By default, the command prompt uses the space between words to separate the various inputs of a command for all commands, not just `mkdir`. Even though we advise you to avoid using spaces when naming stuff, you may come across something created by someone who didn't think about this issue. In that case, you have no choice but to use the quotation-marks technique.

As with most commands, you can specify options to use with the `mkdir` command. The most useful one is `-p`, which enables you to create multiple directories within directories in a single line of code. Also, the `-v` option displays some additional information about the command you used, such as when each step of the command is completed. The following example illustrates these two options in action:

```
debian@beaglebone:~/project$ mkdir -vp
        stuff/schematics/datasheets
mkdir: created directory 'stuff'
mkdir: created directory 'stuff/schematics'
mkdir: created directory 'stuff/schematics/datasheets'
```

Naming conventions

The best way to deal with the difficulty of multi-word naming is to concatenate multiple words into a single word. Running words together can make them hard to read, however, as in this example: `anamelikethisquickly becomesconfusing`. It's useful to be able to distinguish each word in the name. Every programmer has a preferred method. Possible conventions include using uppercase letters or underscores, as in `aNameLikeThis IsNoLongerConfusing` or `a_name_ like_this_is_not_confusing_ either`. Use the technique that feels most comfortable to you. You can also use hyphens, but that's a less-common convention among programmers.

You can add multiple options to a command by concatenating them, as you saw in the preceding example.

Without the −p option, the shell would attempt to create the directory `datasheets` inside the `stuff/schematics` directory. Because this directory wouldn't exist yet, an error would have resulted.

Take a moment to appreciate this use of `mkdir`. In standard use of a computer with a GUI, you'd have to go through the trouble of creating a folder, going inside it, creating another, and so on. Using the command line, however, you create a folder and a subfolder by typing a single line command. In many other situations, you can accomplish what would normally be tedious tasks simply in this straightforward fashion. As mentioned at the beginning of this chapter, at first glance using the Linux command line may seem to be less user-friendly and more confusing than using a GUI, but you can't deny the added velocity at which you can complete simple tasks when you know your way around and understand the commands.

Creating, editing, and viewing text files

You can create an empty file by using the `touch` command, as shown here:

```
debian@beaglebone:~/project$ touch hello.txt
debian@beaglebone:~/project$ ls
circuitSchematic        hello.txt         stuff
Code_for_the_project    ListOfMaterials   theoretical_stuff
```

After you create the empty file, you can open it by using a text editor such as nano:

```
debian@beaglebone:~/project$ nano hello.txt
```

As expected, `hello.txt` is empty — that is, it has no text in it. Naturally, you can write whatever text you want, but leave well enough alone for now. You're about to find out how to add text to a file by using — you guessed it — the command line. For now, exit nano by pressing Ctrl+X.

To store text in a file, use the following command:

```
debian@beaglebone:~/project$ echo 'Hello World!' > hello.txt
```

The `touch` command may seem to be a bit redundant when you're dealing with `.txt` files because both of the preceding commands — writing something on nano or using `echo` — create a file if it doesn't exist already, as shown in the following example:

```
debian@beaglebone:~/project$ echo 'Hello World!!' >
          hello2.txt
debian@beaglebone:~/project$ nano hello3.txt
debian@beaglebone:~/project$ ls
circuitSchematic        hello3.txt          stuff
Code_for_the_project    hello.txt           theoretical_stuff
hello2.txt              ListOfMaterials
```

Note that `hello3.txt` appears only if you write something in it before exiting nano. If you don't write something in the file before exiting nano, the file isn't created.

To look at the contents of a file rather than opening it with a text editor such as nano, you can use the `cat` command as follows:

```
debian@beaglebone:~/project$ cat hello.txt
Hello World!
```

To append text to the end of a file, use the `echo` command as shown here:

```
debian@beaglebone:~/project$ echo 'Pleased to meet you!'
          >> hello.txt
debian@beaglebone:~/project$ cat hello.txt
Hello World!
Pleased to meet you!
```

To break down these last few new commands, the `echo` command is used to display on the terminal the text that follows it. Had you simply used it with text following it, you'd get a result like the following:

```
debian@beaglebone:~/project$ echo 'Hello!'
Hello!
```

In this example, no file is specified for saving the text, so the output is sent to the *standard output,* which is the terminal. The greater-than sign (>) is used to redirect that output where you want, such as to the beginning of an existing file or a file you want to create. Using two greater-than signs (>>) means that you want to redirect the output to the end of the specified file.

Finally, you should know that the real use of the command cat is to concatenate files and print the output. If you concatenate a file with nothing, as we've done thus far, cat simply outputs that file.

The following examples show you how you can use the cat command for what it was born to do:

```
debian@beaglebone:~/project$ echo 'Good bye!' > bye.txt
debian@beaglebone:~/project$ cat hello.txt bye.txt
Hello World!
Pleased to meet you!
Good bye!
```

You can redirect the output of a command by using the > sign, as follows:

```
debian@beaglebone:~/project$ cat hello.txt bye.txt > helloAndBye.txt
debian@beaglebone:~/project$ cat helloAndBye.txt
Hello World!
Pleased to meet you!
Good bye!
```

As with mkdir, commands aren't limited to one file. You can specify them to work with as many files as you want, and the files are processed in order, as shown in the next succession of commands.

It's interesting to note that the concept of redirecting your output applies to all commands. That means that any command that prints words in the terminal (the standard output) can be saved in a .txt file with the use of the > sign:

```
debian@beaglebone:~/project$ echo 'Hello!' 'Everything ok?' 'Bye!'
Hello! Everything ok? Bye!
debian@beaglebone:~/project$ echo 'Hello!' > hello2.txt 'How are you?' >
                hello3.txt 'See you later!' > bye2.txt
debian@beaglebone:~/project$ cat hello2.txt hello3.txt bye2.txt
Hello! How are you? See you later!
debian@beaglebone:~/project$ ls
bye2.txt            hello3.txt        stuff
bye.txt             helloAndBye.txt   teste2.txt
circuitSchematic    hello.txt         teste.txt
Code_for_the_project  ListOfMaterials  theoretical_stuff
hello2.txt
```

```
debian@beaglebone:~/project$ ls > list.txt
debian@beaglebone:~/project$ cat list.txt
bye2.txt
bye.txt
circuitSchematic
Code_for_the_project
hello2.txt
hello3.txt
helloAndBye.txt
hello.txt
ListOfMaterials
list.txt
stuff
teste2.txt
teste.txt
theoretical_stuff
```

Using the commands covered in this section, you can manipulate and work with files fairly easily. Sometimes, though, you may want to open the file and use a more direct approach to edit it; that's what text editors are for. Try using nano again to view the contents of a text file (see Figure 4-3).

```
debian@beaglebone:~/project$ nano helloAndBye.txt
```

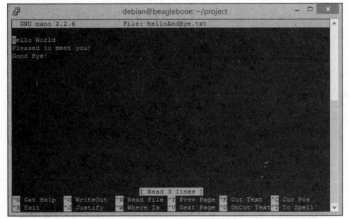

Figure 4-3:
Editing a file by using nano.

Use the arrow keys to move around the file and make whatever alterations you want. You can save by pressing Ctrl+O or exit by pressing Ctrl+X. If you attempt to exit without saving, nano asks you whether you want to save; type **Y** for yes or **N** for no and then press Enter or Return. There are plenty of other tools within nano, but we don't go into them all here. Press Ctrl+G to access the Get Help information.

Removing files and directories

To remove files, you can use the `rm` command:

```
debian@beaglebone:~/project$ ls
bye2.txt          Code_for_the_project  helloAndBye.txt list.txt
bye.txt           hello2.txt            hello.txt       stuff
CircuitSchematic  hello3.txt            ListOfMaterials TheoreticalStuff
debian@beaglebone:~/project$ rm hello.txt
debian@beaglebone:~/project$ ls
bye2.txt              hello3.txt        stuff
bye.txt               helloAndBye.txt   teste2.txt
circuitSchematic      hello.txt         teste.txt
Code_for_the_project  ListOfMaterials   theoretical_stuff
hello2.txt            list.txt
```

There's no way to undelete files and directories when you delete them this way, so be cautious! The `rm` command also works for directories, but special care is required when you use it for that purpose; directories are special files, after all. If you attempt to remove a directory through the normal use of `rm`, this message would be the result:

```
debian@beaglebone:~/project$ rm ListOfMaterials
rm: cannot remove 'ListOfMaterials': Is a directory
```

This message means that you need to use `rm` with some of the available options to remove directories. You can use three options with the `rm` command:

- ✔ `-r`, which recursively (hence the name) removes the contents of directories from bottom to top to ensure that no files are left without a directory to reside in

- ✔ `-i`, which prompts the user to confirm each deletion

- ✔ `-f`, which forces its way down, overriding any confirmation prompts that may occur for some specific files

Use the following command remove the `stuff` folder created in earlier examples in this chapter:

```
debian@beaglebone:~/project$ rm -rfi stuff
rm: descend into directory 'stuff'? y
rm: descend into directory 'stuff/schematics'? y
rm: remove directory 'stuff/schematics/datasheets'? y
rm: remove directory 'stuff/schematics'? y
rm: remove directory 'stuff'? y
```

The `-i` and `-f` options are sort of contradictory, and the one that comes last is the one that's dominant. In other words, `rm -rif` would be quite different from `rm -rfi`, which is used in the preceding example. The `-i` option would be ignored, and everything would be removed right away. Most of the time, using either `rm -rf` or `-ri` makes more sense.

Naturally, you can use each of these options independently. If you don't use `-i`, everything is deleted without asking for permission; if you don't use `-f`, you'd probably see no difference, because there are no files in that folder you need to force to be deleted; and if you don't use `-r`, you get the error message shown earlier in this section.

Another way to remove a directory safely is to use the `rmdir` command, which forbids you from deleting folders that still have content. The following example illustrate how this command works in a new folder:

```
debian@beaglebone:~/project$ mkdir toBeDeleted
debian@beaglebone:~/project$ cd toBeDeleted
debian@beaglebone:~/project/toBeDeleted$ touch file1 file2 file3
debian@beaglebone:~/project/toBeDeleted$ ls
file1 file2 file3
debian@beaglebone:~/project/toBeDeleted$ cd ..
debian@beaglebone:~/project$ rmdir toBeDeleted
rmdir: failed to remove 'toBeDeleted': Directory not empty
debian@beaglebone:~/project$ cd toBeDeleted
debian@beaglebone:~/project/toBeDeleted$ rm file1 file2 file3
debian@beaglebone:~/project/toBeDeleted$ ls
debian@beaglebone:~/project/toBeDeleted$ cd ..
debian@beaglebone:~/project$ rmdir toBeDeleted
debian@beaglebone:~/project$ ls
bye2.txt            hello3.txt          teste2.txt
bye.txt             helloAndBye.txt     teste.txt
circuitSchematic    hello.txt           theoretical_stuff
Code_for_the_project ListOfMaterials
hello2.txt          list.txt
```

Note that we didn't specify a file type, such as `.txt`, with `touch`. The truth is, for simple text files, specifying a file type doesn't matter. By definition, an empty file or blank file is a file with the size of 0 bytes, which is what an empty `.txt` file is.

You can delete a directory while you're still inside it. When you do that, the prompt still tells you that you're inside that directory, but when you leave it, you realize that the directory has ceased to exist:

```
debian@beaglebone:~/project$ mkdir toBeDeleted
debian@beaglebone:~/project$ cd toBeDeleted
debian@beaglebone:~/project/toBeDeleted$ rmdir ../toBeDeleted
debian@beaglebone:~/project/toBeDeleted$ cd ..
debian@beaglebone:~/project$ ls
bye2.txt            hello3.txt          teste2.txt
bye.txt             helloAndBye.txt     teste.txt
circuitSchematic    hello.txt           theoretical_stuff
Code_for_the_project ListOfMaterials
hello2.txt          list.txt
```

When you type a command without specifying a path, the shell assumes that you're talking about a file inside your current directory. In the preceding example, there's no toBeDeleted directory inside toBeDeleted, which is why you need to use rmdir with the relative path ../toBeDeleted.

Copying and renaming files

Copying and renaming files are common tasks, no matter what OS you use. In Linux, you can perform these tasks by using pretty straightforward commands. For copying, you use the following command:

```
cp [OPTIONS] <copy_from> <copy_to>
```

copy_from is the name of the file from which you want to copy a file, and copy_to is where you want to save the copied file. The following code illustrates this command, starting by creating a <copy_to> folder:

```
debian@beaglebone:~/project$ mkdir importantFiles
debian@beaglebone:~/project$ cp hello2.txt importantFiles
```

The syntax for moving a file with the mv command is the same as the syntax for the cp command:

```
debian@beaglebone:~/project$ mv bye.txt importantFiles
```

If the importantFiles directory didn't exist, the mv command would rename the file bye.txt, making it importantFiles. Although this renaming may lead to confusion and unexpected errors, use the following technique to rename files from the command prompt:

```
debian@beaglebone:~/project$ cd importantFiles
debian@beaglebone:~/project/importantFiles mv hello2.txt greetings.txt
debian@beaglebone:~/project/importantFiles cd ..
```

Now confirm the results of what you just typed :

```
debian@beaglebone:~/project$ ls importantFiles
bye.txt   greetings.txt
```

The `mv` command means either "move a file" or "rename a file," depending on whether its second input is a directory that already exists.

If the destination folder already has a file with the same name as the file you're copying, that file will be overwritten!

You can use several options with these commands, two of which are quite useful and probably familiar to you. One option is `-i`, which protects you from overwriting files in the same way that you're protected from deleting files with `rm`; you're prompted to confirm before the file is overwritten. The other option is `-v`, which describes what's going on, just like when it's used with `mkdir`.

Selecting multiple files in Linux

Sometimes, you need to select multiple files, but without a GUI, dragging the mouse won't do. When you use the command line, you can select multiple files by using wildcards.

The name does them justice, as *wildcards* are special characters that can be used to represent any character in different ways. Rather than providing a filename for your command to work with, you provide a pattern. The best way to explain this concept is to provide examples.

Start by creating a new folder (for matters of organization) and filling it with files of a similar name:

```
debian@beaglebone:~/project$ mkdir Hellos
debian@beaglebone:~/project$ cd Hellos
debian@beaglebone:~/project/Hellos$ touch hello1.txt hello2.txt hello3.txt
              hello4.txt
debian@beaglebone:~/project/Hellos$ ls
hello1.txt hello2.txt hello3.txt hello4.txt
```

Naturally, the patterns here are `hello` and `.txt`. You can use three wildcards.

The question-mark (?) wildcard replaces one single character, so `hello?.txt` refers to all those `hellos`. Try it with the `file` command:

```
debian@beaglebone:~/project/Hellos file hello?.txt
hello1.txt: empty
hello2.txt: empty
hello3.txt: empty
hello4.txt: empty
```

Note, however, that the ? wildcard replaces just one character. If you had more than ten hellos, this code would select only the first nine:

```
debian@beaglebone:~/project/Hellos touch hello12.txt
debian@beaglebone:~/project/Hellos file hello?.txt
hello1.txt: empty
hello2.txt: empty
hello3.txt: empty
hello4.txt: empty
```

This example is where the asterisk (*) wildcard comes in. Rather than replacing just one single character, it replaces any number of characters. hello* selects everything that starts with hello; *.txt selects everything that ends in .txt; and *hello* selects everything that has the word *hello* in it:

```
debian@beaglebone:~/project/Hellos touch oh_hello.txt helloBuddy.txt
debian@beaglebone:~/project/Hellos file hello*
hello12.txt:      empty
hello1.txt:       empty
hello2.txt:       empty
hello3.txt:       empty
hello4.txt:       empty
helloBuddy.txt:  empty
```

```
debian@beaglebone:~/project/Hellos file *.txt
hello12.txt:      empty
hello1.txt:       empty
hello2.txt:       empty
hello3.txt:       empty
hello4.txt:       empty
helloBuddy.txt:  empty
oh_hello.txt:    empty
```

```
debian@beaglebone:~/project/Hellos file *hello*
hello12.txt:      empty
hello1.txt:       empty
hello2.txt:       empty
hello3.txt:       empty
hello4.txt:       empty
helloBuddy.txt:  empty
oh_hello.txt:    empty
```

As expected, file hello* won't return information about the oh_hello.txt file, and file *hello* and file *.txt won't miss any file. Note, however, that if you had files with the names bye.txt and hello.jpg in there, these two commands would yield different results: file *hello* would ignore bye.txt, and file *.txt would ignore hello.jpg.

The last wildcard is square brackets ([ ]), which replaces a character with a set of specific letters. To select all files whose names start with a, b, or c, for example, you can use [abc]*:

```
debian@beaglebone:~/project/Hellos touch awesome beaglebone can do
                extremely fantastic gigs
debian@beaglebone:~/project/Hellos file [abc]*
awesome:     empty
beaglebone: empty
can:         empty
```

You can also use [ ] the other way around, to select files that don't not start with the specified characters, by using the ^ character:

```
debian@beaglebone:~/project/Hellos file [^abc]*
do:               empty
extremely:        empty
fantastic:        empty
gigs:             empty
hello12.txt:      empty
hello1.txt:       empty
hello2.txt:       empty
hello3.txt:       empty
hello4.txt:       empty
helloBuddy.txt:  empty
oh_hello.txt:    empty
```

Finally, you can specify a range by using [ ] and a hyphen, like so:

```
debian@beaglebone:~/project/Hellos file [b-e]*
beaglebone: empty
can:         empty
do:          empty
extremely:   empty
```

Wildcards may be a bit confusing, but all you need to remember is the rule of thumb that a wildcard replaces one or more characters, allowing you to narrow or broaden the number of files you want to select. Playing around with wildcards is the best way to get a feel for how to use them. Following are some more examples, the first two of which deserve special attention and explanation:

```
debian@beaglebone:~/project/Hellos touch hello23.txt
debian@beaglebone:~/project/Hellos file hello[23].txt
hello2.txt: empty
hello3.txt: empty
```

hello23.txt doesn't appear when you use file hello[23].txt. Weird, huh? This result is due to the fact that what's inside the brackets is a list of *one* possible character to substitute for *one* character immediately next to hello and before .txt. file hello[23][23].txt or hello[32][32].txt or any other combination, would display hello23. txt but not hello2.txt or hello3.txt because it's looking for *two* characters before .txt:

```
debian@beaglebone:~/project/Hellos touch A
debian@beaglebone:~/project/Hellos file *a*
awesome:        empty
beaglebone:     empty
can:            empty
fantastic:      empty
```

In this example, you're selecting all files whose names contain a. The file A doesn't appear due to the fact that, as stated earlier in this chapter, Linux is case-sensitive. The letter a and the letter A are completely different characters.

Here are some more examples to help you get familiar with how wildcards work:

```
debian@beaglebone:~/project/Hellos file hello[2-4].txt
hello2.txt: empty
hello3.txt: empty
hello4.txt: empty
debian@beaglebone:~/project/Hellos file hello??.txt
hello12.txt:   empty
debian@beaglebone:~/project/Hellos file hello[^23]*
hello12.txt:       empty
hello1.txt:        empty
hello4.txt:        empty
helloBuddy.txt: empty
debian@beaglebone:~/project/Hellos file ?
A: empty
debian@beaglebone:~/project/Hellos file *
A:              empty
awesome:        empty
beaglebone:     empty
can:            empty
do:             empty
extremely:      empty
fantastic:      empty
gigs:           empty
hello12.txt:    empty
hello1.txt:     empty
hello23.txt:    empty
hello2.txt:     empty
hello3.txt:     empty
hello4.txt:     empty
helloBuddy.txt: empty
oh_hello.txt:   empty
```

You can use wildcards with any other commands, just as you'd use the name of a file. As proof, bid adieu to the `Hellos` directory as follows:

```
debian@beaglebone:~/project/Hellos rm -v *hello*
removed 'hello12.txt'
removed 'hello1.txt'
removed 'hello2.txt'
removed 'hello3.txt'
removed 'hello4.txt'
removed 'helloBuddy.txt'
removed 'oh_hello.txt'
debian@beaglebone:~/project/Hellos ls
A  awesome  beaglebone  can  do  extremely  fantastic  gigs
```

You could simply have deleted everything right away by using the * wildcard because it replaces any number of characters. The following code does that:

```
debian@beaglebone:~/project/Hellos$ rm -v *
removed 'A'
removed 'awesome'
removed 'beaglebone'
removed 'can'
removed 'do'
removed 'extremely'
removed 'fantastic'
removed 'gigs'
debian@beaglebone:~/project/Hellos$ ls
debian@beaglebone:~/project/Hellos$ cd ..
debian@beaglebone:~/project$ rmdir Hellos
```

The computer uses spaces to separate the inputs of commands! That said, when you're using asterisks, an accidental space could lead to catastrophic results. Suppose that you want to delete all the `.jpg` files you have inside a folder. To do that, you could use

```
rm *.jpg
```

Had you unwittingly placed an extra space in the command, as in

```
rm * .jpg
```

the shell would interpret this command as a direction to remove * — which means *remove everything* — and *then* attempt to remove a file named `.jpg`. You may unwittingly delete a very important file in that directory, and there's no "undelete" option. One solution would be to use the `-i` option whenever you decide to delete many files, but having to confirm each deletion would be tedious and would defeat the purpose of using wildcards. The best solution is simply to be very cautious whenever you're deleting files — and to double that caution if you're doing so by resorting to wildcards.

You should always be cautious when deleting files. If, for any specific project you may encounter in the future, you find yourself working as a superuser, that caution should be much greater. Nothing can hold you back from deleting everything on the computer, leading to a system crash due to the deletion of a crucial file, directory, or whatever. The command that causes this problem is `rm -rf /*` issued by someone who's logged in as superuser. We're exposing you to this command because someone, somewhere may claim that it's the solution to the problem you're having. Now you're prepared for this claim, and you can ignore it. You can also laugh and say, "Ah, almost got me there!"

Using long-listing format and permissions

Earlier in this chapter, in the section "Listing files and directories," we introduce the long-listing format of the `ls` command, which is displayed when you use it with the `-l` option. This format offers quite a bit of information about the files in the directory you list:

```
debian@beaglebone:~/project$ ls -l
total 32
-rw-r--r-- 1 debian debian   32 Jul  1 00:11 bye2.txt
drwxr-xr-x 2 debian debian 4096 Jun 30 23:58 CircuitSchematic
drwxr-xr-x 2 debian debian 4096 Jun 30 23:58 Code_for_the_project
-rw-r--r-- 1 debian debian    0 Jul  1 00:11 hello2.txt

-rw-r--r-- 1 debian debian    0 Jul  1 00:11 hello3.txt
-rw-r--r-- 1 debian debian   43 Jul  1 00:09 helloAndBye.txt
drwxr-xr-x 2 debian debian 4096 Jul  1 00:43 importantFiles
drwxr-xr-x 2 debian debian 4096 Jun 30 23:58 ListOfMaterials
-rw-r--r-- 1 debian debian   18 Jul  1 00:15 list.txt
drwxr-xr-x 2 debian debian 4096 Jun 30 23:58 TheoreticalStuff
```

You should dissect these lines for the information they contain. Starting from the right (because those commands are the most intuitive and the easiest to explain), you have the following:

- ✔ **The filename** (`bye2.txt`): Remember that the names of directories are also filenames.

- ✔ **The time and date of the last modification** (`Jul 1 00:11`): If you had an older file, this format would change slightly. Rather than showing the time when you last altered the file, the year in which you modified it would be displayed.

- ✔ **The size of the file, measured in bytes** (`32` or `4096`): One important thing to note is that for the directories, this number is the size of the file that represents the directory, not the sum of the contents of the directory. Thus, all directories display a size of 4096 bytes, regardless of whether they are empty. To have the sizes of the contents printed in units that make more sense (such as 1K, 120M, and 2G), use the `-h` (human-readable) option.

✔ **The owner of the file and the group that owns it** (`debian debian`): The two columns that feature `debian` represent, from left to right, the owner of the file and the group that owns it. Thus, the second column could be something like LabPCs.

✔ **The number of hard links to the file** (1 or 2): The number before `debian` represents the number of hard links to the file. In the case of a directory, that number is the number of immediate subdirectories it contains, as well as the directory itself and the parent directory. Therefore, a directory with no subdirectories has at least two hard links to it.

The remaining columns consist of information regarding permissions; they provide insight into who is able to use the files and in which ways. You can do three things with a file: read it (`r`), write in it (`w`), and execute it (`x`). Also, there are three groups of people, from the point of view of your computer: the owner, the group, and the world.

That information is provided in the leftmost part of each line and is always a combination of ten characters. To understand this code, you can break it into four parts: one for the size of one character and three for the sizes of three characters:

✔ The first character tells you what kind of file you're dealing with: a regular file (`-`) or a directory (`d`).

✔ Next are the permissions for the owner (the first three characters), the group (the next three characters), and everyone else (the last three characters). For a specific file, someone who has read permission can open the contents of the file or list a directory; someone who has write permission can change the contents of the file and of a directory (such as by creating or deleting files); and someone who has execute permission for a regular file can use it as a program and run it, or enter a directory.

Typically, you see `-rw-r--r--` in a file. This code means that the owner can read it and write in it, and everyone else (the group and the world) can read it but not make any changes. The code is always `rwx`, so if you see a hyphen in the place of one of these letters, the file doesn't give that specific permission to that group of people.

For a directory, you often see `drwxr-xr-x`. Here's the letter-by-letter translation:

✔ It's a directory (`d`).

✔ The owner can read, write, and execute it (`rwx`). Because this item is a directory, the owner can see its contents with the `ls` command or when using a GUI (read permission), add files to or delete files from it (write permission), and get inside the directory (execute permission).

✔ The group can read and execute it (`r-x`) but not write in it, meaning that they can list its contents (read permission) and also get inside it (execute permission), but they can't create or delete any files (no write permission).

✔ Everyone else has the same permissions as the group — that is, they can check the contents without messing around with them.

Two small details are worth noting:

✔ Even if a file gives you write permission, it still answers to the directory that contains it. Even though you can alter the file itself, you can rename or delete it only if you have write permission for its directory.

✔ In reality, you can't do anything in a directory if you don't have the execute permission, so a three-character indicator such as rw- doesn't allow you to do anything. Most things that you try to do result in a Permission denied error.

The chmod command enables you to change a file's permissions. You have many ways to use this command, but perhaps the most intuitive way is to use the sum (+) and subtraction (−) operators, along with the people or groups to which you want to give or remove permissions: the user (the owner of the file), the group, the world (other users), or all of these by using u, g, o, or a, respectively.

In the following example a command removes write permission from hello2.txt for the user, gives write permission to the group for bye2.txt, and grants execute permission to the world for hello3.txt:

```
debian@beaglebone:~/project$ ls -l
total 32
-rw-r--r-- 1 debian debian   32 Jul  1 00:11 bye2.txt
drwxr-xr-x 2 debian debian 4096 Jun 30 23:58 CircuitSchematic
drwxr-xr-x 2 debian debian 4096 Jun 30 23:58 Code_for_the_project
-rw-r--r-- 1 debian debian    0 Jul  1 00:11 hello2.txt
-rw-r--r-- 1 debian debian    0 Jul  1 00:11 hello3.txt
-rw-r--r-- 1 debian debian   43 Jul  1 00:09 helloAndBye.txt
drwxr-xr-x 2 debian debian 4096 Jul  1 00:43 importantFiles
drwxr-xr-x 2 debian debian 4096 Jun 30 23:58 ListOfMaterials
-rw-r--r-- 1 debian debian   18 Jul  1 00:15 list.txt
drwxr-xr-x 2 debian root   4096 Jun 30 23:58 TheoreticalStuff
debian@beaglebone:~/project$ chmod u-w hello2.txt
debian@beaglebone:~/project$ chmod g+w bye2.txt
debian@beaglebone:~/project$ chmod o+x hello3.txt
debian@beaglebone:~/project$ ls -l
total 44
drwxr-xr-x 2 debian debian 4096 Apr 23  2014 Code_for_the_project
drwxr-xr-x 2 debian debian 4096 Apr 23  2014 ListOfMaterials
-rw-r--r-- 1 debian debian   10 Apr 23  2014 bye.txt
-r--rw-r-- 1 debian debian   35 Apr 23  2014 bye2.txt
drwxr-xr-x 2 debian debian 4096 Apr 23  2014 circuitSchematic
-rw-r--r-- 1 debian debian   33 Apr 23  2014 hello.txt
-r--r--r-- 1 debian debian    0 Apr 23  2014 hello2.txt
-r--r--r-x 1 debian debian    0 Apr 23  2014 hello3.txt
```

```
-rw-r--r-- 1 debian debian   43 Apr 23  2014 helloAndBye.txt
-rw-r--r-- 1 debian debian  173 Apr 23  2014 list.txt
-rw-r--r-- 1 debian debian    9 Apr 23  2014 teste.txt
-rw-r--r-- 1 debian debian    9 Apr 23  2014 teste2.txt
drwxr-xr-x 2 debian debian 4096 Apr 23  2014 theoretical_stuff
```

As you can verify, the user lost his or her permission to write in the file
hello2.txt. To confirm, use the echo command:

```
debian@beaglebone:~/project$ echo 'This will not work' > hell
o2.txt
-bash: hello2.txt: Permission denied
```

For bye2.txt, even though you can't readily test it, you can check the list
to see that the group was given write permission for it. The same applies to
hello3.txt, which now shows an x that wasn't there earlier.

Managing Software on Your BeagleBone

When you know your way around the command line, downloading and
installing new software on a computer or device running the Linux OS is quite
easy and straightforward. The software comes in what are called *packages* —
software programs that can be downloaded from the Internet and installed
simply by typing a command in the prompt.

To download and install these packages, you normally use a *package manager,* which downloads and installs not only the software you requested, but
also all other required software, known as *dependencies*. The Debian distribution uses a package manager called apt.

If you read other literature about the BeagleBone, you may find that you should
use the opkg utility as the package manager. As mentioned in Chapter 2, up until
recently, the standard distribution used by the BeagleBone was Ångström. The
examples in this book use the Debian distribution, so apt is the way to go.

To manage your software, you need the authorization of the administrator,
whom you already know as the superuser. Being logged in as root is often
considered to be unsafe, as the computer becomes vulnerable not only to
its user (who may unwittingly make undesired changes in the file system),
but also to malicious software that may have gotten inside. With that in
mind, you can carry out a command with the authorization of the root
user without being logged in as such. To do so, type **sudo** (superuser do)
before a command.

In any other situation, if you get an error message telling you that the command you typed can be executed only with the authorization of root, try using sudo before it. Be cautious, though. If the command is telling you that it needs the authorization of root, it's probably because something serious is involved!

First and foremost, you have to update the list of available package versions that your package manager is aware of. (The package manager keeps such a list in the BeagleBone's file system.) Type the following command:

```
sudo apt-get update
```

You need to be connected to the Internet for this command to work.

Text scrolls by after you type the command, giving information about the newest listings.

Next, you should update the software, which you can achieve by commanding apt to upgrade. This command upgrades all the packages you've installed to their most recent versions:

```
sudo apt-get upgrade
```

In terms of wording, the difference between updating and upgrading is subtle, but what they do is quite different (even though they're usually done together). sudo apt-get update updates the list of available package versions but doesn't install or upgrade any of them, whereas sudo apt-get upgrade updates the packages themselves, checking the list to do so. For that reason, you should always run update before upgrade.

Installing software

To install a package for which you already know the name, you have to type the following command:

```
sudo apt-get install <desired application>
```

To see how this process works, use the following command to install the Midnight Commander application, which is a visual file manager:

```
sudo apt-get install mc
```

This command downloads the package from the Internet and installs it, as well as any dependencies it requires to work properly.

Always run sudo apt-get update before installing software.

Running software

To run programs directly from the prompt, simply type their names, as shown in the following command and in Figure 4-4:

```
debian@beaglebone:~$ mc
```

Figure 4-4:
Running
Midnight
Commander
through
PuTTY.

Updating software

You can update the latest versions of your software by typing the upgrade command:

```
sudo apt-get upgrade
```

Generally, though, you want to update the list of available package versions before you upgrade to ensure that apt gets you the most recent updates for your installed software.

In the "Installing software" section, we show you how to get updates and upgrades by writing the commands separately, but you can write them both in a single line as follows:

```
sudo apt-get update && sudo apt-get upgrade
```

The && is a binary operator that means AND. The AND operator is commonly used in programming to test for multiple conditions. For now, keep in mind that its use ensures that the second command executes only if the first succeeds. If your update fails for some reason (maybe because you lack an Internet connection), the system won't even attempt to upgrade.

This process (specifically, the upgrading part) can take a very long time, which can be troublesome if you want to update a single application. Fortunately, you can do so by typing the `install` command again, remembering to update the list of available package versions first:

```
sudo apt-get update && sudo apt-get install mc
```

This command doesn't install the software all over again. Instead, the package manager first checks for updates and installs them. If updates aren't available, the package manager displays a message that the software is already up to date.

Removing software

To remove software from your BeagleBone, you resort once more to the apt package manager. Here's an example:

```
sudo apt-get remove mc
```

This command, however, leaves behind files that are somehow related to the software, such as configuration files and logs. If you don't intend to use those files in any way, you can remove everything by using `purge`:

```
sudo apt-get purge mc
```

You can also direct the system to check for unnecessary packages and/or files and remove them automatically.

The package manager downloads and installs not only the requested package, but also any other packages that it may depend on. Thus, if you delete some software, its dependencies may stay behind. The apt package manager deems the dependencies unnecessary and deletes them automatically when you issue the following command:

```
sudo apt-get autoremove
```

Don't fret about giving so much power to the package manager. Before deletion, you see a list of the packages that will be removed, and you're prompted to press Y to confirm that you do want those packages removed. You also see how much space will be freed.

To remove all files that are undoubtedly unnecessary, you can type the following command:

```
sudo apt-get clean
```

These files are usually installation files. They remain on your computer after the installation of a program, even though they're no longer needed. Removing them isn't an issue. If you decide to reinstall a package, you can simply do so as previously described in the "Installing software" section. The installation file downloads again.

We highly recommend not removing any package that you didn't install yourself unless you're absolutely certain that you know what it's for. It may be a necessary package that comes with the Linux OS, and removing it may lead to a system crash.

Seeing what's installed on your BeagleBone

To see a list of installed packages on your BeagleBone, type the following command:

```
dpkg --list
```

Note that this command doesn't require root authorization. After all, you aren't messing around with the software; you're just listing it. Consequently, it's not necessary to use sudo.

To see whether a specific package is installed, as well as a more detailed description about it, you can use the following command:

```
dpkg --status <nameOfThePackage>
```

Changing the Hostname and Password

Currently, the hostname of your BeagleBone is, rather boringly, beaglebone. You may want to change it to something more personal. Doing so is also useful when you start to use more than one BeagleBone on the same network, because the hostname is the name that's displayed to all the other users on that network.

If you want to change the hostname, start by typing the following command:

```
debian@beaglebone:~$ sudo echo 'newHostName' > /etc/hostname
```

Your hostname is changed to the one that you prefer. The BeagleBone won't recognize this "host," however, so you need to edit the `hosts` file. To open and edit it, follow these steps:

1. **Type the following in a text editor such as nano:**

   ```
   debian@beaglebone:~$ sudo nano /etc/hosts
   ```

2. **On the line that reads `127.0.0.1 beaglebone`, change `beaglebone` to your new hostname**

3. **Save the file, and quit nano.**

4. **Reboot your BeagleBone.**

   Your new hostname should appear during your next login.

Use the arrow keys to navigate nano, and press Ctrl+O to save and Ctrl+X to exit. If you attempt to exit without saving, you're prompted to press Y if you want to save or N if you don't.

The default debian user password is `temppwd`. If you want to change it, simply type the command `passwd` and follow the steps printed in the terminal:

```
debian@beaglebone:~$ passwd
Changing password for debian.
(current) UNIX password:
Enter new UNIX password:
Retype new UNIX password:
passwd: password updated successfully
debian@beaglebone:~$
```

The text is hidden while you write the passwords.

Shutting Down and Rebooting

There are better ways to shut down and reboot your BeagleBone than simply unplugging it. Unceremoniously unplugging your BeagleBone is the equivalent of shutting down your computer by pressing the power button or even removing its power source, which sometimes leads to complications such as file corruption.

To shut down your BeagleBone, simply type this command on the command line:

```
debian@beaglebone:~$ sudo shutdown -h now
```

You see the following information after you use the `shutdown` command:

```
Broadcast message from root@beaglebone (pts/0) (Thu Jul  3 18:50:09 2014):
The system is going down for system halt NOW!
debian@beaglebone:~$
```

To reboot, type this:

```
debian@beaglebone:~$ sudo reboot
```

This is the result:

```
Broadcast message from root@beaglebone (pts/0) (Thu Jul  3 18:44:29 2014):
The system is going down for reboot NOW!
```

You need to log in again through SSH after rebooting.

Commanding the Prompt Like a Jedi Master

This section provides a few tips and tricks that maximize the efficiency with which you use the Linux OS. This material won't help you save the galaxy or show you how to fetch the TV remote with telekinesis, but it should help you navigate the prompt much faster than before — and with a lot more style.

Recalling previous commands

You can easily recall the commands you've used previously by pressing the up- and down-arrow keys. Imagine that you listed the contents of a file by using `ls -l`; then you created a directory and a file inside this new directory. You want to see the list again to see the default permissions of this new directory. Rather than keying in `ls -l` again, you can simply press the up-arrow key twice.

Next, imagine that you want to list the contents of this new folder to see the file inside it, but you want to add the `-h` option. Simply press the up-arrow key to bring `ls -l` onscreen once more; you can use the left and right arrow keys to navigate through that line and then add the `-h` option and the name of the new directory. You can tell that this method saves some work.

Now imagine repeating the entire process for someplace other than your working directory, a place with a very long absolute path, such as this:

```
ls -l /home/debian/Desktop/project/aFolder/aDeeperFolder/
          anEvenDeeperFolder/theDeepestFolder
```

In fact, create this folder now for the sake of further exemplification:

```
debian@beaglebone:~/Desktop$ mkdir -p aFolder/aDeeperFolder/
          anEvenDeeperFolder/theDeepestFolder
```

Autocompleting commands

After writing the first letters of a line, press Tab to command the shell to try to guess what you meant to write and to autocomplete it. Naturally, this feature is most useful when you want to access long filenames. If it fails, write a little more to give the shell a better hint. You can try it by typing the following at the Desktop and then pressing the Tab key:

```
debian@beaglebone:~/Desktop$ cd aF
```

The shell completes the line with cd aFolder/.

Note the slash at the end. When you used cd to access a directory in the previous sections, you never placed a slash at the end of its name. Placing or not placing a slash is exactly the same. Why does the autocompletion add a slash, then? That's because it's ready to continue guessing the names of files within that directory. If you keep pressing the Tab key, you eventually end up with the following command:

```
debian@beaglebone:~/Desktop$ cd aFolder/aDeeperFolder/anEvenDeeperFolder/
          theDeepestFolder
```

Because nothing else was inside any of those folders, it was quite easy for the shell to autocomplete your command even without having hints; there was only one option, after all. Otherwise, the prompt prints a list of possible files, asking you to write a few more letters. The following example illustrates that:

```
debian@beaglebone:~/Desktop/aFolder/aDeeperFolder/anEvenDeeperFolder/
          theDeepestFolder$ touch heyJohn heyMarie heyCarl
```

If you type **file** and then press Tab repeatedly, you see the following:

```
debian@beaglebone:~/Desktop/aFolder/aDeeperFolder/anEvenDeeperFolder/
          theDeepestFolder$ file hey
```

Continue pressing Tab. The prompt suggests all the possibilities:

```
debian@beaglebone:~/Desktop/aFolder/aDeeperFolder/anEvenDeeperFolder/
          theDeepestFolder$ file hey
heyCarl    heyJohn    heyMarie
debian@beaglebone:~/Desktop/aFolder/aDeeperFolder/anEvenDeeperFolder/
          theDeepestFolder$ file hey
```

If you give the prompt a better hint, such as this,

```
debian@beaglebone:~/Desktop/aFolder/aDeeperFolder/anEvenDeeperFolder/
          theDeepestFolder$ file heyJ
```

when you press Tab again, you see the result:

```
debian@beaglebone:~/Desktop/aFolder/aDeeperFolder/anEvenDeeperFolder/
          theDeepestFolder$ file heyJohn
```

Using keyboard shortcuts

You have ways to navigate the command line other than pressing the left- and right-arrow keys, which sometimes seem to take forever to get you some-where. Following are some useful keyboard shortcuts:

- ✔ Ctrl+A and Ctrl+E do the same thing as the Home and End keys — that is, they bring you to the beginning and the end of the current command, respectively.

- ✔ Ctrl+Left and Ctrl+Right jump between inputs (arguments) in a command; the cursor jumps from a space or a slash to the next.

- ✔ Ctrl+U clears the entire line.

- ✔ Ctrl+K deletes everything from the position of the cursor to the end of the line.

- ✔ Ctrl+W deletes a single word before the cursor.

- ✔ Ctrl+R allows you to search your command history. If you press Ctrl+R and then type **cd**, for example, your most recent command involving cd appears on the command line. Pressing Ctrl+R again shows you the cd command before that, and so on. Press the left- or right-arrow key when you find the one you want.

  This search finds characters, not commands. If you had a command such as `mkdir photos_from_cd`, you could use Ctrl+R with cd to find it.

Using these Ctrl shortcuts helps you jump around quite fast. Suppose that you want to copy a file from the Desktop to the anEvenDeeperFolder directory. First, create the file by using the touch command:

```
debian@beaglebone:~/Desktop$ touch hello.txt
```

To copy the file, you would have to type the following cumbersome command:

```
debian@beaglebone:~/Desktop$ cp hello.txt /home/debian/Desktop/aFolder/
        aDeeperFolder/anEvenDeeperFolder
```

What a chore! Instead, you can achieve the same result by following these steps:

1. **Press Ctrl+R and then type** mkdir:

   ```
   (reverse-i-search)'mkdir': [m]kdir -p aFolder/aDeeperFolder/
           anEvenDeeperFolder/theDeepestFolder
   ```

   The preceding example and those that follow are all about showing you how to have your cursor jumping around in a line by using keyboard shortcuts. In the examples, the terminal cursor is represented with closed brackets ([]). If your cursor is somewhere else and you press the keyboard shortcuts you'll get different results.

2. **Press Ctrl+right arrow until your cursor is right before the directory you want to eliminate from the path:**

   ```
   debian@beaglebone:~/Desktop$ mkdir -p aFolder/aDeeperFolder/
           anEvenDeeperFolder[/]theDeepestFolder
   ```

3. **Press Ctrl+K to get rid of** theDeepestFolder/:

   ```
   debian@beaglebone:~/Desktop$ mkdir -p aFolder/aDeeperFolder/
           anEvenDeeperFolder[]
   ```

4. **Press Ctrl+A to go to the beginning of the line:**

   ```
   debian@beaglebone:~/Desktop$ [m]kdir -p aFolder/aDeeperFolder/
           anEvenDeeperFolder
   ```

5. **Press Ctrl+right arrow twice.**

   Your cursor is now after–p:

   ```
   debian@beaglebone:~/Desktop$ mkdir -p[]aFolder/aDeeperFolder/
           anEvenDeeperFolder
   ```

6. **Press Ctrl+W twice to erase** mkdir -p,**and then type** cp hello.txt:

   ```
   debian@beaglebone:~/Desktop$  []aFolder/aDeeperFolder/anEvenDeeperFolder
   ```

Alternatively, you can type something like **cp he** and then press Tab:

```
debian@beaglebone:~/Desktop$  cp he[]aFolder/aDeeperFolder/
         anEvenDeeperFolder[
```

7. **Press Tab:**

```
debian@beaglebone:~/Desktop$  cp hello.txt[]aFolder/aDeeperFolder/
         anEvenDeeperFolder
```

Keeping everything clean

Typing the command `clear` or pressing Ctrl+L quickly clears the screen, but it doesn't clear the terminal window. In fact, the result is like pressing Enter or Return many times: If you scroll up, you still see the commands you used previously. If you truly want to clear everything, you can use the `reset` command.

The `reset` command reinitializes the terminal window, so that it appears to have just started (and, thus, has nothing in it). The command doesn't reinitiate the shell, however, so it doesn't alter the shell's state. In layman's terms, the shell's state is the same, so you can still access your command history.

Taking things further

The Linux OS offers a world of possibilities. It allows you to do plenty of things and gives you a degree of freedom, versatility, and customizability that is rare in any OS. This chapter should be enough to get you started using Linux on the BeagleBone, but if you're interested in finding out more, you can grab a copy of *Linux For Dummies,* 9th Edition, by Richard Blum (John Wiley & Sons, Inc.).

Also, Linux is open-source software, so consulting the web is often a good way to find out more. You can find many friendly Linux users who are more than happy to share some of their knowledge and resources. If you search for the specific problem that you encounter, there is bound to be someone who has had the exact same problem — and someone who has explained how to solve it.

Additionally, `www.linux.com/learn`, `http://linuxsurvival.com`, and `http://elinux.org` are great resources to find out more about Linux. Elinux is a website destined specifically for embedded systems that run Linux, such as the BeagleBone.

Chapter 5

Designing Circuits

• •

• •

*T*his chapter gets you up to speed regarding the most basic principles of electricity so that you can understand what is happening on the circuits you build to interact with your BeagleBone. It introduces you to the fundamentals of electricity. We explain new techniques, rules, and/or new circuit components and their respective symbols throughout the remainder of the book where those concepts are most appropriate.

The study of the phenomena that deal with electricity is complex and vast. Deep down, things such as your phone, your computer, and your BeagleBone are nothing but a great deal of electric components manipulating electricity. You don't need to understand how these components work to use those devices. Because you'll make electronic circuits of your own that use the BeagleBone as support, however, you should understand some basic principles of electricity.

Introducing Electricity

Ah, electricity. Most people know what it is but have no idea what it *really* is. It's been around since the dawn of the universe, and some sources say that the ancients actually believed it was some kind of magic. Thunder is a manifestation of electricity. Rubbing a pencil on your hair and then using it to attract pieces of paper is also electricity. When you press a few keys on your keyboard, what makes them show up on your screen? Again, electricity.

Electricity appears as a form of energy due to the existence of electrically charged particles (protons and electrons; see Figure 5-1) on the structure of an atom — the foundation of all matter.

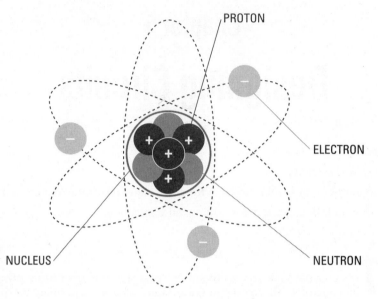

Figure 5-1:
The struc-
ture of an
atom.

Voltage, current, and resistance

This energy can appear as a static accumulation of electrical charge — an electric potential or *voltage* — or as a dynamic flow of electrons — an electric *current* (see Figure 5-2).

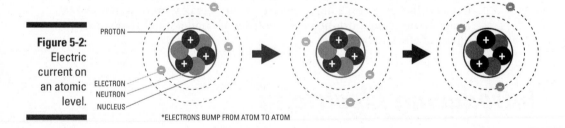

Figure 5-2:
Electric
current on
an atomic
level.

An electric current is basically electrons bumping from atom to atom. This phenomenon happens only in some materials. The atoms that make up rubber, for example, are too posh to engage in this kind of behavior. Copper atoms, however, are party animals that get down on the dance floor for some bumping action with just the slightest motivation. Elements such as copper are defined as good *conductors*. They still need some motivation, though, some sort of energy to get them moving. That energy is known as *voltage,* and thus there must be a *voltage source* to provide that energy. In a sense, voltage is the force that pushes the electric current forward.

Generally, you don't need to know any of this mumbo-jumbo about how voltage and current exists. Long story short, applying a voltage to a conductive material gets an electrical current flowing. You do need to know how voltage and current behave and how they can be manipulated, however.

The electrical wires mentioned in Chapter 1 usually have copper in them to get the current flowing. This copper is covered by a nonconductive material — an *insulator* — so that the copper where the current flows is protected.

The third concept you need to be aware of is *electrical resistance.* All electronic components exhibit some sort of *resistance,* which is a material's capacity to resist electric current. For the current to get through this material, the current needs to be pushed through; it needs a voltage. What we call a *voltage drop* occurs at the resistive component.

In the next section, you find out about mathematizing these values by using three very simple equations, so it's important to know the following:

- ✔ **Voltage** is measured in volts (V). A 1.5V AA battery, for example, is a 1.5V voltage source.

- ✔ **Current** is measured in amperes, or amps for short (A). The variable used to represent it, however, is often I (from current intensity).

- ✔ **Resistance** is measured in ohms (Ω) and is represented as R.

The symbol for resistance, Ω, is the uppercase Greek letter omega. One of the side effects of taking an electronics course is that you may end up knowing pretty much the entire Greek alphabet.

The water analogy

It's much easier to understand electrical phenomena when you compare electric current with water flow. Imagine a system of plumbing pipes through which water flows. Some sort of force has to drive the water, such as a water pump, which is analogous to a voltage source. Also imagine that one section of the pipes has a much smaller diameter than the rest of the system. This section exhibits much higher resistance to the flow of water, so for the water current to pass at the same speed, more force is required.

A basic circuit example

The simple circuit shown in Figure 5-3 consists of a voltage source, a resistor, and a light-emitting diode (LED) connected with wires made of copper or any other conductive material.

Figure 5-3:
A basic
circuit that
lights up an
LED.

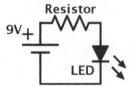

The voltage source — typically, a battery, such as the 9V battery in Figure 5-3 — supplies voltage to the circuit, which draws current from the battery. The relationship between the value of the battery and the current that's drawn from it is called *power,* which is measured in watts (W).

All electronic circuits are . . . well, circuits: They're always a closed loop. Current must always return to its source. That said, the voltage supplied by the battery drops along the circuit. Each component eats up a slice of those tasty 9V due to the resistance they exhibit, *and the voltage dropped along the entire circuit must always equal the amount of voltage supplied.*

Copper wires exhibit resistance, but that resistance is so ridiculously low that you can pretend it isn't there at all for most applications. Consequently, you can assume that no voltage drop whatsoever occurs along the wires.

When a circuit has no resistive components, the voltage can't drop before the current goes back into the battery again. This type of circuit is called a *short-circuit* and is often harmful to your circuit and its components. Don't test this at home, but if you connect a battery's positive (+) pole to its negative (–) pole with a wire, the battery would become really hot and lose all its energy very quickly. Such is the effect of a short-circuit.

Some components are very specific to the amount of voltage that they need to work, which is why it's important to understand the concepts presented in this chapter. If you apply the 9V directly to the LED, the LED would blow up. Well, actually, just the filament inside would burn up, so the event really wouldn't be a fun one. The LED would light up for a brief moment; then there would be some smoke and a nasty smell. On the other hand, if you apply less voltage to the LED than is specified, the light won't reach its full brightness or may even not light at all. That's why a resistor is close to it. If the LED needs 2V and draws about 0.03A to work properly, the circuit somehow needs to get rid of the extra 7V that come from the battery. Determining these values is what the next section is about.

The current along a closed loop is the same through all components. The voltage drop varies from component to component in the circuit.

Examining the Equations

This section describes the equations that govern the electrical phenomena that are introduced in this chapter. If math is generally a nightmare for you, do not worry; these are all pretty straightforward calculations.

Ohm's Law

Ohm's Law — the bread and butter of all things electric — describes the mathematical relationship among voltage, current, and resistance. Its name derives from the German physicist who discovered it in 1827: Georg Simon Ohm. The equation for Ohm's Law is

$$V = I \times R$$

The relationship is a simple one: The voltage drop on a resistive component is proportional to its resistance and the current flowing through it.

Suppose that you want to get a current of 2A through two different resistances: one with the value of 1 Ω and another with the value of 3 Ω. Because the second resistance has a higher value, it resists the current in a more significant way. Thus, you need more force to push the current through; you need a higher voltage. Here are the equations for those two situations:

$$2 \times 1 = 2V$$
$$2 \times 3 = 6V$$

Using algebra, you can rearrange the equation of Ohm's Law to obtain any value provided that you know the other two.

To know how much current will go through a resistance when you know the voltage drop, you use this equation:

$$I = V/R$$

To find out the resistance you need to get a specific value for voltage drop and current, use this equation:

$$R = V/I$$

To figure out the value of the resistor that would get rid of the extra 7V (9V from the voltage source minus 2V that the LED needs) from the earlier example, the equation is this:

$$R = 7/0.03 \approx 233\,\Omega$$

The equal sign with the wiggly dashes, $\approx$, means *approximately equal to.*

Power calculations

Power (P) is the amount of energy per second that your circuit consumes. It's calculated as follows:

$$P = V \times I$$

Naturally, you can rearrange this equation with algebra, leading to the following alternatives:

$$I = P/V$$
$$V = P/I$$

The power provided by a voltage source must always be used up in its entirety throughout the circuit. Mathematically, this means that for the circuit example, the power dissipated at the resistance plus the power dissipated at the LED equals the power supplied by the voltage source:

$$P_{source} = 9 \times 0.03 = 0.27W$$
$$P_{resistor} + P_{LED} = 7 \times 0.03 + 2 \times 0.03 = 0.27W$$

A voltage supply provides power; circuit components use it.

Joule's Law

A few years after Ohm came up with his law relating resistance, current, and voltage, the English physicist James Prescott Joule decided to relate Ohm's Law to the concept of power. Joule's Law was derived as

$V = I \times R$ (Ohm's Law)

and

$P = V \times I$ (calculating power)

Thus,

$P = I \times R \times I = I^2 \times R$ (Joule's Law)

Joule's Law can be rearranged as

$R = P/I^2$

By using any of the rearranged forms of Ohm's Law and the equation for power calculation, you can find out different relationships. In the end, though, the values must always be the same:

$I = V/R$ (Ohm's Law)

and

$P = V \times I$ (calculating power)

Thus,

$P = V \times V/R = V^2/R$ (Joule's Law)

which can be rearranged as

$R = V^2/P$

Units of measurement

In the world of electronics, you often deal with very small numbers, such as currents of 0.0001A, or resistances of very high values, such as 10000000Ω.

For convenience, these numbers can be shortened with prefixes, as shown in Table 5-1.

Table 5-1	Units of Measurement	
Prefix	*Symbol*	*Multiplier*
Tera	T	10^{12}
Giga	G	10^9
Mega	M	10^6
Kilo	K	10^3
Mili	M	10^{-3}
Micro	μ	10^{-6}
Nano	N	10^{-9}
Pico	P	10^{-12}

The two values used in this section's introduction could be written like so:

✔ 0.0001A = 100 μA

✔ 1000000 Ω = 1 MΩ

Working with Circuits

This section explains the different basic electrical components, as well as the rules and standards on how to represent them in an electric circuit.

Circuit diagrams

Circuit diagrams are collections of standardized symbols and sets of rules used throughout the world of electronics to represent electronic circuits. Figure 5-3, earlier in this chapter, shows an example of a circuit diagram. This section explains the symbols in the diagrams.

DC Voltage source/DC power supply/battery

The DC *voltage source* (which can also be called the DC power supply or battery) powers up your circuit, feeding it the current that it needs for operation. The required voltage depends on the application. An electric DC motor usually requires a larger amount of voltage than lighting an LED, for example. The symbol for the DC voltage source is shown in Figure 5-4.

Figure 5-4:
DC Voltage
source.

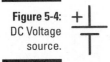

Resistor

The *resistor* is the most basic, most common electronic component of simple electronic circuits. It's there to control the voltage and current supplied to the components that use the energy to do something, such as lighting up. Figure 5-5 shows the symbol for a resistor.

Figure 5-5:
Resistor.

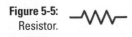

Diodes

Diodes are components used to force the current to flow in only one direction, which is why the circuit symbol displays an arrow, as shown on the left side of Figure 5-6. An LED is simply a diode that also happens to light up. The circuit symbols for the two are very similar except for the two arrows on an LED, as shown on the right side of Figure 5-6.

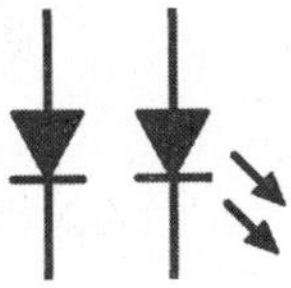

Figure 5-6:
The symbol
on the left is
for a diode.
On the
right is the
symbol for
an LED.

Unlike resistors, diodes have polarities, and the direction of current flow is always from the anode (+) pin to the cathode (–) pin. Therefore, the tip of the arrow is the (–) side of the diode. Figure 5-7 illustrates diode polarity on an LED.

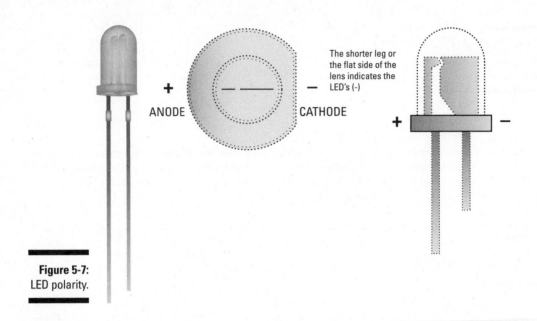

The shorter leg or the flat side of the lens indicates the LED's (-)

ANODE   CATHODE

Figure 5-7:
LED polarity.

If you slightly change the circuit in Figure 5-3 by flipping the LED around as shown in Figure 5-8, the circuit wouldn't work. The LED wouldn't light up because it would be blocking current flow. Remember that the current supplied by the battery goes from its (+) to its (–) pin. Be careful whenever you work with components that have polarities!

Figure 5-8:
A nonfunctioning circuit, with its LED orientation reversed.

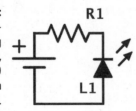

The alternative configuration shown in Figure 5-9 — in which the battery has been inverted — does work.

Nothing is wrong with the configuration in Figure 5-9 as far as science is concerned, but having the power source's (+) pin pointing upward has been known as a good practice for organization for a very long time. Generally, you want your circuit's current to go around in a clockwise fashion.

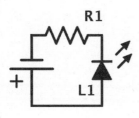

Switches

The example circuit has a somewhat significant issue: Unless you unplug the battery, the LED will always be lit until the battery discharges. A very simple, yet quite useful way to add control to your circuit is to use switches, as shown in Figure 5-10.

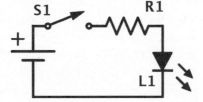

When you use a switch, you either make a metallic connection (enabling current to go through) or you break one. In the example circuit, the switch functions as an on/off switch.

When it comes to drawing a circuit diagram, the term *switch* refers to pushbuttons as well as actual switches.

Capacitors

We state earlier in this chapter that resistors are the most common components of electronic circuits. Capacitors run a close second. *Capacitors* are electronic components that can store energy electrostatically. The mathematics and possible applications of this capability go beyond the scope of this book, but because capacitors are such common components of circuits, we needed to at least expose you to its symbol, shown in Figure 5-11. It's just a matter of time until you meet a schematic that features this symbol.

Figure 5-11:
The two equivalent circuit symbols for a capacitor.

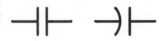

Capacitors come in two main types: ceramic and electrolytic (see Figure 5-12). An electrolytic capacitor exhibits polarity in the same way that diodes do. Generally, you want to connect the (+) pin to the side that current is coming from.

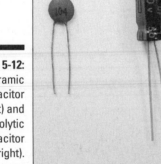

Figure 5-12:
Ceramic capacitor (left) and electrolytic capacitor (right).

To know which pin is the anode (+) and which pin is the cathode (–), you have two options:

- The (–) pin should always be the shorter leg. One of the legs may have been trimmed, however, so this feature isn't the most reliable determinant.
- The (–) pin is the one below the band white stripe as shown in Figure 5-13.

Figure 5-13:
The cathode (–) on an electrolytic capacitor.

The capacitance of a capacitor is measured in farads, and the most common values are on the order of μF (microfarads), nF (nanofarads), and pF (picofarads).

Integrated circuit (IC) chips

You can combine electrical components in a million ways to achieve different results. At their core, your calculator, your car, your computer, and your BeagleBone all boil down to the same thing: a great many transistors along with some resistors, capacitors, and whatever other basic components they need. In that sense, integrated circuit (IC) chips appeared on the scene to simplify matters. An integrated circuit is a fully functioning circuit inside a small plate of (normally) silicon. It can feature up to several billion transistors along with other components while being the size of your fingernail. Figure 5-14 shows just one example.

The black squares on your BeagleBone are IC chips. Each one is responsible for a different task on the board.

Color coding

Color coding is an important technique in building an electronic circuit, especially the further you progress in terms of complexity. As you may have noticed, wires come in different colors, albeit there is absolutely no difference among them in purely electric terms. The colors exist to help you with organizing your circuit, which is really, really handy if the wiring on it is abundant. Also, if you're working on a project with some other person, establishing a code can greatly help each of you understand what each person has done without much of a headache.

Transistors

The transistor is a tiny electric component featuring three pins rather than two. The voltage between a pair of these pins controls the current flowing through the other two. It's funny that this simple capability makes it the heart of all modern electronics.

The first computer created was the size of a football stadium. The development of the transistor made it possible to shrink computers to the size of your desk or even your palm.

To be honest, you most likely won't ever feature a transistor on the circuits you build, but that's because someone already did all the hard work for you. The BeagleBone is made up of billions of transistors. Even though you don't really need to know about the transistor to carry on using this book, we think it's important that you at least know what it is. The things we talk about in this book wouldn't even exist if not for the transistor.

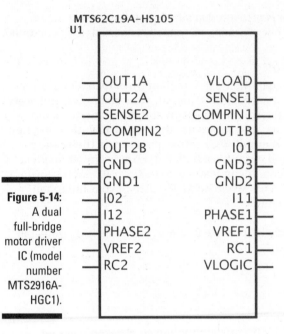

Figure 5-14:
A dual
full-bridge
motor driver
IC (model
number
MTS2916A-
HGC1).

You can use whatever color code you want. Following is a common standard:

- Red for positive power supply (+)
- Black/white for circuit ground (−)
- A different color for every part of your circuit

    You can call a part of a circuit whatever you want and organize accordingly. Here are a few examples:

    - All wires that come directly from a BeagleBone pin are blue; everything else (apart from the power supply) is green.

    - The wires that deal with the resistive network of the circuit are yellow, whereas those related to the left DC motor are green, and those related to the right DC motor are white.

    - The wires that come into the Bluetooth device are blue; those that come out of the device are green; all wires related to the LCD display are yellow.

For very simple circuits, this technique doesn't make much of a difference, but it's a good idea for you to start having it in mind. When you reach a higher degree of complexity, you'll be able to work with a procedure with which you're already comfortable. Organization, communication with a partner, and debugging become much simpler.

Resistor color charts

The resistance of a resistor is determined by the color bands that appear along it. The bands are read from left to right. What is left, though, and what is right? In Figure 5-15, the three bands on the right are separated by gaps of equal size, whereas the separation to the fourth band is larger. This arrangement means that you should flip your resistor. The order of the bands in Figure 5-15 is Red Red Red Gold — not Gold Red Red Red!

Figure 5-15:
A resistor.

The first two bands represent the numbers of the first two digits, whereas the third represents the number of zeros after those digits — its *multiplier*. The fourth band is the tolerance of this value.

Table 5-2 provides an explanation of the color codes.

Table 5-2		Resistor Color Chart	
Color	*Value*	*Multiplier*	*Tolerance*
Black	0	$\times 10^0$	–
Brown	1	$\times 10^1$	±1%
Red	2	$\times 10^2$	±2%
Orange	3	$\times 10^3$	–
Yellow	4	$\times 10^4$	±5%
Green	5	$\times 10^5$	±0.5%
Blue	6	$\times 10^6$	±0.25%
Violet	7	$\times 10^7$	±0.1%
Gray	8	$\times 10^8$	±0.05%
White	9	$\times 10^9$	–
Gold	-	$\times 10^{-1}$	±5%
Silver	-	$\times 10^{-2}$	±10%

In Figure 5-15, in which the code is Red Red Red Gold, the value is determined as follows:

$$2 \quad 2 \quad \times 10^2 \pm 5\% = 2200 \pm 5\% \; \Omega$$

The tolerance means that the value isn't precisely 2200 Ω, but somewhere between 2200 × (1+0.05) = 2310 Ω and 2200 × (1–0.05) = 2090 Ω.

Keep yourself organized! As you may have noticed, finding out the value of a resistor can be somewhat tedious. Keeping different resistors separated and labeled may save you some time. The same applies to other components, such as capacitors.

Because resistor values are based on a color code, naturally, it's hard to have every single resistance value available. If you use Ohm's Law for some application and realize you need a resistor value that doesn't exist, using the closest existing value shouldn't be an issue. If your calculations lead you to a resistance value of 233 Ω, a 220 Ω or 270 Ω resistor should be okay — the 270 Ω value is preferred to avoid feeding more current than you should; values other than these may not work for your circuit.

If you find yourself looking at a circuit diagram that needs a specific value for a resistor that you don't have at the moment, you have two options:

✔ Make a trip to your closest electronics store.

✔ Combine the resistors that you have handy.

If you have to exercise the option of combining resistors, you can connect them in two different ways so that their equivalent resistance, which is labeled Req, will either increase (series connection) or decrease (parallel connection), as shown in Figure 5-16 and Figure 5-17.

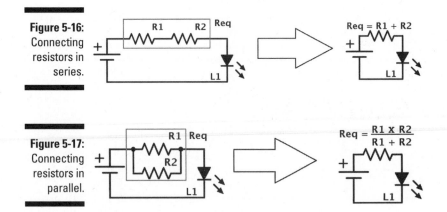

Figure 5-16: Connecting resistors in series.

Figure 5-17: Connecting resistors in parallel.

You can see these techniques at work in the following examples:

- ✔ **Series connection:** A 270 Ω resistor connected in series with a 220 Ω is *exactly the same* as if you'd used a single 490 Ω resistor.

- ✔ **Parallel connection:** A 1200 Ω resistor connected in parallel with a 800 Ω *is exactly the same* as if you'd used a single 720 Ω resistor.

Datasheets

A datasheet is basically — you guessed it! — a sheet containing data about a certain electrical component.

Datasheets are particularly useful when you use an IC because you don't need to know about the circuit inside it. Circuits for which you don't need to know what is going on inside is what electronic enthusiasts normally call a *black box.* You simply need to know what goes in (the input pins) and what comes out (the output pins), which you do by consulting its datasheet. Consider Figure 5-18.

Figure 5-18:
An ATMEGA
328P-PU IC
chip.

The simplest way to access a component's datasheet is to do an online search for something along the lines of *"ATMEGA328P-PU datasheet,"* where ATMEGA328P-PU is the model number. Some PDF files should be among the results of the search; open one to access a great deal of information about your chip.

A datasheet needs to be extremely detailed, featuring things like the circuit inside the IC chip and the highest level of humidity that the device can handle. Generally, you don't need to worry about these details unless you're working on some high-end, very specific project. Often, you need to be concerned only about the page that contains the *pinout:* the information about the IC's pins.

It's important to note that we've merely scratched the surface of the theory of circuit design. For a more detailed approach, feel free to consult *Electronics For Dummies,* by Gordon McComb and Earl Boysen (John Wiley & Sons, Inc.).

Chapter 6

Introducing Digital Electronics with the BeagleBone

In This Chapter

▶ Finding out about the tools of the trade for electronic projects

▶ Discovering several electrical components for your circuits

▶ Getting acquainted with the GPIO pins

▶ Controlling the BeagleBone's Output and Input pins by writing into and reading from files

▶ Figuring out what PWM is and how you can employ it using the BeagleBone

▶ Augmenting the BeagleBone's capabilities with capes

*T*his chapter is where working with the BeagleBone starts to get cool. If you've worked through the chapters consecutively, you understand how to use Linux and play around with the command-line prompt, and you have a grasp of the basics of electronics. For the remainder of this book, you use this combined knowledge to unlock the BeagleBone's full potential.

Besides the outstanding computational power that the BeagleBone offers, it also boasts many capabilities for interfacing with electrical devices and components. There are two sets of headers along its edges that host 46 pins each, allowing you to easily — yet awesomely — create electronics projects. All these pins apparently are the same, but they can be programmed to do a wide range of tasks. Reading from sensors, lighting up light-emitting diodes (LEDs), and wiring up motors are some of the possible applications. This chapter introduces you to the various tools necessary to start building electronic circuits; explains the general purpose input/output (GPIO) mode of the BeagleBone's pins; illustrates how to use these pins in GPIO mode; and explores the use of *capes,* which are plug-in boards that expand the BeagleBone's capabilities.

Looking for the Right Tools

This section describes the most important tools you need to start creating prototypes of your projects. After you have a diagram and the necessary components, you need to know how to connect the whole thing — easy to do with a breadboard, jumper wires, and a pair of needle-nose pliers.

Breadboards

Simply put, the breadboard (see Figure 6-1) is what allows you to create prototypes so that you can test and experiment with them without making permanent connections that you can't undo. With a breadboard, you can reuse the components of your circuit without any kind of setback.

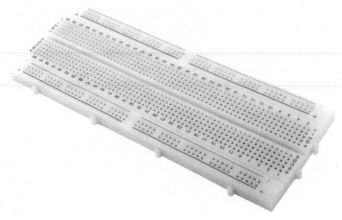

Figure 6-1:
Breadboard.

What makes the breadboard so special? Beneath all the holes in it are copper tracks (see Figure 6-2), which enable you to create metallic connections for current to pass through without committing to more permanent solutions (such as soldering).

There are many sizes and types of breadboards, but the concept is always the same: If you plug a wire into one of the holes in a breadboard, you connect the wire to a copper track that keeps all the holes in its row connected.

The copper tracks are normally covered by a plastic coating. If you're looking at a breadboard and can't see the copper, trust us when we say that it would look the same as Figure 6-2. Don't try removing the plastic coating to check it out for yourself!

Figure 6-2:
The copper
tracks of a
breadboard.

To better understand the connections within the board, refer to Figure 6-1. On the long sides of the board are two lines of holes separated from the central holes. On most boards, these holes are delimited by a red (+) and a blue (–) line, which suggests that you use them as a positive power source (+) and a negative power source (–), respectively. The copper tracks beneath those holes are *horizontal* and are broken at the center. If you connect the positive side of a 9V battery to one of those tracks, any electrical component leading to the same track will be fed with 9V.

Some breadboards don't have the red and blue lines, whereas others don't exhibit the break at the center of the horizontal lines, but their layout is still exactly the same as in Figure 6-1.

At the center of the breadboard are shorter lines in parallel with the short side of the board. The tracks there are *vertical* and are also broken at the center. For components with multiple legs, such as integrated circuits (IC) and pushbuttons, this trench in the center prevents the legs on one side from connecting to the other. (Some tiny breadboards have only the vertical copper tracks.)

In a sense, the horizontal and vertical lines are the same things — copper tracks — so you can connect things however you want, such as connecting the battery to a vertical line. Conventions exist for a reason, however; they're often guidelines to the easiest way to accomplish a task and also ways to keep you organized.

Thus, we advise you to follow this convention: Horizontal is for power and ground; vertical is for everything else.

Figure 6-3 shows how to connect a circuit on a breadboard by using a 9V battery, a pushbutton, a 470Ω resistor, and a light-emitting diode (LED).

Figure 6-3: A pushbutton circuit with an LED and a 9V battery.

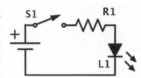

 Components in the world of electronics are very, very tiny. Using needle-nose pliers (see Figure 6-4) to plug your resistors, LEDs and ICs into your breadboard can save you lots of time and protect your sanity, since using human hands alone often becomes a headache — especially as the breadboard becomes clustered.

Figure 6-4: Needle-nose pliers.

 For a typical LED, 220Ω to 470Ω usually is good enough to protect the LED from burning up without reducing its brightness too much, even if different LEDs differ slightly in terms of necessary current and voltage. Naturally, you can also calculate the necessary resistor value for a LED using Ohm's Law (see Chapter 5), but there's no need to do so for most LEDs.

Jumper wires

Jumper wires (which are also known as *jump wires* or simply *jumpers)* are usually used with a breadboard because they're easy to plug into holes. These wires consist of copper, an insulator so that the electric signal is protected, and a connector. Figure 6-5 shows a collection of jumper wires.

Figure 6-5:
An assortment of jumper wires.

Depending on the type of connector on the ends of the wires, jumper wires can be female/female, female/male, or male/male. Male connectors are exposed, unshielded electrical terminals that can be easily inserted into a receptacle, such as the BeagleBone, the breadboard, or a female connector to ensure a robust electrical connection. Since you will be prototyping on a breadboard, for the remainder of this book only male-male jumper wires are necessary.

Jumper wires are definitely the easiest way to establish communication among your LEDs, sensors, resistors, and other electrical components and the BeagleBone. There's no need to cut, trim, or bend them; they're ready to use from the moment you get them!

There are several more tools used in circuit design, but there isn't space in this book to cover them all. The tools presented in this chapter are all that you need to start having some fun with the BeagleBone. You can read about several other tools that are useful for an electronics enthusiast at www. dummies.com/go/beaglebone/webextras.

Essential Components and Parts

Although thousands upon thousands of electrical components make up many projects, a few could be called essential because of the frequency at which they're employed in circuits. They're also good candidates for playing around with on the BeagleBone and learning how to properly use the board, and we recommend them that you get them as soon as possible. You can see plenty of them in Figure 6-6.

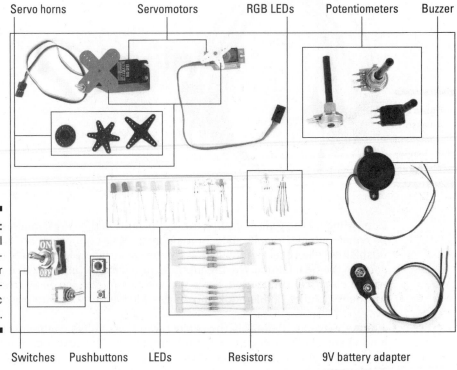

Servo horns   Servomotors   RGB LEDs   Potentiometers   Buzzer

Switches   Pushbuttons   LEDs   Resistors   9V battery adapter

Figure 6-6: Essential components for understanding basic electronics.

To get through the remainder of this book, you should have these components:

- ✔ **Resistors:** Resistors are extremely cheap, and you can buy lots of them at a time. The values you'll use the most are 220Ω , 470Ω, 1k Ω, and 10k Ω, but buying an assorted pack of plenty of resistor values is definitely the best idea.

- ✔ **LEDs:** Get a few of them, in various colors!

- ✔ **RGB LEDs:** These LEDs differ slightly from the previous ones due to the fact that their colors can vary.

✓ **Pushbuttons:** Pushbuttons are the best way to add controllability to your projects. You use them for when you want stuff to happen only when you press the button.

✓ **Switches:** Similarly to pushbuttons, switches are used to control a circuit's behavior. Unlike pushbuttons, the switch stays in the same position until you toggle it again, whereas you have to keep pressing a pushbutton to engage it.

✓ **Buzzers:** Buzzers are very simple electronic devices that output sound when a voltage is applied to them.

✓ **9V battery adapter:** For projects where you need to use a 9V battery, you require an adapter to connect the battery's poles to a breadboard.

✓ **Variable resistors (potentiometers):** We recommend that you get at least a 2K and a 10K potentiometer.

✓ **Servomotor:** Servomotors are usually tiny, slow-rotating motors that require a small amount of current to do their jobs, which makes them ideal to use with development boards such as the BeagleBone.

✓ **Servo horn:** Servo horns are small plastic components that are attached to your servomotor to suit different needs.

 Although you can use other kinds of motors with the BeagleBone, such as DC motors, they require external circuitry to amplify the low current that's drawn from the BeagleBone's pins.

 Most online electronics shops feature starter kits, which may be the easiest way to get launched into circuit design. Purchasing a starter kit usually ensures that you get a good deal, because buying all the components separately is more expensive. You can read more about starter kits in Chapter 18.

The components we have just talked about are essential to get started, and will be the basic building blocks of many of your circuits. This book features projects that use some more advanced components that are used for specific applications — we will tell you to get these when the time comes.

Getting to Know the GPIO

GPIO stands for *general purpose input/output,* which sums up what pins in this mode can do quite well: They can be either inputs or outputs for the vast majority of applications.

In the digital world of electronics, electricity happens in a binary way. In that sense, GPIO pins are either HIGH or LOW. In HIGH state, the pin is connected to 3.3 volts (V). In LOW state, the pin is connected to ground.

Saying that a pin is HIGH or LOW is equivalent to saying that it's on or off. In computer science, these two states are often called true and false or 1 and 0. You use these designations to control the GPIOs. HIGH and LOW, dear reader, sum up the world of digital electronics. Whatever you do in your computer is translated into a set of HIGH and LOW voltages along its hardware to carry out the task you requested. It's beautiful how such complex systems can be designed through such a simple concept. The following sections give you a glimpse of what you can do with just HIGH and LOW.

Understanding How GPIOs Work

In Chapter 4, we say that for the Linux operating system (OS), everything is a file. We weren't exaggerating with the term *everything:* files are also how you control the GPIOs: by reading from and writing into files in the BeagleBone's file system.

Chapters 7 through 11 show you how to control the GPIOs in a simpler yet more abstract way by using libraries for the BoneScript and Python programming languages. But it's important, useful, and insightful to understand how to control the GPIOs via a more direct approach: manipulating those files directly from the command-line prompt.

If you're acquainted with programming, you should know that you can control the GPIOs with any language that allows you to open, read, and write into files, such as C.

To work along with the examples in the following sections, make sure that you have the following items on hand:

- ✔ Breadboard
- ✔ Jumper wires
- ✔ 220 Ω or 470 Ω and 10K Ω resistors
- ✔ Pushbutton or toggle switch
- ✔ LEDs

Viewing the GPIO pins layout

Figure 6-7 shows the *default* GPIO pins. Besides those pins, the figure shows eight ground (GND) pins, two 3.3V pins, and four 5V pins; virtually, you can use these pins as power sources. Other pins labeled in the figure are useful in later chapters.

P9

GND	1	2	GND
3.3V (VDD)	3	4	3.3V (VDD)
5V (VDD)	5	6	5V (VDD)
5V (SYS)	7	8	5V (SYS)
	9	10	
GPIO 30	11	12	GPIO 60
GPIO 31	13	14	GPIO 40 (PWM)
GPIO 48	15	16	GPIO 51 (PWM)
GPIO 4	17	18	GPIO 5
	19	20	
GPIO 3 (PWM)	21	22	GPIO 2 (PWM)
GPIO 49	23	24	GPIO 15
GPIO 117	25	26	GPIO 14
GPIO 125	27	28	
	29	30	GPIO 122
	31	32	VDD_ADC
AIN4	33	34	GND_ADC
AIN6	35	36	AIN5
AIN2	37	38	AIN3
AIN0	39	40	AIN1
GPIO 20	41	42	GPIO 7 (PWM)
GND	43	44	GND
GND	45	46	GND

P8

GND	1	2	GND
	3	4	
	5	6	
GPIO 66	7	8	GPIO 67
GPIO 69	9	10	GPIO 68
GPIO 45	11	12	GPIO 44
GPIO 23 (PWM)	13	14	GPIO 26
GPIO 47	15	16	GPIO 46
GPIO 27	17	18	GPIO 65
GPIO 22 (PWM)	19	20	
	21	22	
	23	24	
	25	26	GPIO 61
	27	28	
	29	30	
	31	32	
	33	34	
	35	36	
	37	38	
	39	40	
	41	42	
	43	44	
	45	46	

Figure 6-7:
The layout of the GPIO pins on the BeagleBone.

The pins that aren't labeled in the figure are, by default, in a mode different from GPIO. Some of those pins can be put in GPIO mode, up to a total of 65 possible digital inputs and outputs. Doing so isn't really necessary, though, as there are already quite a lot of pins set in GPIO mode by default.

The BeagleBone's pins are rated at 3.3V, which means that connecting 5V to them could be extremely hazardous to your board — to the point of blowing up the processor and permanently ruining the board. You need to be extremely careful whenever you need 5V for some components in your circuit and make sure that 5V never reaches any of the BeagleBone's pins.

If you're curious about the complete capabilities of the expansive headers, visit `http://beagleboard.org/Support/bone101` for more information.

Setting GPIOs as Outputs

Often, the best way to get acquainted with a new working platform is to light up and turn off an LED on command. To do so, you set a GPIO as output; you want to control the state of a component.

Wiring the circuit for an LED

First, you set up the circuitry. Use the following steps to wire your circuit as shown in Figure 6-8. For the locations of the pins used in the following steps, refer to Figure 6-7.

1. **Turn off the BeagleBone.**

   Before plugging things into the BeagleBone, it's generally a good idea to shut it down (as described in Chapter 4) and remove the power source from it.

2. **Power up the breadboard.**

   Using a jumper wire, connect the BeagleBone's 3.3V source — pins 3 or 4 on header P9 — to the breadboard's positive track.

3. **Set up your ground.**

   Connect the BeagleBone's GND pin — for example, pins 1 and 2 on both headers — to the breadboard's negative track.

4. **Connect a GPIO pin to the board.**

   This example uses GPIO 40 — pin 14 on the P9 header. Use a jumper to connect it to a vertical row on your breadboard.

5. **Connect a resistor.**

   Without a resistor, an LED burns up easily. A 220 Ω or 470 Ω resistor should drop enough voltage without reducing the LED's brightness too much. Connect the resistor to the jumper you pulled from pin 14, effectively connecting the resistor to GPIO 40.

6. **Connect the LED.**

   Connect the LED's negative leg — the cathode, which is usually the shorter leg — to the breadboard's negative track where you connected ground in Step 3. Connect the positive leg — the anode — to the resistor.

The circuit you've just built is similar to the one used in Chapter 5 to explain the concepts of circuit design. There's one small difference, though: The power comes from GPIO 40 rather than a battery, which you turn on and off by writing into the command prompt.

Adafruit and Fritzing

Throughout this book, you see circuits similar to the one in Figure 6-8. They were drawn using Adafruit's Fritzing library. Fritzing is an open source software that makes it easy to draw circuits. Adafruit is a company that sells electronics kits and components. Adafruit is also well-known for creating learning guides and contributing to open source projects, and Adafruit designed the BeagleBone Black part for the Fritzing software.

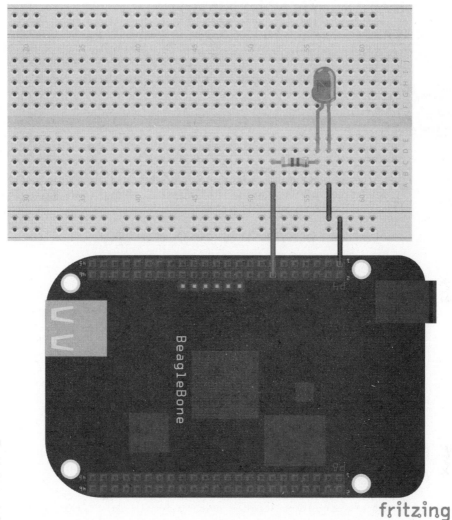

Figure 6-8:
Wiring up
an LED on a
breadboard.

In Step 2, you connect the BeagleBone's 3.3V pin to the breadboard. In reality, for this specific project, making that connection serves no purpose. It's generally good practice, however, to always have the horizontal tracks on your breadboard powered with a constant voltage and with a circuit ground. If you were to connect the resistor to the positive rail on your breadboard, the LED would light up, but you'd have no control over it. Feel free to try it out!

Controlling the GPIO

Because pin 14 is already a GPIO pin by default, you can set it as output. After you've done that, you can easily control whether you want the LED to be on or off by setting the pin to HIGH or LOW, respectively.

You need to be logged in as the root user to access the GPIOs. If you're currently logged in as debian, you can easily change to root as follows:

```
debian@beaglebone:~$ sudo su
```

On the command line, after connecting to your BeagleBone (using your preferred method, as described in Chapter 2), change to the gpio directory with the following command:

```
root@beaglebone:~# cd /sys/class/gpio
```

If you list the contents of this directory, you can see that gpio40 isn't there:

```
root@beaglebone:/sys/class/gpio# ls
export  gpiochip0  gpiochip32  gpiochip64  gpiochip96  unexport
```

You have to export it first by writing in the export file, which creates a folder containing files that can be altered to control the pin's state. On the command line, type the following:

```
root@beaglebone:/sys/class/gpio# echo 40 > export
root@beaglebone:/sys/class/gpio# ls
export  gpio40  gpiochip0  gpiochip32  gpiochip64  gpiochip96  unexport
```

To control the pin's state, change to the newly created gpio40 directory:

```
root@beaglebone:/sys/class/gpio# cd gpio40
root@beaglebone:/sys/class/gpio/gpio40# ls
active_LOW  direction  edge  power  subsystem  uevent  value
```

The *direction* file defines whether this GPIO pin functions as an input or output pin. Because you want to control its state by writing into it, your pin is supposed to be an output:

```
root@beaglebone:/sys/class/gpio/gpio40# echo out > direction
```

The *value* file holds the value of the GPIO: HIGH (1) or LOW (0). Thus, to turn the LED on, enter the following command:

```
root@beaglebone:/sys/class/gpio/gpio40# echo 1 > value
```

Now your LED should be on, as shown in Figure 6-9.

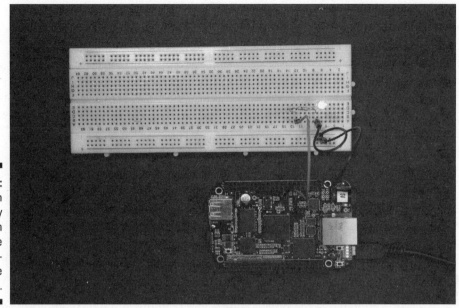

Figure 6-9:
You turn on the LED by typing in files in the Beagle-Bone's file system.

If the LED seems dim, try a lower resistance value. We recommend that you not go lower than 220Ω, though.

To turn it off, use the following command:

```
root@beaglebone:/sys/class/gpio/gpio40# echo 0 > value
```

When you're done with a pin, it's often a good idea to unexport it so that it becomes available for different purposes. You unexport the pin by writing into the unexport file. The following succession of commands unexports gpio40 and shows that its directory has been eliminated.

```
root@beaglebone:/sys/class/gpio/gpio40# cd ..
root@beaglebone:/sys/class/gpio# ls
export  gpio40  gpiochip0  gpiochip32  gpiochip64  gpiochip96  unexport
root@beaglebone:/sys/class/gpio# echo 40 > unexport
root@beaglebone:/sys/class/gpio# ls
export  gpiochip0  gpiochip32  gpiochip64  gpiochip96  unexport
```

If you're successful in controlling the LED, you may have just taken your first big step into digital electronics. Although lighting up an LED may not seem like much, the concept behind it is pretty much the same as controlling a motor, a buzzer, or an LCD screen!

Feel free to play around with the other GPIOs shown in Figure 6-7 earlier in this chapter.

Setting GPIOs as Inputs

The procedure for setting a GPIO pin as input is very similar to the technique in the "Setting GPIOs as outputs" section earlier in this chapter. The key difference is that you *read from* the `value` file rather than writing in it. To verify this difference, you need to build the circuit shown in Figure 6-9. Grab a pushbutton and follow these steps:

Wiring the circuit for a pushbutton

To wire up a pushbutton to the BeagleBone, follow these steps and refer to the diagram for the circuit in Figure 6-10. For the locations of the pins referred to in the following steps, refer to Figure 6-7 earlier in this chapter.

If you still have the circuit from the preceding example, you can skip Step 2.

1. **Turn off the BeagleBone.**

   Remove the power source and shut down the BeagleBoard through the command line, as described in Chapter 4.

2. **Power up the breadboard, and set up the ground.**

   Using jumper wires, you can connect pin 1 or 2 of either header to the negative track — these pins provide ground — and connect pin 3 or 4 of header P9 to the positive track — these provide 3.3V.

   The BeagleBone pins aren't 5V tolerant! Be careful to connect pin 3 or 4 of header P9, *not* pins 5, 6, 7, and 8.

3. **Connect a GPIO pin to the breadboard.**

   You can use any of the pins that are labeled as GPIOs. This example uses GPIO 45, which is pin 11 of header P8. Connect it to a vertical row on the breadboard through the use of a jumper.

4. **Place your pushbutton on the breadboard.**

   If you're using a pushbutton, you should place it at the center of the breadboard to separate the pairs of legs.

5. **Connect one of the pushbutton's legs to the positive rail.**

   Use a jumper to establish this connection.

6. **Connect the other leg to the input pin.**

   Connect it to the jumper that comes from the BeagleBone pin of the GPIO that you are using — pin 11 of header P8 in this example.

7. **Connect a pull-down resistor.**

A *pull-down resistor* is a resistor used to prevent the existence of a short circuit when the pushbutton is closed. Connect it from the ground track to the leg of the pushbutton that connects to the input pin. A 10K Ω resistor should do the job.

When the pushbutton is closed (which is the same as saying that the pushbutton is pressed), having a pull-down resistor makes the current — which follows the path of least resistance, according to Ohm's Law — go to the input pin rather than to the ground. Thus, there is a voltage reading at the input pin.

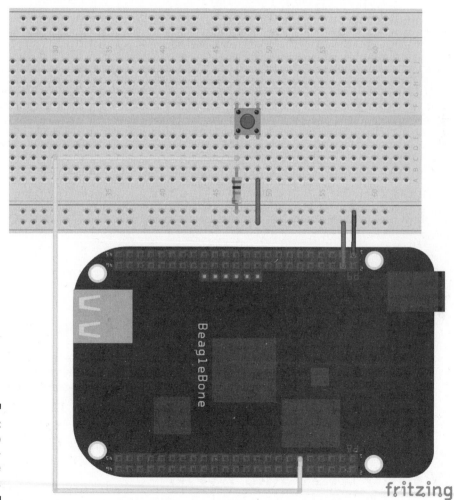

Figure 6-10: Wiring up a pushbutton on the breadboard.

Controlling the GPIO

When you're done with the circuitry, you can move on to the command line. Start by exporting the pin that you use as an input by typing the following commands:

```
root@beaglebone:/sys/class/gpio# echo 45 > export
root@beaglebone:/sys/class/gpio# ls
export  gpio45  gpiochip0  gpiochip32  gpiochip64  gpiochip96  unexport
```

Then set the pin as input by writing into the `direction` file:

```
root@beaglebone:/sys/class/gpio# cd gpio45
root@beaglebone:/sys/class/gpio/gpio45# echo in > direction
```

If the button isn't pressed, the 3.3V from the positive track of your breadboard has no way of reaching the GPIO pin, so if you read from the `value` file, you should get 0 because the pin is connected to ground:

```
root@beaglebone:/sys/class/gpio/gpio45# cat value
0
```

If you're pressing the button, however, the `value` file should hold 1, indicating that the pin is in the HIGH state:

```
root@beaglebone:/sys/class/gpio/gpio45# cat value
1
```

Unexport the pin when you're done:

```
root@beaglebone:/sys/class/gpio/gpio45# cd ..
root@beaglebone:/sys/class/gpio# echo 45 > unexport
root@beaglebone:/sys/class/gpio# ls
export  gpiochip0  gpiochip32  gpiochip64  gpiochip96  unexport
```

By itself, reading the state of a button (pressed or not pressed, HIGH or LOW) doesn't sound very exciting. Throughout this book, though, you use input pins to control outputs. You instruct your BeagleBone to read from a pin and then follow directions such as "If it's HIGH, do `<something>`; if it's LOW, do `<something else>`."

Setting GPIOs as PWM

Digital electronics are weird. How can everything be programmed with a fixed binary (HIGH and LOW) set of values? Suppose that you want to create a circuit to sound a buzzer. Are you stuck with either an ear-deafening sound or no sound at all? Is there no middle level?

Scientifically speaking, the answer is "Nope, no middle level." Your voltage output is always either 3.3V or 0V, and that's what you're stuck with. In reality, though, techniques are available that enable you to produce "fake" mid-level voltages. That's where pulse-width modulation (PWM) comes in.

PWM is a digital electronics technique that relies on the fact that instantaneity is a lie. There are no instantaneous phenomena in life — only very, very fast phenomena.

Practically speaking, if you alternate an LED's voltage between LOW (0V) and HIGH (3.3V) very, very fast, the human eye — which is a slower system than the rate of this change — won't be able to keep up with the speed at which the LED goes on and off. Instead, it sees some mid-level brightness.

The same applies to buzzers and servo motors: If you set the frequency at which the PWM changes from LOW to HIGH to very high, they won't be able to keep up with this rate of change. Because their speed/volume doesn't change instantaneously according to the voltage, they instead sound or rotate at a level somewhere in the middle.

PWM is a way to create a fake analog output from your BeagleBone. A good analogy to distinguish analog from digital is to think of lamps. A lamp that simply allows you to turn it on or off is a digital system; a lamp that features a brightness-selection dial is an analog system.

You have ways to produce real analog outputs from the BeagleBone, but doing so requires external components called digital-to-analog converters (DACs), which are seldom necessary except for specific applications. Analog inputs are often needed for projects, however, so the BeagleBone features internal analog-to-digital converters (ADCs), which we cover in Chapter 9.

Specifically, when you use PWM, you're doing several things (see Figure 6-11):

- ✔ Generating a square wave that changes between LOW and HIGH at a very high frequency. Its *period* — the time it takes until it repeats itself — is very short.

- ✔ Setting its duty cycle. The *duty cycle* is the fraction of the period at which the pin stays HIGH. A duty cycle of 50 percent results in an LED at 50 percent brightness.

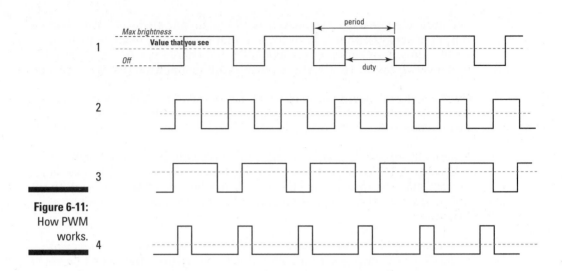

Figure 6-11:
How PWM
works.

Wiring the circuit for a brightness-regulated LED

To illustrate how you can set a GPIO as PWM, grab an LED, a resistor and a few jumpers, and build the same circuit shown in the section "Setting GPIOs as Outputs" and Figure 6-8 earlier in this chapter. The circuit is the same, but pin 14 on header P9 is configured quite differently.

Controlling the GPIO

On the command line, follow these steps:

1. **Activate** pwm:

```
root@beaglebone:~# echo am33xx_pwm > /sys/devices/bone_capemgr.9/
        slots
```

Your bone_capemgr.# directory may have a number different from 9. Check ahead by using ls, or simply press Tab after typing **bone** to auto-complete the directory name.

2. **Set** P9_14 **as** pwm:

```
root@beaglebone:~# echo bone_pwm_P9_14 > /sys/devices/bone_
        capemgr.9/slots
```

As in the earlier examples, you can access a directory with a couple of files that you can write in so you can control pin P9_14.

3. **Change to the /sys/devices/ocp.3/pwm_test_P9_14.15 directory and list it:**

```
root@beaglebone:~# cd /sys/devices/ocp.3/pwm_test_P9_14.15
root@beaglebone:/sys/devices/ocp.3/pwm_test_P9_14.15# ls
driver  duty  modalias  period  polarity  power  run  subsystem  uevent
```

The `ocp.#` folder may also have a different number, and `pwm_test_P9_14.15` may or may not have `.15`. Again, autocompletion is your friend: Simply press Tab after typing **ocp** and after typing **pwm**.

4. **Change the polarity to 0:**

```
echo 0 > polarity
```

Having the polarity set to 1 implies thinking in reverse. A higher duty cycle means lower voltage (brightness for the LED's case), which is why it's preferable to set it to 0. It's more intuitive: A higher duty cycle means higher voltage.

5. **Define the period in nanoseconds:**

```
echo 1000 > period
```

6. **Define the duty cycle in nanoseconds:**

```
echo 500 > duty
```

Play around with different periods/duty cycles to get the gist of using GPIOs as PWM! In the values used as examples, the LED should be at 50 percent brightness. Try changing the duty cycle to other values, and notice how the brightness of the LED changes:

```
echo 250 > duty
echo 100 > duty
echo 750 > duty
echo 900 > duty
```

The values of `period` and `duty` by themselves don't hold much meaning. What matters is the relative proportion of the `duty` toward the `period`. A period of 1,000 nanoseconds with a duty cycle of 500 nanoseconds would have the same brightness as a 2,000 period and 1,000 duty. The duty cycle is 50 percent of the period in both cases.

The PWM must always change between HIGH and LOW much faster than the system does. Thus, the value you set for `period` depends on the component you're using. Checking the component's datasheet can often help in this regard. If you can't find any information, though, you can always try different values until you get the right one.

Trying out PWM with a buzzer and a servomotor

You can experiment with PWM by using a servo motor and/or a buzzer if you have one handy. The wiring of the buzzer is very similar to that of the LED in Figure 6-8, but it doesn't require a resistor (see Figure 6-12).

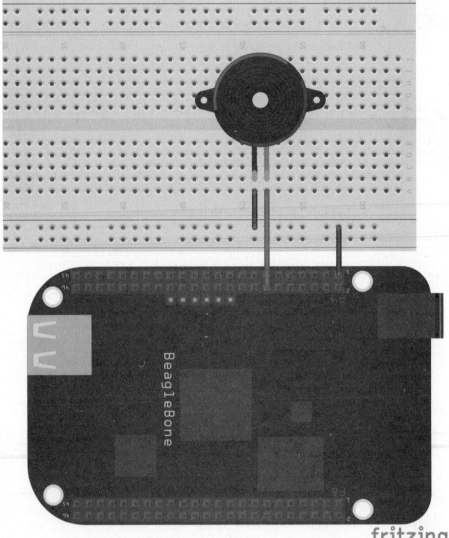

Figure 6-12:
Wiring a
buzzer to
control it
with PWM.

fritzing

The wiring of the servomotor is similar, but the servomotor has two wires that need to be connected to 3.3V (red) and ground (black), and the middle wire (usually yellow or orange) should be connected to the digital pin. You can use pin P9_3 or P9_4 as a constant 3.3V DC source. Figure 6-13 shows the circuit.

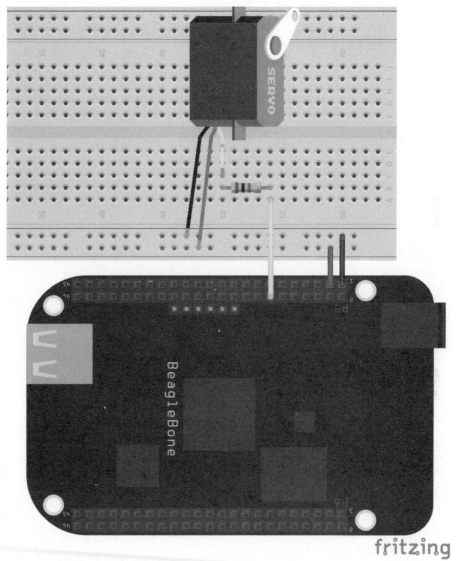

Figure 6-13: Wiring a servo to control it with PWM.

Play around with these three circuits by trying different `period` and `duty` values!

Creating shell scripts

A *shell script* is a way to memorize several lines of commands, in a sequential fashion, and use them whenever you please. Consider the example of lighting an LED. The full list of commands, from exporting to writing into the value of the GPIO, is as follows:

```
echo 40 > /sys/class/gpio/export
echo out > /sys/class/gpio/gpio40/direction
echo 1 > /sys/class/gpio/gpio40/value
```

You can simply put all these commands into a shell script that you can use for future reference. Using nano, create a .sh file as follows:

```
root@beaglebone:~# nano exportAndON.sh
```

To create a shell script, all you have to do is write the lines of commands, in the correct sequence, just as you did before. The first line should always be #!/bin/bash. Simply write this code in the nano text editor:

```
#!bin/bash
echo 40 > /sys/class/gpio/export
echo out > /sys/class/gpio/gpio40/direction
echo 1 > /sys/class/gpio/gpio40/value
```

Close nano by pressing Ctrl+X and then press Y to save. Your shell script is created! It isn't ready to use yet, however, because it doesn't have execute permission. You can change that situation with the chmod command:

```
root@beaglebone:~# chmod +x exportAndON.sh
```

Now you can go through the entire process of exporting gpio40, setting it as output, and turning it on by typing the following:

```
root@beaglebone:~# ./exportAndON.sh
```

The first line of a script is called a *shebang* and always starts as #!. If you don't include this line in the script, you can still run it by typing bash <scriptname.sh>. ./<scriptname.sh>, however, won't work.

You can create shell scripts for whatever you want. Feel free to experiment!

Adding Capes to the BeagleBone

Capes are plug-in boards that you can plug on top of the BeagleBone computer to add extended capabilities to it in a simple manner. Capes give you quick access to some easy-to-use systems such as LCD screens, GPS modules, and motor controllers. Some of these are introduced in this section; if you're interested in checking out the enormous list of capes, visit `http://elinux.org/Beagleboard:BeagleBone_Capes`.

Some capes aren't compatible with both the Original BeagleBone and the BeagleBone Black. Always check ahead or ask the manufacturer before making a purchase.

BeagleBone Proto Cape

The BeagleBone Proto Cape is a simple cape that fits atop your BeagleBone. It contains through-hold solder points and two 46-pin headers that connect directly to the BeagleBone. Its simplicity and accessibility make it a great workspace for creating prototypes after the breadboard phase.

Some Proto Capes, such as the ones from Tigal KG (see Figure 6-14), also exhibit extra useful circuitry such as LEDs and switches. Visit `https://www.tigal.com/product/2413` for more information.

Figure 6-14:
BeagleBone
Proto Cape
from Tigal.

Photo courtesy of Tigal

BeagleBone Power Cape

You can use the Power Cape to supply power in a flexible way. When the Power Cape is plugged in to your BeagleBone, if the BeagleBone isn't being fed by any other source (such as an USB cable), the Power Cape supplies the necessary power through its lithium battery. Conversely, if 4.5V or higher DC power is available from other sources, the lithium battery recharges, even if the BeagleBone is off.

The Power Cape provides two interesting features:

✔ An onboard power monitor (INA219), which allows you to monitor the voltage of the battery and the current it supplies.

✔ A scheduling feature that enables you to designate when to turn your BeagleBone on. You can schedule your BeagleBone to start feeding off the battery at a desired time, which may be interesting for automation projects.

You can visit `http://andicelabs.com/shop/andicelabs/beaglebone-power-cape/` for more information.

BeagleBone Motor Cape

Motor Capes make the whole deal of using motors much easier and straight-forward. Because the BeagleBone's GPIO pins can drive a current of only 6 milliamps (mA) maximum, they don't have the kick to get powerful motors running without some external help.

By using a Motor Cape, you can drive up to eight DC brush motors going at 500 mA per motor — quite the power-up!

The vendors of this cape sell it with NXT connectors or screw terminal blocks. The latter type usually are the easiest to work with in most standard electrical projects.

Visit `http://elinux.org/CircuitCo:BeagleBone_Motor_w/_Screw_Blocks` for more information.

BeagleBone mikroBUS Cape

The BeagleBone mikroBUS Cape (see Figure 6-15) is a plug-in board that enables you to connect up to four MikroElektronika Click Boards to the BeagleBone in the easiest way possible.

Photo courtesy of Tigal

Click Boards are tiny plug-and-play devices that require minimal settings. The idea is simple: Create small boards that have the same pinout standard, which allows boards with completely different functionalities to be connected in the same fashion. A microSD slot, an MP3 board, and a Bluetooth module are all connected in the same way, and all of them can easily fit on the BeagleBone mikroBUS cape.

Currently, more than 70 Click Boards are available, and the list keeps growing. Visit www.mikroe.com/mikrobus for more information on this new concept.

BeagleBone GPS/GPRS Cape

As its name suggests, this cape adds GPS (Global Positioning System) and GPRS (General Packet Radio Service) functionality to the BeagleBone, allowing you to track your position and use the GPRS for straightforward machine-to-machine (M2M) communication.

It's a good idea to buy an external antenna with this cape, because the board doesn't feature one. Visit the manufacturer's page at www.exploitsys.com/ENG/GPS_GPRS%20BB%20Cape.html for more information.

BeagleBone LCD Cape

Plenty of LCD capes are available for the BeagleBone. These caps sit nicely atop your board while adding touchscreen capability to it. Resolution varies from 480x272 pixels to 800x480 pixels. Figure 6-16 shows one such cape.

With this cape, you can interact directly with the BeagleBone through touch and through the buttons located in positions that enable easy use. The cape also feature expansion connectors so that you can easily access the GPIO that are still free after the cape has been plugged in.

Visit `https://www.tigal.com/product/4269` for more information.

Figure 6-16: BeagleBone Black 5.0 Display Cape from Chipsee.

Photo courtesy of Tigal

BeagleBone HD Camera Cape

RadiumBoard's HD Camera Cape provides an easy way to use your BeagleBone Black with a high-resolution mobile camera. This cape is divided into two parts: an expansion board that manages the data and a board with the necessary sensors for imaging and optics.

This cape isn't compatible with the Original BeagleBone!

If you're a camera enthusiast, a rundown of the cape's key features may be important for you. Visit the following link for the details: `http://elinux.org/Beagleboard:BeagleBone_HD_Camera_Cape`.

Part III
Programming with BoneScript

Visit www.dummies.com/go/beaglebone/webextras to read an article about using keyboard shortcuts with the Cloud9 IDE.

In this part . . .

- ✔ Launching the Cloud9 integrated development environment (IDE) for the first time

- ✔ Experimenting with BoneScript and writing your first script

- ✔ Understanding general programming concepts, such as variables, `if` statements, and `while` loops

- ✔ Playing around with a three-color LED, some buttons, and a motion sensor

Chapter 7

Introducing BoneScript

. . . .

In This Chapter

▶ Getting familiar with JavaScript, Node.js, and BoneScript

▶ Launching and exploring Cloud9 IDE

▶ Writing your first script from scratch with BoneScript

▶ Wiring an LED and a resistor and blinking more LEDs

. . . .

*O*ne of the coolest things that the BeagleBone enables you to do is watch the code you write become projects that interact with the real world. Chapter 6 gives you a glimpse of that world, but it really merely scratches the surface.

This chapter introduces BoneScript, a library containing functions specially created for the BeagleBone. This library greatly simplifies the process of configuring the pins of your BeagleBone; tasks such as blinking a light-emitting diode (LED), reading a button, controlling a servomotor, and reading a sensor are quite easy with BoneScript.

You get into programming just as you get the hang of riding a bike — by practicing — and that's exactly what this chapter helps you do. This chapter introduces new concepts with examples whose results you can promptly watch in the real world. We greatly encourage you to try them yourself and, after you feel confident, add a twist of your own.

Introducing JavaScript, Node.js, and BoneScript

JavaScript is a programming language that is most commonly used on websites. If you've ever visited a website with really cool things, such as interactive buttons, slideshow animations, alert messages, or pop-up windows, some sort of JavaScript certainly was working on the back end. JavaScript is used in web browsers, and it allows interactions with the clients without talking to the server.

JavaScript communication is done asynchronously. This means that data isn't transmitted at regular intervals, which makes it different than several communication protocols.

`Node.js` is a framework that allows applications written in JavaScript to run applications outside the web browser and interact directly with the server. BoneScript is a `Node.js` library that makes reading and controlling the GPIOs (general purpose inputs/outputs; see Chapter 6) of your BeagleBone a no-brainer.

One thing that makes JavaScript really powerful is the fact that unlike in other programming languages, your code won't wait to run each line sequentially. Some lines are skipped and then wait for an event such as a button press. For this reason, people often say that this language is much faster than usual. This language contrasts with Python, the other GPIO-controlling language covered in this book, in which all lines of code run one after another, each line waiting for the previous one to complete before doing its task.

Introducing Cloud9 IDE

The Cloud9 integrated development environment (IDE) is an open-source web-based programming platform that supports several programming languages. This great piece of software comes installed on your BeagleBone by default. Its greatest advantage is that the code you write on your desktop computer is immediately passed to your BeagleBone through the SSH (Secure Shell).

Cloud9 also comes with some features that make every programmer's life a little bit easier:

- ✔ **Code completion:** After you start typing a command, if you hover your mouse over what you've typed, you see suggestions for autocompleting your command.

- ✔ **Functions:** The code editor comes with search, a `goto` file, themes, and much more.

- ✔ **Drag-and-drop functionality:** It's easy to move folders and files within your workspace.

- ✔ **Programming:** Cloud9 supports several programming languages, such as JavaScript, Python, HTML, Ruby, and C.

- ✔ **SSH and FTP:** You can access your own server with SSH (the process is similar to the one described in Chapter 3, but done in a browser) and connect to your FTP server to edit your projects.

- ✔ **Collaborative:** Cloud9 enables you to work with other developers to edit the same code and chat in real time.

Visit the official Cloud9 IDE website at `https://c9.io` to find out more about this software.

Launching the Cloud9 IDE

Grab your BeagleBone and connect it to your computer through a Mini USB cable. After the board boots up, open your web browser, and type **192.168.7.2:3000** in the address bar. You see something similar to Figure 7-1 when the page loads.

You can also access the Cloud 9 IDE via Ethernet. Power up your BeagleBone, and connect an Ethernet cable from your BeagleBone to your router. Open your web browser, and type **beaglebone:3000**. You see a page that looks like the one shown in Figure 7-1.

If you've changed your hostname as discussed in Chapter 4, in your web browser's address bar, type *<yourhostname>*:**3000**.

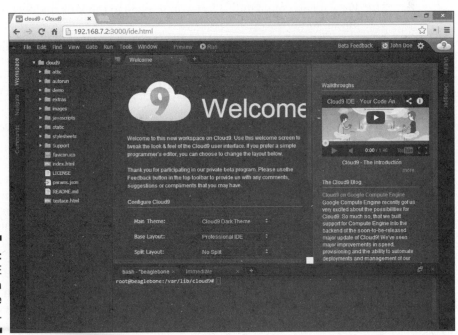

Figure 7-1: Cloud9 IDE running on a BeagleBone Black.

Exploring the Cloud9 IDE

When you open the Cloud9 IDE for the first time, you may feel intimidated. There are so many menus, submenus, options, and tabs!

To get started with your first project, you need to know about only a few of the windows of the Cloud9 IDE. The following sections give you a closer look at the six main areas of the Cloud9 IDE.

Menus tab

If you've ever used any computer application, you'll find that the menus in the Cloud9 IDE are organized in a very familiar way:

- ✔ **File** menu commands create, open, save, and close files.
- ✔ **Edit** menu commands give you the option to undo or redo a task, as well as cut, copy, paste, and edit your files. You can use the typical Ctrl or Cmd key shortcuts with these tools.
- ✔ **Find** menu commands make it easy to find or replace words in your code.
- ✔ **View** menu commands allow you to change the look and feel of your editor window.
- ✔ **Goto** menu commands provide fast ways to access the right file.
- ✔ **Run** menu commands are used to run and build your scripts.
- ✔ **Tools** menu commands are used to format your code, rename variables, and play macros.
- ✔ **Window** menu commands enable you to select the windows you want to open or close.

Workspace

You can access all your folders and files with the workspace window (see Figure 7-2). Just like in your computer's file system, everything is organized in a hierarchy. You can drag and drop to move files, and creating folders and files is quite easy.

Editor

The first time you open the Cloud9 IDE, the Preferences tab is open in the editor window (refer to Figure 7-1 earlier in this chapter). You can close that tab because by default, Cloud9 is preconfigured.

As soon as you open one of your scripts, the editor window looks like the one shown in "Creating a folder and .js file" later in this chapter. This window is where you write all your code. The editor highlights the functions according to the syntax of the programming of the file you have open, which is decided by its file extension.

Menus tab   Address bar   Editor

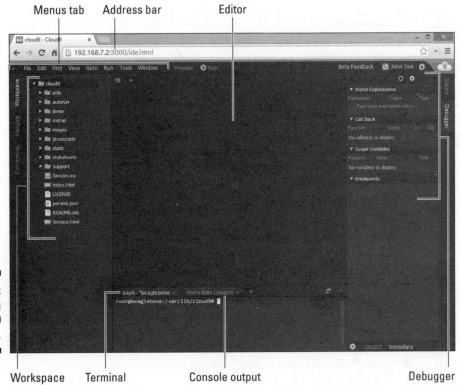

Figure 7-2:
Exploring
the Cloud9
IDE.

Workspace   Terminal   Console output   Debugger

Console

When you run a script, the console prints the output of your application (refer to Figure 7-2 earlier in this chapter). If you're running a web server, for example, the console tells you the URL of the page that is being served. You can also print messages — using the JavaScript function `console.log('<Your message>')`. Those messages are commonly used to debug your code.

Debugger

The debugger is the perfect way to see exactly what is happening when you run your scripts (refer to Figure 7-2 earlier in this chapter). You can create a breakpoint so that your code runs only to a certain line that you define. You can also see which functions your code is calling and which values are stored in your variables.

Terminal

Terminal allows you to run commands as described in Chapter 4 and Chapter 7. You can control your BeagleBone directly from the web browser, meaning that you can update or install new software, move files, and perform other commands. By default, you're logged in as `root`, so you have full access to all commands that can be performed on your board.

Be careful when you are logged in as root! As the administrator — or, as the Linux community usually calls it, superuser — you have the permissions to execute commands that would actually mess up the BeagleBone. Refer to Chapter 4 for more on the root user.

Creating a folder and .js file

With the Cloud9 IDE open, you can create a folder and file in your workspace. Follow these steps:

1. **Right-click the `cloud9` folder and choose New Folder from the short-cut menu.**

    A new folder is created inside the `cloud9` folder.

2. **Name the new folder `Projects`.**

    The new folder is named `Projects` because that's where all projects in future chapters will be stored. Naturally, you can name yours whatever you want.

3. **Right-click the `Projects` folder and choose New File from the short-cut menu.**

    This step creates a new file inside your `Projects` folder.

4. **Name your file `blink.js`.**

    Your file must end with the extension `.js` (JavaScript) because it will run a JavaScript script.

    The result should be similar to Figure 7-3.

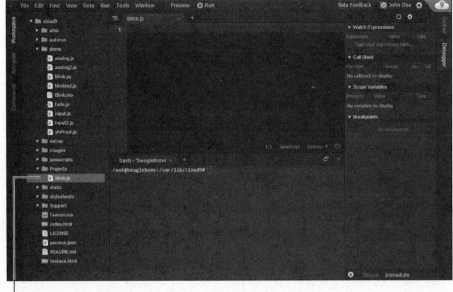

Figure 7-3:
Projects
folder and
a new file
called
blink.js.

The new file

Blinking an Onboard LED with BoneScript

This section shows you how to write your first script from scratch to blink an onboard LED. There's a popular saying in the digital electronics world: If you can blink an LED, you can do anything. It's true. The difference between controlling an LED to controlling, say, the outlet that controls your toaster is almost nonexistent. Don't underestimate this project just because it's a simple one.

If you followed the instructions in the preceding sections, at this moment you have your first folder and a `.js` file created.

When you get done with writing the program in this section, it will look like this:

```
/*
        Blink
        Turns an onboard LED on and off continuously,
        with intervals of 1 second.
*/
// Load BoneScript module
var b = require('bonescript');
```

```
// Create a variable called led, which refers to the onboard USR3 LED
var led = "USR3";
// Initialize the led as an OUTPUT
b.pinMode(led, b.OUTPUT);
// Create a variable called state, which stores the current state of the LED.
var state = b.LOW;
// Set the LED as LOW (off)
b.digitalWrite(led, state);
// Execute the toggle function every one second (1000 milliseconds)
setInterval(toggle, 1000);
// Function that turns the LED either HIGH (on) or LOW (off)
// depending on the parameter state.
function toggle() {
        if(state == b.LOW) state = b.HIGH; // if the LED is LOW (off), change
                the state to HIGH (on)
        else state = b.LOW; // otherwise, if the LED is HIGH (on), change the
                state to LOW (off)
        b.digitalWrite(led, state); // write the new state value to the led pin,
                turning the led on or off
}
```

This script has only a few lines of code, which you can divide, like so:

✔ Commenting

✔ Loading the BoneScript module

✔ Creating variables

✔ Configuring pins

✔ Setting the default pin state

✔ Setting an interval

✔ Creating a function

The following sections describe these groups of code in more detail. Follow along and write the snippets of code to your `blink.js` file.

Commenting

The script starts as follows:

```
/*
        Blink
        Turns an onboard LED on and off continuously,
        with intervals of 1 second.
*/
// Load BoneScript module
```

This group of code is a series of comments. Comments are plain English — or some other language — that explains how the code works. Anything designated as a comment is ignored and won't interfere with your code.

It's important that you use comments frequently so that other people who read your code understand what you're trying to do. Comments are also helpful for reminding yourself what your code did when you open the file a few months later. They're easily the leading tools for organization.

There are two types of comments:

- **Single-line:** The // symbol indicates that anything that follows in that line should be ignored.
- **Multiple-line:** Any text between the /* and */ symbols is a comment written across multiple lines. It's a good practice to start a script with multiple-line comments that include the script name, a brief explanation of what the code does, and some information about the author.

Loading the BoneScript module

Following is the first line of code that runs:

```
var b = require('bonescript');
```

You need to type this line every time you work with BoneScript because it loads the BoneScript module into your script in an object — called b in this case. An *object* is a combination of properties, and a *property* is an association between a name and a value. You control your BeagleBone by changing the values of the object you created.

Creating variables

The next line creates another variable:

```
// Create a variable called led, which refers to the onboard USR3 LED
var led = "USR3";
```

This line creates a variable called led to store the string "USR3" that refers to your onboard USR3 LED. A *string* is a collection of characters, words, and phrases, written between quotation marks.

JavaScript is case-sensitive. If you define led as your variable, you always need to type **led**, because LeD, LED, and Led are different.

Configuring pins

You need to initialize the LED as an output:

```
// Initialize the led as an OUTPUT
b.pinMode(led, b.OUTPUT);
```

To configure a pin to act as an output or input, you use the function pinMode(), which takes two parameters:

```
pinMode(<GPIO>, <mode>)
```

The two parameters are

- ✔ **GPIO:** The string of the pin you want to define — in this case, USR3, which is defined as led.

- ✔ **mode:** This argument sets the GPIO as an OUTPUT or as an INPUT. An LED is always an OUTPUT.

This function can take four more parameters — mux, pullup, slew, and callback — but they're optional, and we don't use them in the following examples.

Setting the default pin state

Create a variable called state, and set the default state to your LED:

```
// Create a variable called state, which stores the current state of the LED.
var state = b.LOW;
// Set the LED as LOW (off)
b.digitalWrite(led, state);
// Execute the toggle function every one second (1000 milliseconds)
```

You use the digitalWrite() function to write HIGH or LOW to your GPIO:

```
digitalWrite(<GPIO>, <value>, [callback])
```

This function takes three parameters:

- ✔ **GPIO:** Define the string of the pin you want to define. You want to change the `led` state.
- ✔ **value:** Set as `HIGH` or `LOW`. By default, you want the LED turned off.
- ✔ **callback:** Call a function upon completion. This parameter is optional, and even though you don't need it for this example, you use it frequently when programming in BoneScript.

Setting an interval

The following line is executed every second:

```
// Execute the toggle function every one second (1000 milliseconds)
setInterval(toggle, 1000);
```

To toggle the LED on and off every second, you use a function called `setInterval()`:

```
setInterval(<callback>, <milliseconds>)
```

The two parameters of this function are:

- ✔ **callback:** Calls a function upon completion. In this example, it executes the `toggle()` function.
- ✔ **milliseconds:** Sets the length of time between executions in milliseconds. In this case, the length of time is 1000 milliseconds (1 second).

Creating a function

This section is the most important part of your code, because it's when you create the `toggle()` function that turns your LED on or off:

```
function toggle() {
        if(state == b.LOW) state = b.HIGH; // if the LED is LOW (off), change
                the state to HIGH (on)
        else state = b.LOW; // otherwise, if the LED is HIGH (on), change the
                state to LOW (off)
        b.digitalWrite(led, state); // write the new state value to the led pin,
                turning the led on or off
}
```

Functions are great ways to organize your code. If you want to do something multiple times, instead of repeating your whole code several times, you create a separate function that you can call and execute any time. This is how you create a new function:

```
function toggle() {
// Your code goes here
}
```

Inside the curly braces, you can type what you want your code to do. In this example, you want to see whether the state variable is LOW, which means that the LED is off, so you change the state variable to HIGH. If the LED is HIGH, change state to LOW:

```
if(state == b.LOW) state = b.HIGH; // if the LED is LOW (off), change the state
                 to HIGH (on)
else state = b.LOW; // otherwise, if the LED is HIGH (on), change the state to
                 LOW (off)
```

When setting the value of a variable, you use a single equal sign, such as state = b.HIGH. When you want to check for the value of a variable, as in an if statement, you use two equal signs, as in if(state == b.LOW).

When you know the next state of your LED, you need to use the function digitalWrite() again to change the pin from LOW to HIGH or vice versa, according to the value stored in the state variable:

```
b.digitalWrite(led, state); // write the new state value to the led pin, turning
                 the led on or off
```

Running the script

Before you can run your script, you need to save it. Simply press Ctrl+S or Cmd+S and then click the green Run button at the top of the screen. You should see your USR3 LED blinking every second.

After your script has run for a while, you can stop your program by clicking the Stop button.

If you click the Run button and nothing happens to your board, you're probably running the script in debugger mode. To turn off debugger mode, click the little bug icon shown in Figure 7-4.

Run button

Figure 7-4:
Turning off
debugger
mode.

Debugger mode turned off

Blinking More LEDs with BoneScript

In this section, you see how to design a circuit to introduce a physical LED to the blinking on-board LEDs.

Grab your BeagleBone, a Mini USB cable, a computer, a breadboard, an LED, and a 220 Ω or 470 Ω resistor. That's everything you need for this section.

Wiring the circuit

Before you start wiring your circuit, make sure that your BeagleBone is disconnected from power.

Follow these steps to wire your circuit as shown in Figure 7-5:

1. **Connect the BeagleBone's ground (GND) pin (pins 1 and 2 on both headers) to the breadboard's negative track.**

2. **Use a jumper to connect a BeagleBone pin to a vertical row on your breadboard.**

   This example uses pin 14 on the P9 header.

3. **Connect a 220 Ω or 470 Ω resistor to the jumper you pulled from P9_14.**

   Without a resistor, an LED burns up easily. A 220 Ω or 470 Ω resistor should drop enough voltage without reducing the LED's brightness. If the LED is too dim, use a 220 Ω resistor rather than a 470 Ω resistor.

4. **Connect the LED's negative leg (the cathode, which is usually the shorter leg) to ground, and the positive leg (the anode) to the resistor.**

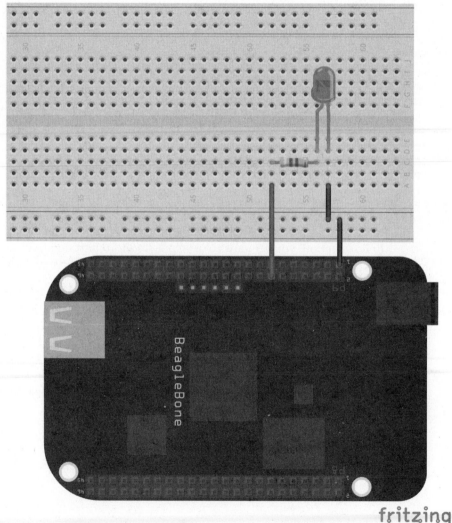

Figure 7-5:
Pin P9_14 attached to an LED and a resistor.

Opening the blinked.js demo

In this section, you don't write code, as there is a built-in demo that does just what you want. Follow these instructions to open the demo:

1. **Connect your BeagleBone to your computer with a Mini USB cable.**

2. **Type** 192.168.7.2:3000 **in the address bar.**

   This text loads the Cloud9 IDE.

3. **Click the folder demos in the workspace.**

4. **Double-click the** blinked.js **file.**

   The file opens, as shown in Figure 7-6.

This code is similar to the code in the "Blinking an onboard LED with BoneScript" section, but it adds a few more concepts, such as arrays and loops, which are covered in the following sections.

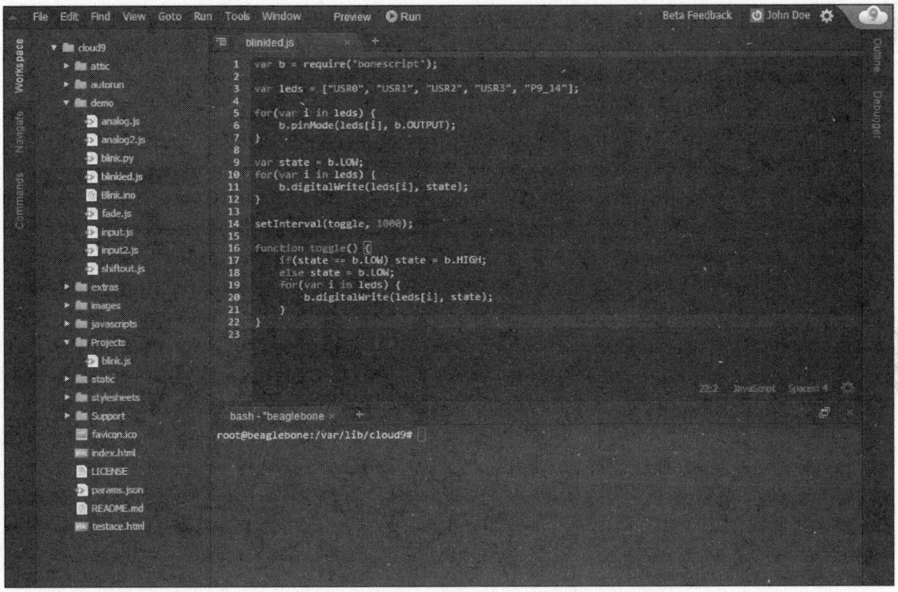

Figure 7-6: Cloud9 IDE with demo file blinked. js open.

Loading a module

When you're programming with BoneScript, the following is always your first line of code:

```
var b = require('bonescript');
```

Creating an array

With an array, you can store multiple values in a single variable:

```
var leds = ["USR0", "USR1", "USR2", "USR3", "P9_14"];
```

You could create five variables to store all those strings:

```
var led0 = "USR0";
var led1 = "USR1";
var led2 = "USR2";
var led3 = "USR3";
var led4 = "P9_14";
```

An array makes your code look nicer and your variables more accessible. They are also very useful to use in loops, which are covered in the next section. If you want to access the elements of your array, such as the "USR0" string, you need to type **leds[0]**. Here's how it works:

```
leds[<index>]
```

REMEMBER

The first element in an array is indexed as 0, the second element is stored in the index 1, and so on.

Creating a loop

You use a for loop when you have a snippet of code that you want to repeat several times:

```
for(var i in leds) {
    b.pinMode(leds[i], b.OUTPUT);
}
```

That for loop goes through all the LED pins — the ones stored in the leds array — and set them as outputs. You could take another approach by configuring the LEDs as outputs if you repeat the code five times:

```
b.pinMode(leds[0], b.OUTPUT);
b.pinMode(leds[1], b.OUTPUT);
b.pinMode(leds[2], b.OUTPUT);
b.pinMode(leds[3], b.OUTPUT);
b.pinMode(leds[4], b.OUTPUT);
```

As you can see, with a for loop, your code looks more organized and less repetitive. Using for loops may seem to add complexity, but imagine having to set up 30 outputs without using a loop.

Setting the default pin state

In this section, you set all pins to LOW as default. The following line creates a variable that stores the current state:

```
var state = b.LOW;
```

Then you use another `for` loop to go through all your five LEDs and turn them off with the `digitalWrite()` function:

```
for(var i in leds) {
    b.digitalWrite(leds[i], state);
}
```

Executing the toggle () function

Using a `setInterval()` function allows you to call the `toggle()` function every second:

```
setInterval(toggle, 1000);
```

The `toggle()` function does exactly what it does in the "Creating a function" section: blinks an onboard LED. But now you're using a `for` loop to change the state of all five LEDs to HIGH or LOW, according to the value stored in the `state` variable:

```
function toggle() {
    if(state == b.LOW) state = b.HIGH;
    else state = b.LOW;
    for(var i in leds) {
        b.digitalWrite(leds[i], state);
    }
}
```

Running the script

At this point, if you've completed all the preceding sections, you should have your circuit wired and a window with the `blinked.js` script open.

You don't need to save your script and delete comma because you haven't edited your code.

Simply click the Run button, and watch all four USR LEDs and the LED blinking at the same time (see Figure 7-7)!

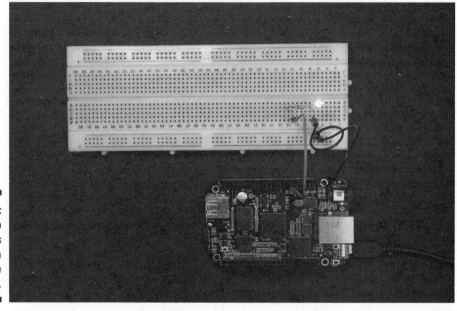

Figure 7-7:
Demo
blinked.js
running on a
BeagleBone
Black.

If your USR LEDs are blinking but the physical LED isn't, you may have wired something wrong. Placing the LED in reverse is quite often the problem. Reread the instructions to confirm that you set things up properly.

More on BoneScript

Chapter 8 covers more BoneScript projects, featuring different electrical components and more BoneScript functions, but if you want to take things even further, check the BoneScript Library page on the official website: `http://beagleboard.org/` `Support/BoneScript`. There, you can find more information about BoneScript functions and other project examples. You can also check Chapter 18 to discover more about this powerful programming language for the BeagleBone.

Chapter 8

Experimenting with BoneScript

In This Chapter

▶ Discovering how to interact with your circuits

▶ Adjusting the brightness of an RGB LED

▶ Moving a servomotor with a potentiometer

▶ Detecting whether someone entered your room

*T*he more you know about BoneScript, the easier it gets to see the endless possibilities for playing around with this programming language. This chapter shows you how to turn on a light by pressing a pushbutton, how to control a motor's rotation through the use of a potentiometer, and how to automatically turn on a light that warns you that someone has entered a room.

At first glance, all the projects in this chapter may seem straightforward and simple, just as most of the electronic devices you engage with are. For example, on a daily basis you encounter things that have buttons, knobs, and sensors that control some output. This chapter walks you through the most basic, yet most important, functions that BoneScript offers. Later, you'll be able to incorporate the building blocks presented in this chapter into your own unique projects.

The instructions in this chapter assume that you can connect your BeagleBone to your computer (see Chapter 3), you already know how to open the Cloud9 integrated development environment (IDE), and you can create a new file inside your Projects folder (see Chapter 7). There are also some BoneScript functions used in this chapter that are covered in Chapter 7, and you should read it if you need an explanation on them.

Reading an Input

In the BoneScript projects in the previous chapter of this book, you work only with outputs, defining a pin as an output and then running a script that set that pin to either HIGH or LOW. The result is a blinking light-emitting diode (LED). You make something happen in the world, which means that your pin works as an output.

At times, though, you want to interact with your circuit. Often, it's desirable for the BeagleBone to *read from* something that happened in the world, process that information, and then make something happen.

When we say that the BeagleBone is *reading from* something, it means that it is using an input to receive information such as sensor data or a button press.

The first step of that process is reading the state of a digital pin that's set as an input. In this example, you use a pushbutton to control whether a pin is HIGH (when the pushbutton is pressed) or LOW (when it isn't pressed) and then make the BeagleBone read that information and output the state of the button to a computer screen.

You need the following supplies to get started:

- A pushbutton
- A 10K Ω resistor
- A breadboard
- Jumper wires

Wiring a pushbutton

Figure 8-1 shows a circuit with a pushbutton and a resistor. Most pushbuttons are designed to be inserted right into the middle gap of the breadboard, just like the one in the schematic. This circuit is pretty easy to assemble.

If you have a pushbutton that's slightly different from the one used in this example, you must test its continuity with a multimeter. (You can read about using a multimeter at www.dummies.com/go/beaglebone/webextras. Test whether the pushbutton leads that you're using are connected when the pushbutton is pressed and disconnected when the pushbutton is released.

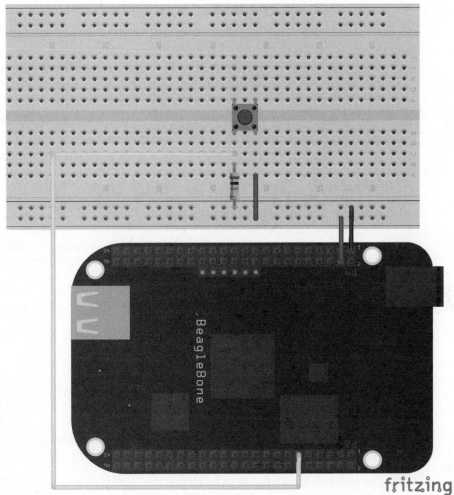

Figure 8-1:
Pushbutton
connected
to the
Beagle-
Bone's input
pin P8_11.

Follow these steps to wire your circuit:

1. **Connect the BeagleBone's ground (GND) — pin P9_1 or P9_2 — to the negative track of the breadboard.**

2. **Use a jumper to connect P8_11 to a vertical row on your breadboard.**

   This pin is the one you'll be using as an input.

3. **Connect the BeagleBone's 3.3V source — pin P9_3 or P9_4 — to the breadboard's positive track.**

4. **Connect the pushbutton.**

   Place it in the center of the board to ensure that each pair of legs is electrically separated.

5. **Using jumpers, connect one of the pushbutton's legs to the positive rail of the breadboard and the other leg to the jumper that comes from P8_11.**

6. **Connect a pull-down resistor between the other leg of the pushbutton and the negative track of the breadboard.**

Writing the code to read the state of a pushbutton

We encourage you to keep all your files inside the `Projects` folder so that everything is well organized. To get started with the code, create a new file called `readButton.js` in your `Projects` folder.

Write the following in your `readButton.js` script:

```
var b = require('bonescript');

var button = 'P8_11';

b.pinMode(button, b.INPUT);
b.digitalRead(button, printStatus);

function printStatus(x) {
    console.log('Button state = ' + x.value);
}
```

The first two lines of code start like all the examples presented in Chapter 7. You're loading the BoneScript module into your script and creating a variable called `button` that refers to P8_11.

On the third line of code, you set the button as an `INPUT` with the function `pinMode()`. Next comes a function that enables you to read the state of your digital pins:

```
digitalRead(<GPIO>, [callback])
```

This function takes two parameters:

✔ **GPIO:** This pin is the one for which you want to know the state. In this case, the pin is P8_11, which you define in the `button` variable.

✔ **callback:** This parameter, called upon completion, returns the button value — HIGH or LOW — stored in the `x.value` variable.

Callbacks are functions that you use frequently when working with JavaScript. In this example, as soon as the digitalRead() function completes its process, it executes the callback function printStatus(). The printStatus(x) function takes a single parameter, which is the returned value from the digitalRead() function, referred by the letter x in parentheses. In the case of digitalRead(), the value returned is either HIGH or LOW.

The last section of code prints on your console the state of your button, which is stored in the x.value variable:

```
function printStatus(x) {
    console.log('Button state = ' + x.value);
}
```

The console.log('<your message>') function is the easiest way to print something to the console. Note that you can print a message you write inside it, such as 'Button state = ', as well as the current value of a variable, such as x.value. You put the message and the variable together with a plus (+).

Apostrophes aren't used to print variable values. Typing **console.log('Button state = ' + 'x.value')**, with the x.value inside apostrophes, prints the line Button state = x.value rather than the actual value of the variable.

The console.log('<your message>') function gives the user some feedback on what's happening while the code is running. It's one of the best tools for debugging your code as you experience later in Chapter 11.

Running the script to read the state of a pushbutton

When you have all the code written, press Ctrl+S or Cmd+S to save it and then click the Run button or press F5 to execute your script.

Take a look at your console output. If you weren't pressing the button, the message Button state = 0 should have been printed.

Conversely, if you run the script again while pressing the button (see Figure 8-2), you see on your screen the line Button state = 1.

The terms HIGH and LOW refer to 1 and 0, respectively.

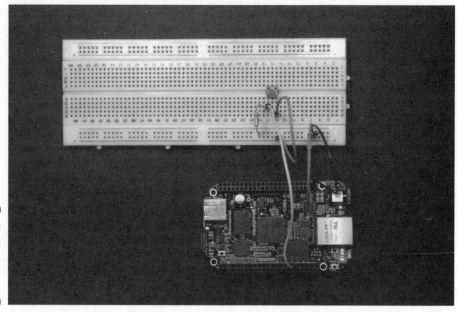

Figure 8-2:
Pushbutton
wired to a
BeagleBone
Black.

Controlling an LED with a Pushbutton

In this project, you find out how to control the state of an output depending on the state of an input — by turning an LED on and off when you press or release a pushbutton. This project also introduces the concept of interrupts.

Interrupts are clever ways to wait for something to change. With the `attachInterrupt()` function, you can create a function that waits for an input pin to change its state by going from LOW to HIGH or the reverse. When that happens, `attachInterrupt()` automatically detects that change and executes a function. This function is useful because it solves some timing issues. The alternative would be to create a script that waits for a button to change, which would be really difficult.

You need the following components:

- ✔ A pushbutton
- ✔ A 10K Ω resistor
- ✔ An LED
- ✔ A 220 Ω or 470 Ω resistor
- ✔ A breadboard
- ✔ Jumper wires

Wiring an LED and a pushbutton

This example is very straightforward to prepare if you've worked through examples in the previous chapter and in the "Reading an Input" section presented earlier in this chapter because you know how to wire an LED and a pushbutton. We won't go into much detail on how to wire this circuit; simply follow the circuit diagram shown in Figure 8-3. You can also follow the steps in the aforementioned sections.

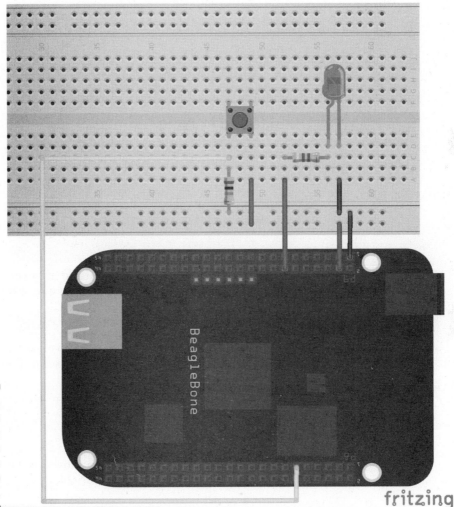

Figure 8-3:
An LED and a pushbutton wired to a BeagleBone Black.

Writing the code

When everything is wired up, power up your BeagleBone, and start coding the next script. Create a new file called buttonLED.js, and type the following code in it:

```
var b = require('bonescript');

var led = "P9_14";
var button = "P8_11";

b.pinMode(led, b.OUTPUT);
b.pinMode(button, b.INPUT);

var state = b.LOW;
b.digitalWrite(led, state);

b.attachInterrupt(button, true, b.CHANGE, toggle);

function toggle(x) {
    if (x.value == b.HIGH) {
        console.log("The button is HIGH");
        b.digitalWrite(led, b.HIGH);
    }
    else {
        console.log("The button is LOW");
        b.digitalWrite(led, b.LOW);
    }
}
```

The first portion of code is identical to what you've used in the previous examples in this chapter. This line is where the code gets interesting:

```
b.attachInterrupt(button, true, b.CHANGE, toggle);
```

You're going to use the attachInterrupt() function to create an interrupt that triggers the toggle() function when someone presses or releases the button:

```
attachInterrupt(<GPIO>, <handler>, <mode>, [callback])
```

This function takes up to four parameters:

✔ GPIO: This pin is the one for which you want to know the state. In this case, the pin is P8_11, defined in the button variable.

✔ **handler:** You can simply set this parameter as `true` so that it always calls the callback if an interrupt occurs. Alternatively, you can set it as a string that's evaluated and, if `true`, it executes the callback. In this example, you don't want to evaluate `handler`'s value; you want it to always be `true` because you want to execute the `toggle()` function every time an interrupt occurs. In fact, this parameter is `true` in most situations.

✔ **mode:** The three types of modes are `RISING`, `FALLING`, and `CHANGE`. In this example, you use `CHANGE` mode, because you want to toggle the LED when the button is pressed and when the button is released. You'd use `RISING` if you only wanted to check for the button's being pressed, whereas `FALLING` refers to the button's being released.

✔ **callback:** This parameter is called upon completion — that is, when a change occurs on the input pin — if the `handler` parameter is `true`.

All the magic happens in the `toggle()` function:

```
function toggle(x) {
    if (x.value == b.HIGH) {
        console.log("The button is HIGH");
        b.digitalWrite(led, b.HIGH);
    }
    else {
        console.log("The button is LOW");
        b.digitalWrite(led, b.LOW);
    }
}
```

When an interrupt occurs, it saves the current state in the `x.value` variable. So if `(x.value == b.HIGH)` — that is, if the button is pressed — you want to toggle the LED to `HIGH`. When another interrupt occurs — when you release the pushbutton — your LED toggles to `LOW`.

Running the script

Save your project and then click Run or press F5.

Your LED should stay on for as long as you hold down the pushbutton (see Figure 8-4), and it should turn off the moment you release the pushbutton.

If the LED is too dim, use a 220 Ω resistor rather than a 470 Ω resistor.

Knowing how to control output pins depending on the state of input pins is a very important asset and one of the most prominent building blocks of advanced electronics projects. Just as your pushbutton controls an LED, you could have an infrared sensor controlling an alarm that goes off whenever someone attempts to raid your fridge. In terms of wiring and coding, the situation is pretty much the same. You have a digital input — HIGH for "fridge door open" and LOW for "fridge door closed" — and a digital output in the form of the alarm.

Adjusting the Brightness with an RGB LED

Everyone loves LEDs. How much cooler could things get with an LED that has three colors and can combine them to create some color effects?

These little pieces of awesomeness are known as RGB (red-green-blue) LEDs. In this project, you find out how to control them by using pulse-width modulation (PWM) with BoneScript and by using interrupts. PWM is covered in more detail in Chapter 6.

The circuit you build in this section consists of an RGB LED whose color and brightness are controlled by pressing a pushbutton.

You need the following components:

- ✔ An RGB common cathode LED
- ✔ 4x 220 Ω or 470 Ω resistors
- ✔ A breadboard
- ✔ Jumper wires

Wiring the RGB LED

There are two types of RGB LEDs:

- ✔ **Common cathode:** The longest lead is connected to the ground pin. Then you connect the other leads to output pins. Except for the longest lead, all leads are associated with different colors; having a lead connected to a pin in the HIGH state lights its color. For leads connected to pins in the LOW state, those colors are off.

- ✔ **Common anode:** The longest lead is connected to the power pin. Then you connect the other leads to output pins, and things work in reverse: LOW values turn a color of the LED on, whereas HIGH turns that color off. If you use a common anode LED, you have to alter your code and wiring according to this reversal of what HIGH and LOW on each lead does.

In the preceding section, we say that you require an RGB common cathode LED. You can use a common anode LED, but keep in mind some things will be slightly different than what's described in this section.

You control the color of an RGB LED by deciding which leads are HIGH and which are LOW.

Follow these steps to wire everything together:

1. **Wire a pushbutton and a pull-down resistor to your breadboard.**

   Refer to Figure 8-1 earlier in this chapter to verify the wiring.

2. **Use a jumper to connect P9_14 to a vertical row on your breadboard.**

   This pin will control the red color of your RGB LED.

3. **Use a jumper to connect P9_16 to a vertical row on your breadboard.**

   This pin will control the green color of your RGB LED.

4. **Use a jumper to connect P8_13 to a vertical row on your breadboard.**

   This pin will control the blue color of your RGB LED.

   Use color coding to keep yourself organized. In this example, using jumper wires that are red for P9_14, green for P9_16, and blue for P8_13 probably would be a good idea.

5. **To each of these jumpers, wire a 200 Ω or 470 Ω resistor.**

6. **Wire the longer lead of your RGB LED to ground (GND) on the bread-board rail.**

7. **Check the schematic in Figure 8-5 to make sure that you have the wiring right.**

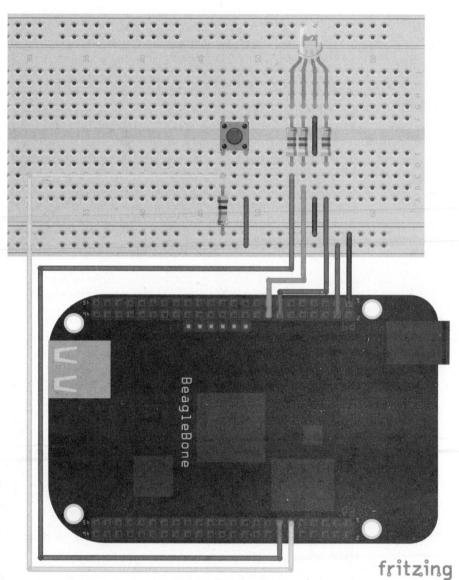

Figure 8-5:
RGB
wired to a
BeagleBone
Black

You can use eight pins use as PWM pins. Refer to Chapter 6 for more information.

Writing the code

Create a new file called RGB.js, and type the following script:

```
var b = require('bonescript');
var RGB = [ "P9_14", "P9_16", "P8_13"];
var button = "P8_11";
var RGB_lead=0;
var brightness=0;

for ( var i = 0; i < 3; i++ ) {
  b.pinMode(RGB[i], b.OUTPUT);
}

b.pinMode(button, b.INPUT);

b.attachInterrupt(button, true, b.RISING, bright);

function bright() {
    if(RGB_lead < 3) { // do this for each color defined by each of the RGB
            LED's leads.
        if(brightness < 1) { //brightness is increased until maximum
            brightness=brightness+0.25; // brightness is increased 25% at  a
            time.
            b.analogWrite(RGB[RGB_lead], brightness, 2000,
                console.log('Brighter')); // write the PWM values into the
                current RGB_lead
        }
        else { //when one of the colors reaches the maximum brightness
            brightness=0; // turn that color off
            b.analogWrite(RGB[RGB_lead], brightness, 2000, console.log('RGB
                lead off'));
            RGB_lead++;
        }
    }
    else { // when the program has gone through the three RGB LED's leads,
            start over
        RGB_lead=0;
    }
}
```

In the first lines of code, you load your BoneScript module, and you create some variables and an array:

```
var b = require('bonescript');
```

```
var RGB = [ "P9_14", "P9_16", "P8_13"];
var button = "P8_11";
var RGB_lead=0;
var brightness=0;
```

Then you configure all pins as outputs with a `for` loop. You also set a button as an input:

```
for ( var i = 0; i < 3; i++ ) {
   b.pinMode(RGB[i], b.OUTPUT);
}
b.pinMode(button, b.INPUT);
```

Next, you create an interrupt that executes every time you press the pushbutton. This interrupt is activated with a `RISING` edge and calls the `bright()` function:

```
b.attachInterrupt(button, true, b.RISING, bright);
```

The `bright()` function is the main character of this code. Spanning the entire function is an `if...else` statement that checks whether the code went through all the RGB LED leads:

```
if(RGB_lead < 3) {
           (...)
}
else {
           (...)
}
```

Inside that main `if`, the program has another `if` statement that checks whether the maximum brightness of 1 has been reached:

```
if(brightness < 1) {
           (...)
}
else {
           (...)
}
```

Before we get into more detail, you need to be aware of the function called `analogWrite()`:

```
analogWrite(<GPIO>, <value>, [freq], [callback])
```

The `analogWrite()` function takes four parameters:

✔ **GPIO:** This pin is the one to apply voltage. In this case, the pins are P9_14, P9_16, and P8_14, which you define in the RGB array.

✔ **value:** The duty cycle of the PWM can be any value between 0 and 1. This value defines the fraction of the duty cycle with regard to the PWM frequency, which in this case defines the LED's brightness.

✔ **freq:** The default frequency of the PWM is 2000 Hz.

✔ **callback:** Call this function upon completion.

See Chapter 6 for the theory behind PWM.

analogWrite() gives a GPIO some voltage between 0V and 3.3V (LOW and HIGH, respectively). In this circuit, it's the function that actually increases the brightness defined by each of the RGB LED's leads:

```
brightness=brightness+0.25;
b.analogWrite(RGB[RGB_lead], brightness, 2000, console.log('Brighter'));
```

The same function is used to turn an RGB LED lead off:

```
brightness=0;
b.analogWrite(RGB[RGB_lead], brightness, 2000, console.log('RGB lead off'));
```

Running the script

Don't forget to save your code before you run it by pressing Ctrl+S or Cmd+S. Then click the green Run button or press F5, and try out your project. When you press the pushbutton, you see the LED's brightness increase, and if you press it a couple of times, the LED goes through all the RGB LEDs colors.

If the LED is too dim, use 220 Ω resistors rather than 470 Ω resistors.

Note: If you press the pushbutton too quickly, brightness may increase by two levels.

You can use the PWM concepts in this project to dim the light on your desk or control a servomotor.

Sweeping a Servo with a Potentiometer

This project shows you how to read analog inputs with yet another extremely useful BoneScript function: analogRead(). As its name suggests, this function allows you to use input pins to read analog values. You also have the opportunity to practice PWM. By putting these two concepts together, you see how you can control the rotation of a servo with a potentiometer.

You need the following components:

- ✔ A servomotor that operates at 3.3V
- ✔ A 1K Ω resistor
- ✔ A 10K Ω potentiometer
- ✔ A breadboard
- ✔ Jumper wires

The next section introduces some important matters regarding analog inputs.

Analog inputs

As mentioned in Chapter 6, PWM produces a "fake" analog signal. In reality, this signal is just a digital signal that alternates between the values HIGH and LOW very quickly, making systems (such as the human eye when it comes to LEDs) perceive that things are working somewhere in the middle. Thus, the BeagleBone doesn't require DACs (digital-to-analog converters) because PWM does the trick just fine.

The real world is an analog world, not a digital one. Therefore, when it comes to reading information from the world, you find that inputs can have a varied range of values, such as temperature, humidity, and light levels or even the resistance of a potentiometer. Due to this fact, analog inputs are necessary, which ultimately led to the BeagleBone's featuring internal ADCs (analog-to-digital converters).

The BeagleBone has seven ADCs and their mission is simple: Read analog voltages between 0V and 1.8V and put them to scale (that is, convert them to values 0 to 1).

Wiring the test circuit

You can verify that an ADC is doing its job by using a very simple circuit and code. All you have to do is wire up a potentiometer (see Figure 8-6) as follows:

- ✔ One of the outer leads goes into GND.
- ✔ The middle lead goes into the P9_40 pin of the BeagleBone. You'll be using this pin for the ADC.
- ✔ The other outer lead goes into P_32. This pin is a 1.8 V source, which is the maximum value that the ADCs on the BeagleBone can handle.

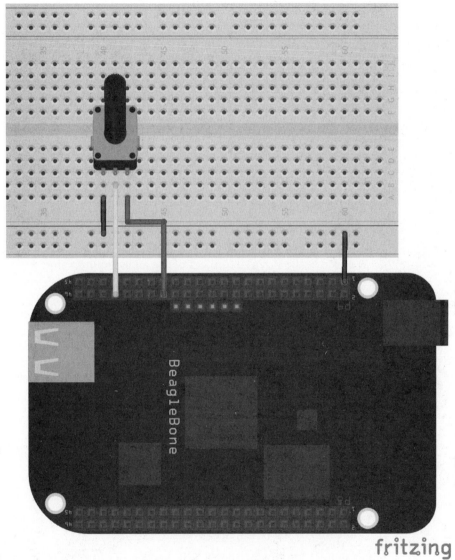

Figure 8-6:
Potentio-
meter
wired to a
BeagleBone
Black.

fritzing

Writing the test code

Create a new file called `potentiometer.js`, and type the following script:

```
var b = require('bonescript');

var pot = 'P9_40';

b.analogRead(pot, printADC);
```

```
function printADC(x) {
    console.log(x.value);
    b.analogRead(pot, printADC);
}
```

This code is quite straightforward. The first `analogRead()` function reads the value of pin P9_40 and then uses a callback to the `printADC()` function, which prints the value of the analog input pin and executes `analogRead()` again. The `analogRead()` function takes two parameters:

```
analogRead(<GPIO>, [callback])
```

The two parameters for the `analogRead()` function are the following:

- ✔ **GPIO:** This pin is the one you want to read the analog input value. In this case, the pin is P8_40, which you define in the `pot` variable.

- ✔ **callback:** Call this parameter upon completion. It returns a value stored in the `x.value` object of the analog input value.

Running the test script

When you run this script, you should see your console output filling with numbers, all of them below 1. As you rotate the knob on the potentiometer, these numbers vary between 0 and 1, depending on the voltage level at the input pin.

The values may never reach 0 or 1, but may be at some values very, very close to those.

Wiring everything together

To build your circuit and connect it to your BeagleBone, you use an analog input pin (see Figure 8-7). Follow these steps:

1. **Connect the BeagleBone's ground (GND) — pin P9_1 or P9_2 — to the negative track of the breadboard.**

2. **Connect the BeagleBone's 3.3V source — pin P9_3 or P9_4 — to the breadboard's positive track.**

3. **Connect the servo brown or black wire to the GND breadboard rail.**

4. **Connect the servo red wire to the 3.3V breadboard rail.**

5. **Place a 1K Ω resistor in your breadboard and then connect the servo orange or yellow wire to the resistor.**

6. **Connect the other lead of the 1K Ω resistor to the P9_14 pin in your BeagleBone.**

7. **Connect the left lead of your potentiometer to the GND breadboard rail.**

8. **Connect the middle lead of your potentiometer to the P9_40 pin in your BeagleBone.**

9. **Connect the right lead of your potentiometer to the P9_32 pin in your BeagleBone.**

Your ADC pins can handle a maximum 1.8V, which is why you connect the source lead of your potentiometer to pin P9_32.

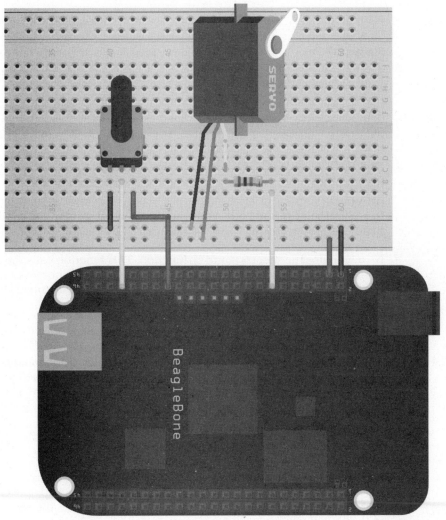

Figure 8-7:
Potentio-
meter
and servo
wired to a
BeagleBone
Black.

Writing the code to sweep a servo with a potentiometer

Create a new file called sweepingServo.js in your Projects folder, and type the following:

```
var b = require('bonescript');
var servo = 'P9_14';
var pot = 'P9_40';
var duty_min = 0.03;

b.pinMode(servo, b.OUTPUT);

b.analogRead(pot, updatePosition);

function updatePosition(x) {
    var position = x.value
    var duty_cycle = (position*0.115) + duty_min;
    b.analogWrite(servo, duty_cycle, 60, nextUpdate);
}

function nextUpdate() {
    b.analogRead(pot, updatePosition);
}
```

In the first five lines of code, you load the BoneScript module, create a few handy variables, and set the servo as an OUTPUT.

Next, you use the analogRead() function. This function calls the updatePosition() function, sending to it the current potentiometer position. This position is stored in the x.value object. As demonstrated in the following code snippet:

```
b.analogRead(pot, updatePosition);
```

Then you create a new variable to store the current position and adjust the duty_cycle. The values 0.115 and duty_min should be used to relate the position of the potentiometer to the duty_cycle of the PWM, and there is no need for you to worry about those. Simply use the following code:

```
var position = x.value
var duty_cycle = (position*0.115) + duty_min;
```

Finally, you move the servo to this new position and execute the nextUpdate() function to check again whether the potentiometer has moved. The code stays in that loop, keeps checking for new movements, and changes the servo according to the potentiometer position:

```
b.analogWrite(servo, duty_cycle, 60, nextUpdate);
```

Running the script to sweep a servo with a potentiometer

After saving and running your project, you should be able to see your servo moving according to the way you move the potentiometer (see Figure 8-8).

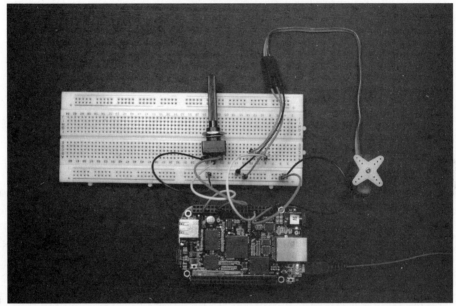

Figure 8-8:
Sweep your servo by rotating your potentio-meter.

You could use a similar approach to control a robot servo with a remote control, which works the same way. Most robots are moved by servomotors, and remote controls have joysticks with potentiometers. If building a robot is something that piques your interest, you're now a little bit closer to that goal!

Most servomotors can rotate only 180 degrees.

Detecting Movement with a Motion Sensor

Have you ever wondered why a light automatically turns on when you arrive in a building or when you enter a public restroom? In this example, you simulate that situation using a PIR (passive infrared) sensor and an LED.

You need the following components:

- A PIR motion sensor
- An LED
- A 220 Ω or 470 Ω resistor
- A breadboard
- Jumper wires

Wiring the motion sensor

You can start by wiring an LED and a 220 Ω or 470 Ω resistor to the same digital pins that you use throughout this chapter. (If the LED is too dim, use a 220 Ω resistor rather than a 470 Ω resistor.) Wire the PIR motion sensor (see Figure 8-9) as follows:

- **VCC:** Connect the sensor red wire to the breadboard rail and then connect the BeagleBone's P9_7 or P9_8 pin to it.

  This PIR motion sensor requires 5V to operate.

- **OUT:** Connect the output orange wire to the P8_19 pin.

- **GND:** Connect the sensor black wire to the GND breadboard rail.

Writing the code for motion detection

Create a new file called motionSensor.js in your Projects folder, and type the following script:

```
var b = require('bonescript');

var led = "P9_14";
var pir = "P8_19";

b.pinMode(led, b.OUTPUT);
b.pinMode(pir, b.INPUT);

b.digitalWrite(led, b.LOW);

setInterval (checkMotion, 2000);

function checkMotion() {
    b.digitalRead(pir, activate);
    function activate(x){
        if (x.value == b.HIGH) {
            b.digitalWrite(led, b.HIGH);
            console.log("Motion detected");
        }
```

```
        else {
            b.digitalWrite(led, b.LOW);
            console.log("No motion detected");
        }
    }
}
```

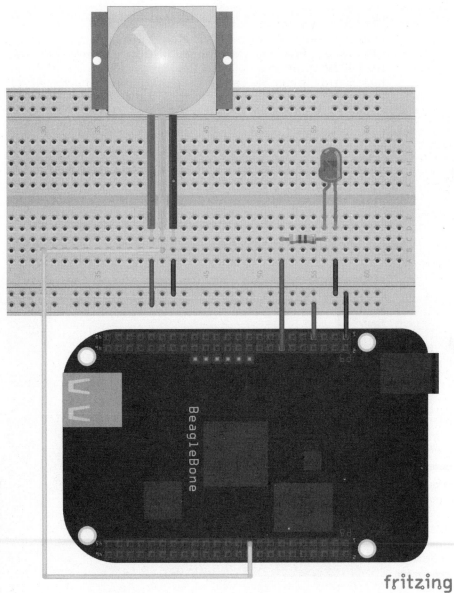

Figure 8-9:
PIR sensor
and LED
wired to a
BeagleBone
Black.

fritzing

As always, you start by loading the BoneScript module and defining variables. Set the pin P9_14, which refers to the LED as an OUTPUT, and set the PIR motion sensor as an INPUT, which refers to the PIR motion sensor's OUT pin.

Next, you use the digitalWrite() function to set the default LED state to LOW. Subsequently, you use the setInterval() function to execute the checkMotion() function every 2 seconds to look for any movement in front of your sensor.

The last step is creating a function called checkMotion(). That function starts by reading the digital value of the PIR motion sensor and then calls the activate() function, which works by checking whether the value read from the PIR INPUT pin is HIGH. If so, the function turns on the LED and prints a message to the console saying that motion has been detected. If the value read from the PIR INPUT pin is LOW, the function turns off the LED and tells the user that no motion was detected.

Running the script for motion detection

When you're running this code, you receive feedback in two ways:

✔ If no motion is detected, the LED remains off, and No motion detected is printed on your console (see Figure 8-10).

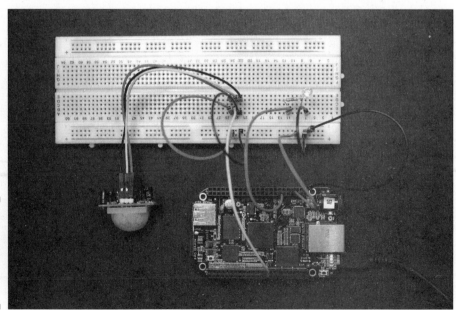

Figure 8-10: The motion sensor circuit with no motion detected.

✔ If motion is detected, the LED lights up, and `Motion detected` is printed on your console (see Figure 8-11).

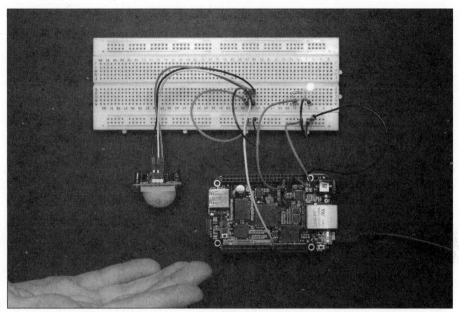

Figure 8-11:
Motion
detected!

Now you know how those automatic lights work and have even built one yourself. If you want the entire building to hear when someone raids your fridge or enters your room, all you have to do is replace the LED with a buzzer, which is wired exactly the same way.

Part IV
Programming with Python

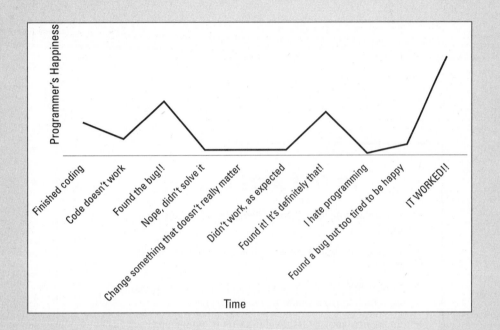

In this part . . .

- ✔ Experimenting with Python, covering the basics on outputs and inputs
- ✔ Finding out about Python's advanced functions for advanced projects
- ✔ Controlling a three-color LED, sending emails automatically, and reading from sensors and devices.
- ✔ Employing good practices for better programming

Chapter 9

Introducing Python

. . . .

In This Chapter

▶ Getting acquainted with Python

▶ Writing your first Python script to blink an LED

▶ Using Python to configure an input pin and test your code with a pushbutton

. . . .

*O*ne of the greatest features of the BeagleBone is the fact that you can program it in several programming languages. After all, the BeagleBone is an embedded Linux system that works just like a computer, with the added perks of input and output pins.

This chapter introduces Python, a powerful programming language that features a dedicated library to interface with the BeagleBone. Python code is easy to understand, and Adafruit's BeagleBone IO (input/output) Python Library that you use in this chapter offers a plethora of functions that enable you to control the BeagleBone's pins in a simple and intuitive way.

This library has conventions that are very similar to the Python library dedicated to Raspberry Pi, the popular RPi.GPIO. Thus, porting projects from one platform to the other should be quite straightforward.

Throughout this chapter, we greatly advise that you use the Cloud9 integrated development environment (IDE) to write the scripts for your projects and test them. Refer to Chapter 8 for more information on how to launch and use it.

Getting Started with Python

Before you get to the fun stuff, you need to be sure that your BeagleBone is set up properly. Installing the operating system is covered in Chapter 2; if you have not already worked through that chapter, go through it now to make sure your BeagleBone is ready to use Python to access its input and output pins.

This section shows you how you can verify whether Python is indeed ready to be used and how to make it ready if it isn't properly set up.

Making sure your libraries are up to date

Before proceeding, you should update and upgrade your software just to make sure you have the latest versions. Use the following command:

```
sudo apt-get update && sudo apt-get upgrade
```

You can test the installation of Adafruit's BeagleBone Input/Output (BBIO) library for Python by executing the following command:

```
sudo python -c "import Adafruit_BBIO.GPIO as GPIO; print GPIO"
```

If everything is working correctly, your console window should print the following line:

```
<module 'Adafruit_BBIO.GPIO' from '/usr/local/lib/python2.7/dist-packages/
          Adafruit_BBIO/GPIO.so'>
```

If so, you can skip the next section.

Comparing Python and BoneScript

If you read Chapters 8 and 9, you should feel relatively comfortable with programming in BoneScript. In many ways, Python and BoneScript are similar. In both languages, you use variables, as well as `if` and `while` statements, and you also control the BeagleBone's pins by changing the values of an object. But you need to be aware of some key differences:

- **The flow of code is different.** Python's interpreter runs each line sequentially. Two programs, one in BoneScript and another in Python, that do the same thing may end up being quite different To verify that difference, compare the section "Blinking an LED with Python" in this chapter with the "Blinking an onboard LED with BoneScript" section in Chapter 8.

- **Indentation is not just organization.** Although you should indent your code as much as possible when you program in BoneScript, indentation is merely a tool — albeit a powerful one — to keep your program organized. In fact, you could write an entire program in a single line of code. In Python, however, indentations tell the interpreter which parts of the code are inside statements such as `if` and `for`.

Installing the libraries

If executing the command in the preceding section results in errors, you need to install the libraries manually. Type the following command:

```
sudo apt-get install build-essential python-dev python-setuptools python-pip
                python-smbus -y
```

Things are always subject to change, and future versions of the Linux kernel may require different libraries, which could make this whole process different. You can bookmark the following link as a reference: `https://learn.adafruit.com/setting-up-io-python-library-on-beaglebone-black/installation-on-ubuntu`. Even though the title mentions Ubuntu, installation in Debian is pretty much the same.

Blinking an LED with Python

Often, it's said that blinking an LED is the foundation of digital electronics. Doing it isn't perceived as simply lighting up a tiny lamp; it's perceived as controlling an output. The gap from blinking an LED to controlling the motors of a quadcopter isn't a big one. Thus, this project helps you get acquainted with Python and Adafruit's BeagleBone IO Library.

Wiring the circuit for an LED

Always make sure that your BeagleBone is disconnected from power before you start wiring!

Follow these instructions to wire your circuit as shown in Figure 9-1:

1. **Connect the BeagleBone's ground (GND) — pins 1 and 2 on both headers — to the negative track of the breadboard.**

2. **Use a jumper to connect P9_14 to a vertical row on your breadboard.**

   This pin is the one you'll be using as an output.

3. **Connect a 220 Ω or 470 Ω resistor to the jumper you pulled from P9_14.**

   This step should ensure that your LED doesn't burn up without reducing its brightness. If the LED is too dim, use a 220 Ω resistor rather than a 470 Ω resistor.

4. **Connect the negative leg of the LED (the cathode, which is usually the shorter leg) to ground and the positive leg (the anode, usually the longer leg) to the resistor.**

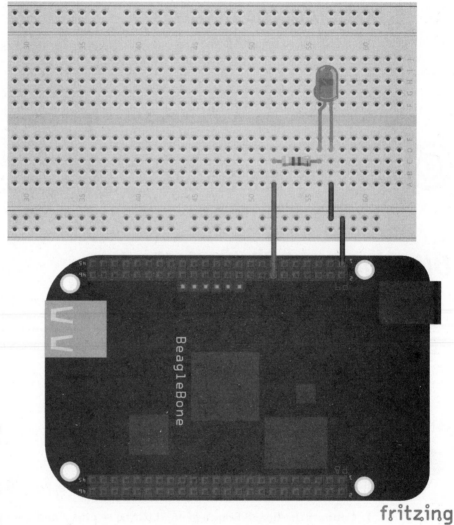

Figure 9-1:
Pin P9_14
attached to
an LED and
a resistor.

fritzing

Writing the code for an LED

Python scripts end with the extension .py, so start by creating a file named blink.py and type the following code:

```
#!/usr/bin/python

"""

        Blink
        Turns an onboard LED on and off continuously,
        with intervals of 1 second.
"""

#import libraries
import Adafruit_BBIO.GPIO as GPIO
import time

#create a variable called led, which refers to the P9_14 pin
led = "P9_14"

#initialize the pin as an OUTPUT
GPIO.setup(led, GPIO.OUT)

#loop forever
while True:
    GPIO.output(led, GPIO.HIGH) #set P9_14 high - turn it on
    time.sleep(1) #stay idle for 1 second
    GPIO.output(led, GPIO.LOW) #set P9_14 low - turn it off
    time.sleep(1) #stay idle for 1 second
```

This script can be divided into several parts, which the following sections cover in detail:

- ✔ Using a shebang
- ✔ Commenting
- ✔ Importing libraries
- ✔ Creating a variable
- ✔ Configuring pins
- ✔ Using a loop
- ✔ Setting the pin state

Using a shebang

A *shebang* is a character sequence starting with the number sign and an exclamation mark (#!). It's not explicitly necessary, but including it on Python scripts is often a good thing to do, so the blink.py file starts with the following line:

```
#!/usr/bin/python
```

We suggest that you use Cloud9 IDE to program the BeagleBone, but you can also run scripts from the command line. To run a Python script, you have to type the following command:

```
python script_name.py
```

However, if you include a shebang in your code, you only have to type:

```
./script_name.py
```

Commenting

Comments are notes that you can write in your script file that don't belong to the code. You include them to help you with organization. The blink.py file includes the following comments:

```
"""
        Blink
        Turns an onboard LED on and off continuously,
        with intervals of 1 second.
"""

#import libraries
```

Python has two types of comments:

- ✔ **Single-line:** A cardinal sign (#) indicates a comment, and the script ignores everything after it until the end of line.
- ✔ **Multiple-line:** Any text between two sets of triple quotation marks (" " ") is ignored, which allows you to use them to create comments that span multiple lines.

Importing libraries

To use the Adafruit library that's installed on your BeagleBone, you have to import it. This library allows you to control the pins of your board in a simple and intuitive way by defining an object. For this example, we call the object GPIO, but you can call it whatever you want. The following line of code imports that library:

```
import Adafruit_BBIO.GPIO as GPIO
```

You can also use Adafruit's library to use pins for uses other than GPIO (general purpose input/output), such as PWM (pulse-width modulation) and analog inputs, in which case you'd import it as

```
import Adafruit_BBIO.PWM as <object_name>
```

or

```
import Adafruit_BBIO.ADC as <object name>
```

The `time` library is a useful library that, as its name implies, provides functions that deal with time. In this project, you use it so you can use the `sleep` function, which halts the program for a set amount of seconds. This is how you import it:

```
import time
```

Creating a variable

Whenever you want to save a value in a variable, simply write the variable's name and make it equal to the value you want to save. In this example, you save the string `"P9_14"` in the `led` variable:

```
#create a variable called led, which refers to the onboard P9_14 LED
led = "P9_14"
```

Configuring pins

In this section, you need to define the pin's job. In this case, you want to control an LED, so you define it as an output:

```
#initialize the LED as an OUTPUT
GPIO.setup(led, GPIO.OUT)
```

For GPIO, the setup function has always two parameters in the following syntax:

```
setup(GPIO, mode)
```

The two parameters are:

- ✔ **GPIO:** The pin you want to control — in this case, `P9_14`, defined in the `led` variable
- ✔ **mode:** `OUT` or `IN`, depending on whether you want to use the pin as an output or input, respectively

The functions that control the pins of the BeagleBone must always be used with the object you defined preceding them!

Using a loop

The `while` loop can be used as follows:

```
while condition:
        <indented code>
```

When you use a `while` loop, the code that's indented below it repeats itself as long as the `while` condition is met — in other words, as long as the condition evaluates as `True`. A condition can be anything. A system controlling a parking lot's gate could be coded like so:

```
while number_of_cars == maximum:
        keep_gate_closed()
```

In the preceding example, assume that `number_of_cars` is a variable that changes according to the current number of cars inside the parking lot. `maximum` is a variable that has a fixed value containing the number of parking spots. `keep_gate_closed()` is a function that does exactly what its name suggests. The chapters in the remainder of this book use variables and functions such as these whose names intuitively suggest their tasks.

The `while` loop in this example continues forever because the condition is defined to be always evaluated as `True`:

```
while True:
     GPIO.output(led, GPIO.HIGH) #set P9_14 high - turn it on
     time.sleep(1) #stay idle for 1 second
     GPIO.output(led, GPIO.LOW) #set P9_14 low - turn it off
     time.sleep(1) #stay idle for 1 second
```

In most programming languages, such as BoneScript, indentation is a great way to make sure that your code is well organized and tidy, but your program still works even if you don't indent any lines of code. In Python, however, your program doesn't work correctly if you don't get the indentation right. For statements such as `while`, the Python interpreter knows what part of the code is included in the statement only by checking the indentation. You can use one or more spaces and tabs, but make sure to maintain consistency throughout the code.

Contrary to JavaScript — and, thus, to BoneScript — Python's code is evaluated from the top of the script in a sequential fashion, one line at a time. That's the reason why a thing such as a loop can exist in this programming language. When the Python interpreter reaches the `while` statement, it knows that the lines indented below it have to run for as long as the condition holds `True`.

Setting the pin state

You use the `output()` function to define whether a pin is `HIGH` or `LOW`. This function is defined as follows:

```
output(GPIO, state)
```

This function has two parameters:

- ✔ **GPIO:** The pin you want to control — in this case, P9_14, defined in the led variable
- ✔ **state:** HIGH or LOW, depending on the state you want the pin to have

In this case, you set the pin's state to HIGH for 1 second and then to LOW for 1 second, and repeat this process indefinitely. You achieve this process by using the time.sleep(seconds) function, which halts the problem for the defined number of seconds (1 second in this case):

```
GPIO.output(led, GPIO.HIGH) #set P9_14 high - turn it on
time.sleep(1) #stay idle for 1 second
GPIO.output(led, GPIO.LOW) #set P9_14 low - turn it off
time.sleep(1) #stay idle for 1 second
```

Running the script for blinking an LED

To see the project working, simply save the script by pressing Ctrl+S or Cmd+S and then click the green Run button. To terminate the program, click Stop or press Ctrl+C.

You should see your LED blinking, such as the one shown in Figure 9-2.

Figure 9-2:
Circuit that blinks an LED controlled by Python code.

Reading a Pushbutton with Python

Digital inputs are just as important as digital outputs. Buttons and sensors that control the outputs of a circuit are the basis of some really great projects.

Wiring the circuit for a pushbutton

Always make sure that your BeagleBone is disconnected from power before you start wiring!

To wire a pushbutton to a BeagleBone, follow these steps:

1. **Connect the BeagleBone's (GND) — pins 1 and 2 on both headers — to the negative track of the breadboard.**

2. **Use a jumper to connect P8_11 to a vertical row on your breadboard.**

   This pin is the one you'll be using as an input.

3. **Connect the BeagleBone's 3.3V source — P9_3 or P9_4 — to the breadboard's positive track.**

   If you are powering your BeagleBone through an external source, the P_5 and P_6 pins of the BeagleBone supply a 5-volt (V) source; if you are powering it through an USB cable, the pins providing 5 V are P9_7 and P9_8. Regardless, you should avoid using any of those four pins as a small mistake might permanently damage your BeagleBone.

4. **Connect the pushbutton.**

   Place the pushbutton at the center of the board to ensure that each pair of legs is electrically separated. Through the use of jumpers, connect one of its legs to the positive rail of the breadboard and the other leg to the jumper that comes from P8_11.

5. **Connect a pull-down resistor between the other leg of the pushbutton and the negative track of the breadboard.**

   Your circuit should look similar to Figure 9-3.

Writing the code and running the script for a pushbutton

After wiring the circuit, create a file named button.py and type the following code:

```
#!/usr/bin/python

#import libraries
import Adafruit_BBIO.GPIO as GPIO
import time

button = "P8_11" create a variable called button, which refers to the P8_11 pin

#initialize the pin as an INPUT
GPIO.setup(button, GPIO.IN) # Initialize P8_11 as an input

#loop forever
while True:
    if GPIO.input(button)  == True: # Checks if the pin is HIGH
        print("HIGH")
    time.sleep(0.01) # In order to not overburden the CPU
```

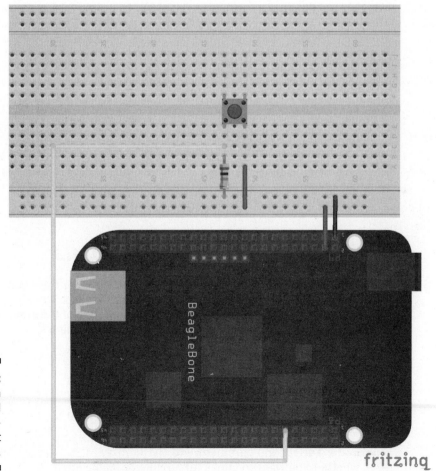

Figure 9-3:
Pushbutton
connected
to Beagle-
Bone's input
pin P8_11.

The terms `HIGH` and `LOW`, `True` and `False`, and `1` and `0` always refer to the same thing, but their use depends on the context.

This code uses concepts from the "Writing the code for an LED" section. It involves two new concepts, however: the `if` statement and the `print()` function. The `print()` function is quite simple and intuitive; the message that makes up its argument is printed on the console. The `if` statement should be read as follows: "If this condition is met, run the indented code below the statement."

Additionally, you use `GPIO.input(GPIO)`, which is a variable that holds the value of the pin — HIGH for when the button is pressed, and LOW for when it isn't.

Test your circuit by clicking Run and then pressing the pushbutton a few times. Whenever you press it, the message `HIGH` should be printed on the console, most likely more than once. It prints several times because the script works as follows: In every cycle of the `while` loop, the script checks whether pin P8_11 is HIGH. If it is, the message prints. Because every cycle of this loop executes extremely fast, the program always reads the value HIGH from P8_11 and prints it several times in less than a second. Even if you're really quick with pressing the button, in reality you are actually very slow from the BeagleBone's point of view, so the board always equates one fast press of the pushbutton as the pushbutton being held down for a while.

This kind of thing can be troublesome. Imagine if your mouse registered multiple clicks when you clicked it only once! Thus, buttons are often used with interrupts. Rather than checking whether the pin is HIGH or LOW, the code checks whether the pin just went from HIGH to LOW (a *falling edge*) or from LOW to HIGH (a *rising edge*). Pressing a button generates a rising edge, whereas releasing it generates a falling edge. Those things happen only once per button press or release.

Writing the code with interrupts

To check for rising and falling edges rather than whether the input pin is HIGH or LOW, the Adafruit library offers the function `wait_for_edge(pin, desired edge)`. When the program reaches that line of the code, the program blocks until the interrupt happens. It is used as follows:

```
wait_for_edge(GPIO, mode)
```

That function takes these parameters:

- ✔ **GPIO:** The first parameter is the input pin you want to check for a rising or falling edge.
- ✔ **mode:** The second parameter is `RISING` or `FALLING`, depending on whether you want to check for a rising or falling edge.

Test your circuit with the following code, and you see that HIGH and LOW should be printed only once per button press or release:

```
#!/usr/bin/python

#import libraries
import Adafruit_BBIO.GPIO as GPIO
import time

button = "P8_11" create a variable called button, which refers to the P8_11 pin

#initialize the pin as an INPUT
GPIO.setup(button, GPIO.IN)

#loop forever
while True:
    GPIO.wait_for_edge(button, GPIO.RISING) #blocks the program until a rising
            edge happens on pin P8_11.
    print("HIGH")
    GPIO.wait_for_edge(button, GPIO.FALLING) #blocks the program until a falling
            edge happens on pin P8_11.
    print("LOW")
```

Introducing if . . . else and if . . . elif statements

if . . . else statements, along with loops, are among the most important coding tools for adding control to your program. if. . . else statements are used as follows

```
if condition:
  do_something()
else
  do_something_else()
```

Their use is just as the words describe them: If a certain condition is met, the indented code below the if runs. Otherwise, the indented code below the else is in the spotlight. If you use only an if, as in the code for the pushbutton, the code after the if runs normally if the pushbutton is pressed. If the pushbutton isn't pressed, the interpreter just skips that part in the code.

With an if, you can also use the elif statement, which can be read as else if:

```
if condition1:
        do_something()
elif condition2:
        do_something_else()
else:
        do_another_something_else()
```

In these situations, the code below the `else` is often the default possibility; `if` and `elif` statements are about particular situations.

You can use an `if` statement alone, with an `elif`, with an `else`, or with both. `else` and `elif`, on the other hand, make no sense without a preceding `if`, and such code would result in an error.

To illustrate the use of an `if . . . elif` statement, you use a button circuit and interrupts, but these interrupts happen in a slightly different way. Rather than using the `wait_for_edge` function, you use two other functions:

- ✔ `add_event_detect(GPIO, event)` defines an event that you want to detect — in this case, a falling or rising edge.

- ✔ `event_detected(GPIO)` is a method that returns `True` whenever the defined event happens.

To test `if. . .elif` and these new functions, you can use the following code:

```
#!/usr/bin/python

#import libraries
import Adafruit_BBIO.GPIO as GPIO
import time

button = "P8_11" # create a variable called button, which refers to the P8_11 pin
count = 0 # create a variable called count and initialize it with the value zero.
          # This variable will count the number of times the button was pressed.

GPIO.setup(button, GPIO.IN) #initialize the pin as an INPUT
GPIO.add_event_detect(button, GPIO.RISING) #adds an event to detect. In this
             case, the rising edge of pin P8_11.

#loop forever
while True:
    if GPIO.event_detected(button) == True: # if a rising edge is detected, run
             the code below
        if count == 0: # if the value of count is zero, run the code below
            print("Button was pressed once!")
            count = count + 1 #increment count
        elif count < 3:
            print("Button was pressed less than three times but more than once!")
            count = count + 1 #increment count
        elif count == 3:
            print("Button was pressed three times!")
            count = count + 1 #increment count
        else:
            print("Button was pressed more than three times!")

    time.sleep(0.01) # in order to not overburden the CPU
```

Unlike the example in the "Writing the code with interrupts" section, in which `wait_for_edge` is used and the program is blocked at that line of code until a pushbutton press occurs, adding an event to detect is a nonblocking technique, which means that your program doesn't block waiting for the pushbutton to be pressed. You can verify by placing a line of code such as `print("test")` at the end of both programs. In the `wait_for_edge` case, `test` is printed only after the pushbutton is pressed and then released, because the interpreter doesn't get to that line of code before the `wait_for_edge` functions unblock. In the `event_detected` case, your screen is filled with the `test` message, because the program still keeps running despite the pushbutton press, which is why this option is called a nonblocking option.

Getting to know the print function

You can use the `print()` function to print the actual value of a variable. We simply wrote the code in the preceding section in a different way to illustrate the use of the `if`, `elif`, and `else` statements. In fact, `print()` is used as follows:

```
print(argument1 + argument2 + argument3 + ...)
```

So far, you've used this function only with strings you place inside it — indicated by the quotation marks — but you can command it to print variables as well. To print both strings and variables that are numbers in the same print command, you have to convert the numbers to a string first. Don't worry! You can do that simply by typing `str(variable)`. You can verify by testing the following code:

```python
#!/usr/bin/python

#import libraries
import Adafruit_BBIO.GPIO as GPIO
import time

button = "P8_11" # create a variable called button, which refers to the P8_11 pin
count = 0 # create a variable called count and initialize it with the value zero.
          # This variable will count the number of times the button was pressed.

GPIO.setup(button, GPIO.IN) #initialize the pin as an INPUT
GPIO.add_event_detect(button, GPIO.RISING) #adds an event to detect. In this
          case, the rising edge of pin P8_11.

#loop forever
while True:
    if GPIO.event_detected(button) == True: # if a rising edge is detected, run
             the code below
        count = count + 1 #increment the variable count
        print("Button was pressed " + str(count) + " times!")

    time.sleep(0.01) # in order to not overburden the CPU
```

The print () function is very useful for receiving feedback from your project, as well as for debugging it.

More on Python

Chapter 11 explores Python's capabilities further with some interesting projects. Still, there's a lot more to this programming language than this book covers. The Internet features a vast number of free tutorials at pages such as http://learnpython.org. You can also check out *Python For Dummies,* by Stef Maruch and Aahz Maruch (John Wiley & Sons, Inc.).

Chapter 10

Experimenting with Python

In this Chapter

▶ Fading an RGB LED using PWM with Adafruit's Python library

▶ Employing the Python library to read analog inputs

▶ Discovering Python's capability for web projects by sending emails automatically

▶ Figuring out how you can use functions to use various projects together

▶ Getting acquainted with the powerful communication protocol UART

C hapter 10 covers Python and Adafruit's BeagleBone Input/Output (BBIO) library, which enables you to control the BeagleBone's General Purpose Input Output (GPIO) pins in a simple and straightforward manner. In this chapter, you get to know functions that allow you to do more complex and useful tasks.

The chapter starts in the analog world. For outputs you get to see Adafruit's Python BBIO functions that deal with pulse-width modulation (PWM) by creating a project to fade an RGB LED. For inputs you find out how to measure analog quantities from temperature sensors. You also get to see the ease with which the BeagleBone can interact with the web, and you explore one of the BeagleBone's communication protocols — UART — that makes data transfer between devices a breeze.

As we preach throughout this book, illustration and practice are great ways to understand and master important digital electronic concepts and the BeagleBone. Gather your tools; it's wiring time!

Fading an RGB LED with Python

Light-emitting diodes (LEDs) are fun. RGB (red-green-blue) LEDs triple the fun with the possibility of creating some sweet color effects with three different colors.

This project consists of controlling which colors of the RGB LED are on and how bright they are through the use of pulse-width modulation (PWM) and Adafruit's BeagleBone I/O Python Library.

If you have enough space to set aside the projects in this chapter without unwiring them, we recommend that you keep them intact. Later in the chapter is a section where you mix various projects together.

You need the following components:

- ✔ An RGB common cathode LED
- ✔ Three 220 Ω or 470 Ω resistors
- ✔ A breadboard
- ✔ Jumper wires

Wiring an RGB LED

This section assumes that you use an RGB common cathode LED. If you have only a common anode LED, your code and your wiring has to be slightly different from what is illustrated in the following sections. See Chapter 8 for a description of RGB common cathode LEDs and RGB common anode LEDs.

The wiring for this project is exactly the same as the wiring for the RGB project in Chapter 8, but the project itself is quite different.

To wire everything together, follow these steps:

1. **Use a jumper to connect P9_14 to a vertical row on your breadboard.**

   This pin is the one you use to control the red color of your RGB LED.

2. **Use a jumper to connect P9_16 to a vertical row on your breadboard.**

   This pin is the one you use to control the green color of your RGB LED.

3. **Use a jumper to connect P8_13 to a vertical row on your breadboard.**

   This pin is the one you use to control the blue color of your RGB LED.

   Use color coding to keep yourself organized. In this scenario, using red jumper wires for P9_14, green jumper wires for P9_16, and blue jumper wires for P8_13 probably would be a good idea.

4. **To each of these jumpers, wire a 220 Ω or 470 Ω resistor.**

5. **Wire the longer lead of your RGB LED to ground (GND) on the bread-board rail.**

   Figure 10-1 illustrates the correct wiring.

Trimming the long lead might make it easier to plug the RGB LED into the bread-board. If you do that, you can distinguish the GND lead by looking at the LED's lens. The biggest chunk of lead inside the lens corresponds to the GND lead.

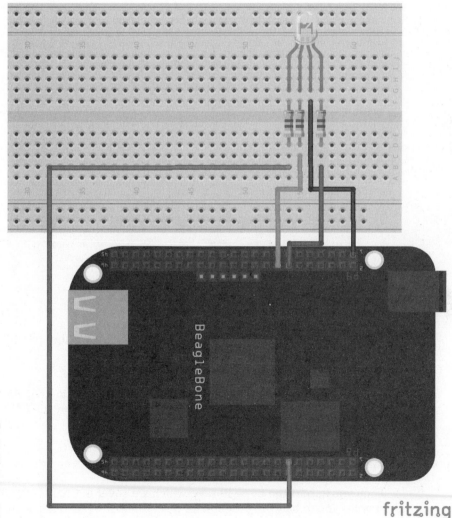

Figure 10-1:
RGB
wired to
BeagleBone
Black.

fritzing

You can use eight pins as PWM pins. Read Chapter 6 for more information about the PWM pins.

Writing the code for fading an RGB LED

Create a script named RGB.py, and type the following:

```
#!/usr/bin/python
import Adafruit_BBIO.PWM as PWM
import time

RGB = ["P9_14", "P9_16", "P8_13"]
#RGB[0] controls red, RGB[1] controls green, RGB[2]controls blue

for i in range(0, 3): #runs the indented code below 3 times
    PWM.start(RGB[i], 0) #initialize PWM with all leads OFF

#set initial conditions
c_initial = RGB[0]
c_next = RGB[1]
c_off = RGB[2]

while True:
    PWM.set_duty_cycle(c_off, 0)
    for i in range(0, 100):
        PWM.set_duty_cycle(c_initial, 100-i)
        PWM.set_duty_cycle(c_next, i)
        time.sleep(0.05) #change this line for faster/slower fading speed
    #swap the colors in the following order: R->G->B->Repeat
    aux = c_initial
    c_off = c_next
    c_next = c_off
    c_off = aux
```

The following sections break down the code for easier understanding.

Importing libraries

The first step after the shebang in a Python script is importing libraries. In this case, you want to import Adafruit's library and define a PWM object, which you name PWM:

```
import Adafruit_BBIO.PWM as PWM
import time
```

Then you import the time library, which we cover in Chapter 9. This library enables you to halt the program for a set number of seconds, using the sleep() function:

Initializing PWM and setting initial conditions

The following chunk of code contains two Python concepts: lists and `for` loops:

```
RGB = ["P9_14", "P9_16", "P8_13"]
#RGB[0] controls red, RGB[1] controls green, RGB[2]controls blue

for i in range(0, 3): #runs the indented code below 3 times
          PWM.start(RGB[i], 0) #initialize PWM with all leads OFF
```

A list is a compound data type. It's a group of variables. Within a list, you can save more than one value. In this case, you create a list called `RGB` where you save the pins that are used in this project. You can access each individual value within a list by using a subscript. In this case, `RGB[0]` refers to `"P9_14"`, `RGB[1]` refers to `"P9_16"`, and `RGB[2]` refers to `"P8_13"`. You can use each element of a list the same way that you use a regular variable.

In Python, the subscript that refers to the first element of a list is always `0`, not `1`.

You can use lists that consist of both text (strings) and numeric values, such as `someList = [1, "hello" 35.117, 141, "bye"]`. It's often advisable, however, for a list to hold items of the same type.

Next comes the `for` loop:

```
for i in range(0, 3): #runs the indented code below 3 times
          PWM.start(RGB[i], 0) #initialize PWM with all leads OFF
```

`for` loops are of extreme importance in the world of programming because they enable you to do stuff a set number of times while increasing a variable in every iteration of the code.

The code after this `for` loop runs three times, but it isn't always exactly the same code. Because the variable `i` increases by 1 at each iteration, this loop goes through all elements of the RGB list and runs the function `PWM.start(pin, duty)` on each of them:

```
PWM.start(pin, duty)
```

This function takes two parameters:

- ✓ **pin:** The pin that you want to use as PWM.

- ✓ **duty:** The initial duty cycle, which goes from `0` for off to `100` for maximum.

Chapter 6 explains that the BeagleBone's PWM default polarity is HIGH, which is somewhat counterintuitive. In the situation described in Chapter 6, the duty-cycle period is a period in which the voltage is LOW, so by default, setting a higher duty cycle on a BeagleBone PWM pin means a LOW voltage. Adafruit's Python library (and BoneScript) functions work in reverse; the default polarity becomes LOW, so the duty cycle is a period in which the voltage is HIGH.

The default might be different on your BeagleBone, and the functions of the libraries you are using might be of a different version that changed these defaults. That said, if things don't work properly, you may have to reverse all the parts of the code that deal with PWM such that a higher duty cycle means lower brightness (100 is off and 0 is maximum).

Last, you define the initial conditions for the leads of your RGB LED:

```
#set initial conditions
c_initial = RGB[0]
c_next = RGB[1]
c_off = RGB[2]
```

Red is the first color, green is the second, and blue is off initially. Naturally, you can change this order as you want. You can also have the three colors on at the same time for different color effects.

Fading from one color to the next

For the `while` that loops forever, you start by turning one of the lights off; blue is defined as the one that stays off initially. Thus, you set the duty cycle of the PWM that controls blue to 0. Then you have a `for` loop that increments i from 0 to 100 in intervals of 0.05 seconds, increasing c_next's duty cycle with i while c_initial's decreases. This loop makes the RGB LED continually fade from c_initial (initially red) to c_next (initially green). The following snippet of code is responsible for that:

```
while True:
        PWM.set_duty_cycle(c_off, 0)
        for i in range(0, 100):
                PWM.set_duty_cycle(c_initial, 100-i)
                PWM.set_duty_cycle(c_next, i)
                time.sleep(0.05) #change this line for faster/slower fading speed
```

Swapping the variables

Because you want the same code to run over and over with different colors and succession, this part of the code swaps the values of the variables around:

```
#swap the colors in the following order: R->G->B->Repeat
    aux = c_initial
    c_initial = c_next
    c_next = c_off
    c_off = aux
```

`c_initial` gets the value within `c_next`; `c_next` gets `c_off`; and `c_off` gets `c_initial`. An auxiliary variable named `aux` is used so that you don't lose the value within `c_initial` when swapping the values.

Running the script for fading an RGB LED

Save the script, run it, and watch the show! Mess around with your code to see the LED fading faster, slower, and in a different order. Change the way duty cycles vary, and combine the three colors in different ways to create cool light effects.

If your circuit doesn't work, you might need to troubleshoot it with a multimeter. Check `www.dummies.com/go/beaglebone/webextras` to see how to do so.

If the LED is too dim, use a 220 Ω resistor rather than a 470 Ω resistor.

Working with Analog Sensors

Analog sensors measure many types of useful data, such as temperature, humidity, light, and distance. The simplest analog sensors work by outputting a voltage that depends on the data they measure. This relationship is often listed on the datasheet of the device as a mathematical formula or a graphical representation.

You work with different sensors in similar ways, as demonstrated by the two examples in the next sections. All you have to do is connect the sensor to one of the BeagleBone's analog-to-digital converter (ADC) pins and read its voltage. Sometimes, there may be a difference in wiring, but the greatest difference is in the calculation that relates voltage to the data that the sensor measures. Figure 10-2 shows which of the BeagleBone's pins can be used as analog inputs; they're labeled from AIN0 to AIN6.

You need the following components:

- Temperature sensor: TMP36
- Infrared (IR) distance sensor: Sharp GP2Y0A21YK
- Two 10K Ω resistors

✔ A breadboard

✔ Jumper wires

	P9						P8		
GND	1	2	GND			GND	1	2	GND
3.3V (VDD)	3	4	3.3V (VDD)				3	4	
5V (VDD)	5	6	5V (VDD)				5	6	
5V (SYS)	7	8	5V (SYS)			GPIO 66	7	8	GPIO 67
	9	10				GPIO 69	9	10	GPIO 68
GPIO 30	11	12	GPIO 60			GPIO 45	11	12	GPIO 44
GPIO 31	13	14	GPIO 40 (PWM)			GPIO 23 (PWM)	13	14	GPIO 26
GPIO 48	15	16	GPIO 51 (PWM)			GPIO 47	15	16	GPIO 46
GPIO 4	17	18	GPIO 5			GPIO 27	17	18	GPIO 65
	19	20				GPIO 22 (PWM)	19	20	
GPIO 3 (PWM)	21	22	GPIO 2 (PWM)				21	22	
GPIO 49	23	24	GPIO 15				23	24	
GPIO 117	25	26	GPIO 14				25	26	GPIO 61
GPIO 125	27	28					27	28	
	29	30	GPIO 122				29	30	
	31	32	VDD_ADC				31	32	
AIN4	33	34	GND_ADC				33	34	
AIN6	35	36	AIN5				35	36	
AIN2	37	38	AIN3				37	38	
AIN0	39	40	AIN1				39	40	
GPIO 20	41	42	GPIO 7 (PWM)				41	42	
GND	43	44	GND				43	44	
GND	45	46	GND				45	46	

Figure 10-2:
BeagleBone
GPIOs with
the ADC
pins.

If you can read and understand the important information in a datasheet, you should be able to use any other sensors by using the concepts shown in this section.

Using the right voltage for the ADC

The following information is so important that the section is one big Warning. Take heed!

Feeding a voltage higher than 1.8V to an ADC pin of the BeagleBone may be hazardous to your board. This situation is something of a nuisance, because most sensors output voltages up to 3.3V, which means that you can't connect them to the ADC immediately. You need a circuit consisting of two resistances to eat up the extra voltage (see Figure 10-3). This circuit is called a *voltage divider*.

Because the ADC pin is in parallel to one of the resistances, it has the same voltage. When you have two resistors in series, the voltage dropped along one of them is the following:

$$V_{ADC} = \frac{R1}{(R1+R2)} V_{sensor}$$

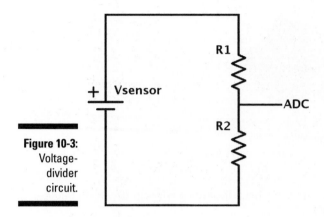

Figure 10-3:
Voltage-
divider
circuit.

The voltage on the resistor is the ratio of the total resistance. Using two equal resistors means that the ADC has 50 percent of the total voltage. If you're dealing with 3.3V, half is 1.65V, which gives you a little leeway. Two 10K Ω resistors should do the trick. Don't use resistors with smaller values!

If you use sensors that output a higher maximum voltage level, it's imperative to determine the ratio of the resistances that you use. For a sensor that outputs 5V, for example, you have the following:

$$1.8 = \frac{R1}{Rtotal} \times 5 \iff \frac{R1}{Rtotal} = 0.36$$

In this case, you should use a pair of resistors where the resistor that is in parallel with the ADC has to have at most 36 percent of the total resistance. You should use a value slightly smaller than the one calculated to have some leeway. A 10K Ω and a 22K Ω resistor achieve a ratio of 31.25 percent, which works just fine by setting the maximum voltage to 1.5625V.

Due to the imprecision of resistors, these values are always slightly different. That's why it's important to calculate for slightly less than 1.8V so that you have some safety margin.

Wiring an IR distance sensor

The IR sensor we use for this project is the Sharp GP2Y0A21YK (see Figure 10-4), due to the fact that it's quite popular and easy to acquire. If you use another sensor, you should consult its datasheet to see which of its pins are GND (ground), Vcc (supply voltage), and Vo or Vout(output voltage). You also need to find the mathematical or graphical relationship between voltage and distance, which affects the last calculation in the code.

Follow these steps to prepare your breadboard to wire up the IR distance sensor Sharp GP2Y0A21YK:

1. **Use a jumper to connect GND — P9_1, P9_2, P8_1, or P8_2 — to a horizontal track on your breadboard.**

2. **Use a jumper to connect 5V to another horizontal track on your breadboard.**

   Use P9_7 and P9_8 if you are powering the BeagleBone via USB and use P9_5 and P9_6 if you are powering it through an external voltage source.

3. **Use a jumper to connect P9_40 to a vertical row on the breadboard.**

   This pin is the one that will read the analog input: AIN 1.

4. **Divide the voltage by connecting two 10K Ω resistors to the jumper that comes from P9_40.**

   One resistor should connect to GND, and the other should connect to the output voltage that comes from the sensor.

To wire up the sensor, you need to know its pinout, which you can find on the datasheet. For the Sharp sensor we're using for this project, refer to Table 10-1. The position described in the table is based on the connectors pointing toward you.

Table 10-1	Pinout of IR Distance Sensor Sharp GP2Y0A21YK	
Position	*Pin Number*	*Signal Name*
Leftmost pin	1	Vo
Middle pin	2	GND
Rightmost pin	3	Vcc

Follow these steps to connect the pins to the jumpers you pulled from the BeagleBone (see Figure 10-5):

1. **Connect pin 1 of the IR sensor to the resistor that connects to P9_40.**
2. **Connect pin 2 of the IR sensor to GND.**
3. **Connect pin 3 of the IR sensor to 5V.**

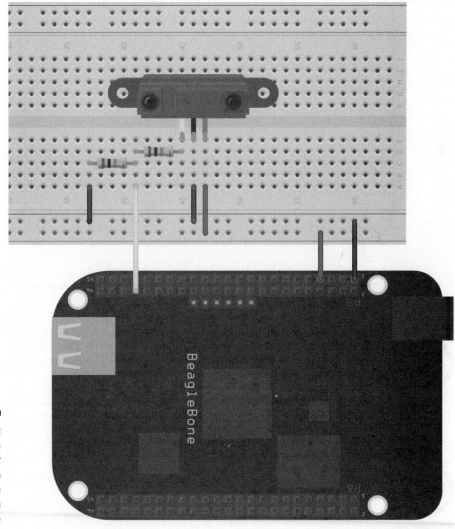

Figure 10-5:
IR distance
sensor
wired to
BeagleBone
Black with
a voltage
divider.

fritzing

Writing the code to measure distance

Create a script named IR.py, and type the following code:

```
#!/usr/bin/python
import Adafruit_BBIO.ADC as ADC
import time
import math


sensor = "P9_40" #or AIN1


ADC.setup()


while True:
    reading = ADC.read(sensor) # values from 0 to 1
    voltage = reading * 1.65 #values from 0 to 1.65V
    distance = 13.93 * pow(voltage, -1.15)
    if distance > 80:
        print("Can't measure more than 80cm!")
    else:
        print("The reading, voltage and distance (in cm) are " + str(reading),
                str(voltage), str(distance))
    time.sleep(0.05) #loop every 50 milliseconds.
```

This code is quite straightforward: It imports an object as ADC to access the ADC pins on the BeagleBone. A new library joins the fray: math. This library includes several functions that simplify complex calculations.

A variable named sensor defines the analog pin to be used, and you use ADC.setup(), which always needs to be present in a program before it starts reading from the ADCs.

You can write AIN0–6 in place of P9_33–40. Note, though, that the order of the numbering of the AINs does not correspond to the numbering of the P9 header: AIN4 is P9_33, and AIN5 is P9_36, for example. Refer to Figure 10-2 earlier in this chapter whenever you're in doubt.

Then comes the while True: loop. The program reads the value of the ADC, which goes from 0 to 1 and represents the fraction of the voltage that's read on the pin. Because that voltage always goes from 0 to 1.65, simply multiplying the reading by 1.65 gets you the real value.

Getting the actual voltage value isn't necessary in many applications. In fact, working with percentages may be much easier.

You convert the voltage reading to the distance in centimeters. This calculation depends on the sensor you use. The pow() function is imported from the math library and calculates voltage to the power of -1.15. It works as follows:

```
result = pow(base, exponent)
```

This function has three variables:

- ✔ **base:** The number you want to elevate to the power of the exponent
- ✔ **exponent:** The exponent's value
- ✔ **result:** The variable where the result will be saved

Python can make that calculation without resorting to functions, but the process is a bit messy and prone to bugs. Also, introducing the math library seems like a good idea, as the library features many other useful mathematical functions, such as sine(), cosine(), and root(). Your program would also work with voltage**-1.15 instead.

Sharp's sensor datasheet provides only a graphical representation to convert voltage into distance, so the formula used in the example is a made-up work-around, which means the following:

- ✔ It isn't 100 percent accurate.
- ✔ The graphic shows that some distances less than 6cm read the same voltage as distances greater than 6cm. Thus, this formula works only for distances greater than 6 cm.
- ✔ The 6cm distance is theoretical. In reality, this value will most likely be different — both because the sensor isn't perfect and because you're using a voltage divider. You can (and should) test what's truly the minimum distance after you run the script.

At the end, you simply print everything and make the program sleep for 0.05 second after each iteration so as to not overburden the central processing unit (CPU).

If you can't find the mathematical relationship for a given graphic, don't fret. You can simply write a program consisting of intervals and if statements. For this project, if you check the IR's datasheet, you see that a sensor output of 1V and 1.5V means a distance between ~15 cm and ~25 cm. Thus, you could create a program that works in the following fashion:

```
if distance > 15 and distance <= 25
        do_something()
elif distance > 25 and distance <= 35
        do_something_else()
#and so on so forth
```

Normally, though, it's easy to find a mathematical relationship. If you don't see it on the datasheet, try an Internet search.

Running the script to measure distance

Save your script by pressing F5 or clicking Run. Move your hand or any other object close to and farther from your sensor to see that the values printed on your screen reflect different distance readings.

Play around with the IR sensor by moving an object very close to it — somewhere between 5cm and 15cm — and use a ruler to check the practical minimum value of distance that you read. This value will be useful in future programs. For us, the distance was a little bit over 9cm, so that's the value we use as minimum.

Wiring a temperature sensor

The wiring for this project is simple. Start by checking your temperature sensor's datasheet to see its pinout. If you're using the TMP36 and looking at it from below, with the curved side facing you, you can refer to Table 10-2.

Table 10-2	Pinout of the Temperature Sensor TMP36	
Position	*Pin Number*	*Signal Name*
Leftmost pin	1	Vcc
Middle pin	2	Vout
Rightmost pin	3	GND

The sensor we used in the example doesn't require a voltage divider because its output surpasses 1.8V only for 266 degrees F (130 degrees C). If the one you use surpasses that voltage at a much lower temperature — or if you're afraid that the TMP36 will read more than 266 degrees F — simply employ a voltage divider as described in the "Using the right voltage for the ADC" section. You can wire it to your circuit exactly as described in the "Writing the code to measure distance" section.

Follow these steps to wire your temperature sensor:

1. **Connect the BeagleBone's GND — pin P9_1, P9_2, P8_1, or P9_2 — to the sensor's GND.**

2. **Connect the BeagleBone's 3.3V supply — pins P9_3 and P9_4 — to the sensor's Vcc.**

3. **Connect the BeagleBone's AIN0 — pin P9_39 — to the sensor's Vout (output).**

Figure 10-6 shows a circuit diagram for this circuit.

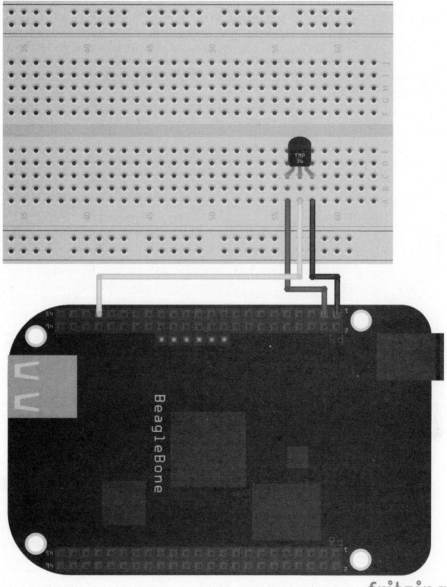

Figure 10-6:
Temperature
sensor
wired to
BeagleBone
Black.

Writing the code to read temperature

As we mention earlier in this chapter, the code you use to read from a sensor is always similar regardless of the type of sensor. The only important differences between this code and the code in the "Writing the code to measure distance" section are the calculations that give the temperature in different units. Refer to "Wiring an IR distance sensor" earlier in this section for a discussion of the code that deals with analog inputs.

To have your BeagleBone print the temperature values that the sensor reads, type the following code:

```
import Adafruit_BBIO.ADC as ADC
import time

sensor = "P9_39"

ADC.setup()

while True:
    reading = ADC.read(sensor) # values from 0 to 1
    voltage = reading * 3.3 #values from 0 to 3.3V, although this only surpasses
            1.8V for temperatures over 266 degrees F

    # the voltage/temperature relationship is as follows:
    # Vo = 1/100 * Temperature + 0.5
    temperatureC = (voltage - 0.5) * 100
    temperatureF = (temperatureC * 9/5) + 32

    print("The reading is: " + str(reading) + "which is, in Volts: " +
            str(voltage))
    print("The temperature in Celsius is: " +  str(temperatureC) + "; and in
            Fahrenheit: " + str(temperatureF))
    time.sleep(0.05) #loop every 50 milliseconds.
```

Running the script to read temperature

Save and run your script, and watch your readings fill the screen. Touch your sensor with your finger, and notice that the values increase. If it's chilly outside, and you're using a laptop, take your circuit for a walk and see the values decreasing. The sensor should detect the temperature quickly.

Simply reading from sensors is fun, but getting stuff running based on readings is what the buzz is all about. Don't unwire this circuit from your breadboard just yet. You use it in another project later in this chapter.

Deriving a formula from a linear graphic

The TMP36's temperature-versus-voltage curve is a nice linear one. If you look at the graphic on its datasheet, and if you remember middle-school algebra, finding out the function that relates those variables isn't hard. To continue reading this part, open TMP36's datasheet and search for the output voltage–versus–temperature graphic.

Many sensors follow relationships like the one for the TMP36, so being able to find the relationship is quite handy. All linear relationships follow the formula y = mx + b. In this case, the value on the y-axis is Vo, and the value on the x-axis is the temperature in Celsius. b is the value that intersects the y-axis, which is 0.5V. m

is the slope, which is the rate with which a variable changes in response to the other. To determine it, you need to choose two (x,y) points, called (x0, y0) and (x1, y2). Then simply employ the following formula:

$$m = \frac{y1 - y0}{x1 - x0}$$

This way, for the TMP36 temperature sensor, you end up with the formula

$$Vo = \frac{1}{100} \times Temperature + 0.5$$

Sending an Email with Python

The BeagleBone is hands-down an exceptional platform for creating web-based projects, due to how easy it is to establish a connection with it. Moreover, Python hosts quite a few functions that greatly simplify matters. For this project, you use Python's email library to create a program that sends emails.

Knowing the prerequisites

Before you get to write the code, there are some prerequisites you need to be aware of.

Finding your email's SMTP server

SMTP stands for *Simple Mail Transfer Protocol,* a standard for email transmission. Each email provider has a different SMTP server, and you have to include the details in your code. The best bet for finding them is searching in the Internet for *<e-mail provider> SMTP;* the necessary details should come up right away.

Reading input from the keyboard

Chapter 9 explains how to read inputs from the world (such as buttons) and how to output text and anything else with the `print` command. To read input from the keyboard, you use the `raw_input (message)` function, which blocks the program until the user types something and presses Enter or Return:

```
data = raw_input(message)
```

Two variables are involved in this function:

- ✓ **input:** The message you want to use to prompt the user to type something
- ✓ **data:** The variable where the input is saved

Writing the code to send an email

Create a file called `emailing.py`, and type the following script:

```
import smtplib
from email.mime.text import MIMEText

my_email = raw_input("Insert your e-mail ")
my_password = raw_input("Insert your e-mail's password ")
subject = raw_input("Insert the subject ")
destination = raw_input("Insert the destination e-mail ")
text = raw_input("Insert the message ")

msg = MIMEText(text)

msg['Subject'] = subject
msg['From'] = my_email
msg['Reply-To'] = my_email
msg['To'] = destination

server = smtplib.SMTP("smtp.gmail.com", 587)
server.starttls()
server.login(my_email, my_password)
server.sendmail(my_email, destination, msg.as_string())
server.quit()

print("Your e-mail has been sent!")
```

The example code features Gmail's SMTP server and port. If you use a different email provider, that part of the code needs to be changed as described in the "Finding your email's SMTP server" section in this chapter.

Don't create a file named `email.py`! This is the name of Python's standard library module for emails, and your script won't work. Avoid creating scripts with names that are too general.

For simplicity, we've broken this program into four parts, which are described in the following sections.

Beware of spam!

A program that automatically sends emails can easily fill your inbox if you're not cautious. Simply creating a loop without any `time.sleep()` or `wait.for.interrupt()` function would result in your program's writing emails as fast as the CPU can handle.

Thousands of emails could be sent in less than a second!

In reality, email providers have defenses against spam, but your account would most likely be suspended, which you don't want to happen.

Importing libraries

The first two lines of code import the required Python libraries to use SMTP and email-related functions. Specifically, `email.mime.text` imports an object (which you name `MIMEText`) that's required to build the email with the correct format:

```
import smtplib
from email.mime.text import MIMEText
```

Getting the email's details

This snippet prompts the user to insert all the required data regarding the email and saves it in variables:

```
my_email = raw_input("Insert your e-mail ")
my_password = raw_input("Insert your e-mail's password ")
subject = raw_input("Insert the subject ")
destination = raw_input("Insert the destination e-mail ")
text = raw_input("Insert the message ")
```

To test this program, you can simply send the email to yourself by writing your own email address in the `destination` variable.

This general program allows you to use whatever emails you want and send whatever messages you want. You could simply use the following in your code:

```
my_email = "myemail@gmail.com"
my_password = "mypassword"
(...)
```

Typing this kind of code is known as *hard-coding*, which often makes things simpler but less general. The trade-off for this simplicity is having to change the code if you want to send a different text or subject, or want to use different email addresses.

If you hard-code, be sure to remove the `while True:` loop. Your program won't block waiting for input, and if you don' remove the loop you'll spam the destination inbox.

Creating the email

The next part starts by creating an object named `msg` that allows you to create the email itself. `MIMEText(text)` takes the email's body as a parameter. Then you build the fields in a standard email with the details that you provided earlier and saved in variables:

```
msg = MIMEText(text)

msg['Subject'] = subject
msg['From'] = my_email
msg['Reply-To'] = my_email
msg['To'] = destination
```

Sending the email

This section is where a connection to an SMTP server is established and the email is sent:

```
server = stmplib.SMTP("smtp.gmail.com", 587)
server.starttls()
server.login(my_email, my_password)
server.sendmail(my_email, destination, msg.as_string())
server.quit()
```

These functions have a few important, not-so-obvious details:

- **`stmplib.SMTP(SMTP server, port)`:** This function connects to the SMTP server provided. Its parameters depend on the email provider you're using.

- **`server.starttls()`:** This function is used for email providers only that use TLS (Transport Layer Security) to encrypt their messages. If yours doesn't, you can simply remove this line of code. Generally, when you search for your email's SMTP server you also find information on whether your email provider uses TLS.

- **`msg.as_string()`:** This function deals with all the complexities regarding the fact that `msg` is an object with multiple parts and isn't defined as a message (that is, a string) to be sent.

Running the script to send an email

You're all set to run the script. Save and simply press F5 or click the Run button, and look at your console. The program is waiting for your input. When you type that input, the program terminates and tells you that the email has been sent. Go check your inbox!

Mixing Up Projects and Creating Functions

The project in "Sending an Email with Python" earlier in this chapter enables you to send emails easily and automatically. Although that's cool, you could easily achieve the same thing by using a standard computer. One thing that makes the BeagleBone awesome is the ease with which your electrical projects in the real world can interact with the Internet. In this section, you see how to put two or more projects together through the use of functions. You can send the data read by the temperature sensor over email, as well as control the brightness and color of an RGB LED through the distance measured by the IR sensor.

Reading a temperature is a program of its own; so is sending an email. The same applies to reading the distance of an IR sensor or controlling the brightness of an RGB LED. These are all independent tasks that can be done without any of the other tasks. That's why creating your own functions with Python is the best course of action here. Rather than creating an entire program in a linear process, you create different pieces of a puzzle and put them together in the end. When programs start to grow in size, it is definitely the best approach to divide the program into several tasks that can be tested independently and then put everything together in the end.

This section assumes you have gone through all the previous sections in this chapter because each independent task is a project built and tested in those sections. Through the use of functions, you add interaction between the different chunks of code.

Creating a function with Python

Functions are extremely useful to define tasks that you do often in your scripts. The following snippet of code shows an example of a good use of functions:

```
def calculator(operand1, operand2, operator):
    print ("Calculating " + str(operand1) + str(operator) + str(operand2))
    if operator == '+':
        return operand1 + operand2
    elif operator == '-':
        return operand1 - operand2
    elif operator == '*':
        return operand1 * operand2
    elif operator == '/':
        return operand1 / operand2
    elif operator == '%':
        return operand1 % operand2
    else:
        return "invalid inputs!"

while True:
    operand1 = raw_input("Introduce first operand ")
    operand2 = raw_input("Introduce second operand ")
    operator = raw_input("Introduce the operator ")
    result = calculator(int(operand1), int(operand2), operator)
    print(result)
```

This code should be quite easy to understand. Note three things, however:

- ✔ raw_input() *always* returns a string. For a computer, the *number* 2 and the *character* 2 are different things. Because strings are collections of characters, the value held in raw_input() is one or more character(s). To make math with that value, you have to convert it to an integer by using int() or to a floating-point number (a number with a decimal point) by using float().

- ✔ Normally, you want to use apostrophes: 'c' when referring to characters and quotation marks and "str" when referring to strings.

- ✔ The operation % is the modulo operation, which determines the remainder of a number when dividing it by another.

When you write a line of code that uses a function, such as my_email = input("Insert your e-mail"), you're executing a *function call,* which asks for a function to be executed. Functions are chunks of code that take parameters, make copies of those parameters, process those copies, and produce return values.

The functions used throughout this book are defined in the libraries you imported at the start of each program. Someone wrote these functions and saved them in those libraries. The projects in Chapter 6 control the GPIOs through writing and reading from files — a fact that's completely transparent to you when you're programming in Python. Someone else wrote the code that deals with the pesky complexities of using files and put it all in a function that anybody can use.

What changes when you mix the programs?

The answer is: very little. We need to note some changes, though. Some of these changes are merely organizational, whereas others are essential. They are

✔ The `while True:` loop must be changed to the main code; otherwise, the program will be stuck in one of the functions forever. This change is essential.

✔ Importing the libraries required for every function usually occurs at the start of the script, before the function definitions. It's common for two different functions to require the same library, which is just a matter of organization.

✔ Normally, initial conditions and initialization of functions such as `PWM()` and `ADC()` are done right after the libraries are imported. Although your code would still work without this change, the change isn't just merely about organization; it improves efficiency because these parts of the code need to happen only once. This function assures that they do indeed run only once instead of at every iteration of the `while True:` loop.

To create a function, use this structure:

```
def function_name(parameter1, parameter2, ...): #the function header
    #all the function code goes here
    return some_variable
```

Remember indentation! If you don't indent when defining a function, the interpreter has no way to distinguish the rest of the code from the function code.

A line such as `some_variable = function_name(parameter1, parameter2)` would do the following:

1. Call your function.

2. Make copies of `parameter1` and `parameter2`.

3. Process the values contained in the copies of `parameter1` and `parameter2`.

4. Return a value that would be saved in `some_variable`.

Functions don't necessarily require the return line or parameters. These functions are used simply to carry out tasks (such as setting some pins to `HIGH` or printing some output), not necessarily to process data and return something to be used in the main part of the code.

Sending temperature readings by email

Because this program is based on the ones in earlier sections of this chapter, the best strategy is to start by copying and pasting them under function definitions. Then move all the library importations to the start of the script. The code for the temperature sensor remains similar, but it doesn't have the `while True:` loop. The function that runs it should return the temperature at the end. The email part requires a slight change; you want to send the sensor temperature, not a message that you write. Besides the libraries imported at the start and `while True:` loop, the main code has two lines of code, consisting of the function calls. Type the following code for the combined programs:

```python
import Adafruit_BBIO.ADC as ADC
import time
import math

import smtplib
from email.mime.text import MIMEText

sensor = "P9_39" #or AIN0

ADC.setup()

def read_temperature():
    reading = ADC.read(sensor) # values from 0 to 1
    voltage = reading * 1.8 #values from 0 to 1.8V

    # the voltage/temperature relationship is as follows:
    # Vo = 1/100 * Temperature + 0.5
    temperature_c = (voltage - 0.5) * 100
    temperature_f = (temperature_c * 9/5) + 32
    return "the temperature in Celsius is" + temperature_c

def send_email(message)

    my_email = raw_input("Insert your e-mail ")
    my_password = raw_input("Insert your e-mail's password ")
    subject = raw_input("Insert the subject ")
    destination = raw_input("Insert the destination e-mail ")
    text = message

    msg = MIMEText(text)

    msg['Subject'] = subject
    msg['From'] = my_email
    msg['Reply-To'] = my_email
    msg['To'] = destination
```

```
    server = smtplib.SMTP("smtp.gmail.com", 587)
    server.starttls()
    server.login(my_email, my_password)
    server.sendmail(my_email, destination, msg.as_string())
    server.quit()

    print("Your e-mail has been sent!")

while True:
    temperature = read_temperature();
    send_email(temperature);
```

Note that the `message` variable of the `send_email()` function holds the same data as the `temperature` variable of the main code. When you send a variable as a parameter, you make a copy of it with whatever name you define in the function header. You're not altering the variable `temperature`! It's very important to remember that the variables within the code of a function are isolated from the rest of the world.

You could use the `send_email()` function with whatever message you desire; the code doesn't care whether the message is a temperature or not. It just takes in a message — any message — and sends it. That's the idea behind functions; they're chunks of code that can be used independently.

Getting lazy

Most likely, you always want to send sensor readings to your own email address and not to someone else's, so having to type all the details is a tad tedious. You can simply hard-code the details in your email function, as follows:

```
def send_email(message)
    my_email = "myEmail@gmail.com"
    my_password = "my_password"
    subject = "Temperature Reading"
    destination = "myEmail@gmail.com"
    text = "The reading is + str(message)" #this is the change

    msg = MIMEText(text)

    msg['Subject'] = subject
    msg['From'] = my_email
    msg['Reply-To'] = my_email
    msg['To'] = destination

    server = stmplib.SMTP('smtp.gmail.com', 587)
    server.starttls()
    server.login(my_email, my_password)
    server.sendmail(my_email, destination, msg.as_string())
    server.quit()

    print("Your e-mail has been sent!")
```

This "lazy" version of the `temperatureEmail.py` script *does not* block waiting for input. It's 100 percent automatic. Thus, it's essential that you remove the `while True:` loop, lest you get your entire inbox spammed with temperature readings — or, more likely, get your email account suspended. Without the loop, the program sends the reading only one time.

Running the script to send the temperature

Save your program by pressing Ctrl+S or Cmd+S and run it by clicking on Run or pressing F5 several times, and see the results. Play around with the temperature sensor as to see different values.

Functions are great ways not only to keep your programs tidy and organized, but also to promote reusability. You could use the `send_email(message)` function to send the data read by a humidity or light sensor, for example. Conversely, you could use the `read_temperature()` function with a program that turns an air conditioner on or off, depending on the temperature.

Functions also make it simpler to work in a team whose members have different tasks. The person who programmed the air conditioner doesn't need to have any clue about how his colleague got the temperature sensor working. Simply knowing what a function returns and what its parameters are gives you enough information to proceed.

Controlling an RGB LED with distance readings

Seeing the RGB LED's brightness and color change as you move your hand around should be a fun thing to do. The good news is that if you've worked through this chapter in order, you already have a great deal of the code required to make this happen.

The circuit for this project is the same as the two circuits in the sections "Wiring an RGB LED" and "Wiring an IR distance sensor." If you didn't unwire them, you're good to go. If you did unwire them, follow the earlier instructions or see Figure 10-7.

This section assumes you are using a common cathode RGB. If that isn't the case, refer to the "Wiring an RGB LED" section to see what changes.

Rather than control the PWM's duty cycle with time, you're going to control it with the distance measured. The function that controls the LED needs to be changed to accommodate this fact. The code that measures distance remains the same as in the "Writing the code to measure distance" section, but no longer has the `while True:` loop. You also need to return the distance at the end of the function that runs the code. The biggest addition is the fact that you need to transform your distance measurement to a percentage; PWM doesn't work with absolute values. That's what the function `absolute_to_percentage()` in the following code is for.

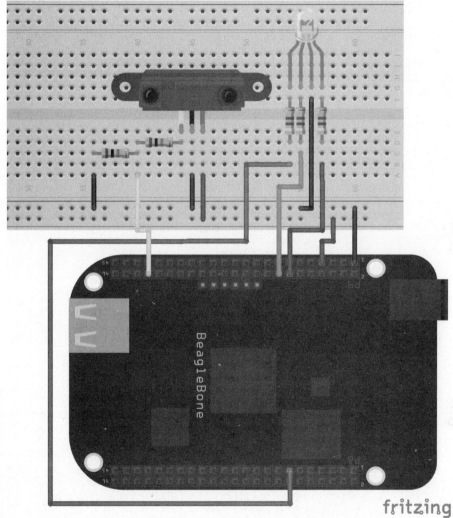

fritzing

Figure 10-7:
RGB and
IR distance
sensor
wired to
BeagleBone
Black.

Using your distance readings

The program works like this:

1. Import libraries.

2. Set initial conditions, and initialize ADC and PWM.

3. Run `read_distance()`, and save the distance measured.

4. Run `absolute_to_percentage()`, which takes the distance value in centimeters and transforms 10 to 80 cm to 0 to 100 percent.

5. Run `control_LED()`, which uses the distance measured to light up the LED.

6. Repeat Steps 3, 4, and 5 until interrupted.

The code is as follows:

```python
#!/usr/bin/python
import Adafruit_BBIO.PWM as PWM
import time
import Adafruit_BBIO.ADC as ADC
import math

#setup RGB
RGB = ["P9_16", "P8_13", "P9_14"]
#RGB[0] controls red, RGB[1] controls green, RGB[2]controls blue

for i in range(0, 3): #runs the indented code below 3 times
    PWM.start(RGB[i], 0) #initialize PWM with all leads OFF

#set initial conditions for RGB
c_initial = RGB[0]
c_next = RGB[1]
c_off = RGB[2]

#setup IR Sensor
sensor = "P9_40" #or AIN1
ADC.setup()

def read_distance():
    reading = ADC.read(sensor) # values from 0 to 1
    voltage = reading * 1.65 #values from 0 to 1.65V
    distance = 13.93 * pow(voltage, -1.15) # values from 10 to 80 cm
              theoretically
    return distance

def absolute_to_percentage(distance, minimum, maximum):
    distance = distance - minimum #shift the 10-80 interval to 0-70
    maximum = maximum - minimum #the maximum value, 80cm, is now 70
    if distance > maximum:   #after 80cm (which is 70 after the shift), values
            start being unreliable
        distance = maximum   #thus, everything after the max is the max itself.
    return distance * 100/maximum # this puts the measured value in terms of
            0 to 100 percent
                            # which is what PWM works with.
def control_LED(distance):
    PWM.set_duty_cycle(c_off, 0)
    for i in range(0, 100):
        PWM.set_duty_cycle(c_initial, 100-distance)
        PWM.set_duty_cycle(c_next, distance)
        time.sleep(0.01)
```

```
while True:
    distance = read_distance()
    distance = absolute_to_percentage(distance, 9, 80)
    print(distance)
    if(distance > 0): #this happens like once in a million, if at all, but the
            program stops when it happens. And at 1GHz, a million is not so
            little!
        control_LED(distance)
        time.sleep(0.05)

    # swap the colors in the following order: R->G->B->Repeat
    aux = c_off
    c_off = c_initial
    c_initial = c_next
    c_next = aux
```

The biggest addition here is the new function `absolute_to_percentage()`, which transforms absolute data readings into values ranging from 0 to 100 percent so that they're ready to be used as PWM duty cycles.

Like any good function, `absolute_to_percentage()` promotes reusability. If you need to do the same thing with data read from any other type of sensor — distance, temperature, light, or whatever — you could use the same function without any changes. The following code includes comments with the values specific to the IR sensor to make it easier to understand:

```
def absolute_to_percentage(distance, minimum, maximum):
    distance = distance - minimum #shift the 9-80 interval to 0-70
    if distance > maximum:    #after 80cm (which is 70 after the shift), values
            start being unreliable
        distance = maximum    #thus, everything after the max is the max itself.
    return distance * 100/maximum # this puts the measured value in terms of 0
            to 100 percent
                        # which is what PWM works with.
```

Note that there should be a minimum distance that the IR distance sensor can read. The way in which you determine this distance is covered in the "Running the script to measure distance" section. For us, this distance was 9 cm, and that's what we use in the example. You can subtract 9 from your distance measured to ensure that the minimum value is `0`. Just remember that the real distance is actually that value plus the minimum (9 in this case). This subtraction makes converting the absolute value of the distance into a percentage much, much easier:

```
distance = distance - minimum #shift the 9-80 interval to 0-70
maximum = maximum - minimum
```

Afterward, you check whether the distance measured is greater than `70` (which would be more than 80 cm). Because the sensor's datasheet shows that values read after 80 cm start being unreliable, you set your maximum as 80 cm:

```
if distance > maximum:    #after 80cm (which is 70 after the shift), values start
                being unreliable
    distance = maximum    #thus, everything after the max is the max itself.
```

Finally, you return a percentage value of the distance measured (with 100 percent being 80 cm *or more)*:

```
return distance * 100/maximum # this puts the measured value in terms of 0 to
                100 percent
```

It's important to note that the variables are swapped outside the function. We do this because variables inside a function are called *local variables.* These variables not only are private to the function itself, but also reset every time the function call terminates.

Otherwise, there aren't many changes in the code you used previously for the RGB, in the "Writing the code for fading an RGB LED" section. One difference is that the duty cycle depends on `distance` rather than `i`, which, in the previous case, was a variable that increments every 0.05 second.

Running the script to fade an RGB LED with an IR distance sensor.

Save the program and start it by clicking Run or pressing F5. Move your hand or an object closer to or farther from the IR sensor, and you should see the brightness of the RGB LED changing accordingly. Its color still changes periodically, though.

What if the LED didn't change color the color periodically? What if everything — the color *and* the brightness — was controlled by your hand? Sound fun? Let's roll.

Enhancing the project

Quite a few parts of this code go beyond gluing the previous two projects together with minor changes, simply due to the fact that we wanted to do a cool thing. Without further ado, here's what the `control_LED()` function for this program does.

You should save the following script in a new file. We named ours `enhRGBInfraRed.py`:

```
#!/usr/bin/python
import Adafruit_BBIO.PWM as PWM
import time
import Adafruit_BBIO.ADC as ADC
import math
```

```
#setup RGB
RGB = ["P9_16", "P8_13", "P9_14"]
#RGB[0] controls red, RGB[1] controls green, RGB[2]controls blue

for i in range(0, 3): #runs the indented code below 3 times
    PWM.start(RGB[i], 0) #initialize PWM with all leads OFF

#set initial conditions for RGB
c_red = RGB[0]
c_green = RGB[1]
c_blue = RGB[2]


#setup IR Sensor
sensor = "P9_40" #or AIN1
ADC.setup()

def read_distance():
    reading = ADC.read(sensor) # values from 0 to 1
    voltage = reading * 1.65 #values from 0 to 1.65V
    distance = 13.93 * pow(voltage, -1.15) # values from 10 to 80 cm
                theoretically
    return distance

def absolute_to_percentage(distance, minimum, maximum):
    distance = distance - minimum #shift the 10-80 interval to 0-70
    maximum = maximum - minimum #the maximum value, 80cm, is now 70
    if distance > maximum:   #after 80cm (which is 70 after the shift), values
                start being unreliable
        distance = maximum   #thus, everything after the max is the max itself.
    return distance * 100/maximum # this puts the measured value in terms of 0
                to 100 percent
                        # which is what PWM works with.


def control_LED(distance):

    if distance <= 33.3:
        PWM.set_duty_cycle(c_red, 100 - distance*3)
        PWM.set_duty_cycle(c_green, distance*3)
        PWM.set_duty_cycle(c_blue, 0)
    elif distance > 33.3 and distance <= 66.7:
        distance = distance - 33.3
        PWM.set_duty_cycle(c_green,   100 - distance*3)
        PWM.set_duty_cycle(c_blue, distance * 3)
        PWM.set_duty_cycle(c_red, 0)
    elif distance > 66.7:
        distance = distance - 66.7
        PWM.set_duty_cycle(c_blue,   100 - distance*3)
        PWM.set_duty_cycle(c_red, distance*3)
        PWM.set_duty_cycle(c_green, 0)
```

```
while True:
    distance = read_distance()
    distance = absolute_to_percentage(distance, 9, 80)
    print(distance)
    if(distance > 0): #this happens like once in a million, if at all, but the
                program stops when it happens. And at 1GHz, a million is not so
                little!
        control_LED(distance)
    time.sleep(0.05)
```

Everything that deals with distance readings is exactly the same. The function that controls the LED, however, has changed significantly:

```
def control_LED(distance):

    if distance <= 33.3:
        PWM.set_duty_cycle(c_red, 100 - distance*3)
        PWM.set_duty_cycle(c_green, distance*3)
        PWM.set_duty_cycle(c_blue, 0)
    elif distance > 33.3 and distance <= 66.7:
        distance = distance - 33.3
        PWM.set_duty_cycle(c_green,   100 - distance*3)
        PWM.set_duty_cycle(c_blue, distance * 3)
        PWM.set_duty_cycle(c_red, 0)
    elif distance > 66.7:
        distance = distance - 66.7
        PWM.set_duty_cycle(c_blue,  100 - distance*3)
        PWM.set_duty_cycle(c_red, distance*3)
        PWM.set_duty_cycle(c_green, 0)
```

This part of the code runs the show. This an enhanced version of the `control_LED()` function receives a value of 0 to 100 to set the PWM of the pins that control the RGB and decides how they're used.

This function could be written in many ways to produce different color effects with the RGB. In this case, the LED fades from one color to the next, depending on the distance from an object. If you place your hand near the sensor and move it away slowly up to 80 cm or more, you should see the LED fade from red to green to blue to red again.

You divide the 0-to-100 interval by 3 so that only two colors are active at any interval. What happens for each interval is decided by `if` and `elif` statements. The first `0if` checks whether the distance measured is less than 33.3 percent of 8 cm. If so, blue is off, and the LED fades from red to green gradually:

```
if distance <= 33.3:
    PWM.set_duty_cycle(c_red, 100 - distance*3)
    PWM.set_duty_cycle(c_green, distance*3)
    PWM.set_duty_cycle(c_blue, 0)
```

Creating permanent connections

If you enjoyed the projects provided throughout this chapter, you may be interested in creating something more permanent than the prototypes you've built with the breadboard. To do so, you need to know how to use a soldering iron. You can learn more about working with a soldering iron at `www.dummies.com/go/beaglebone/webextras`.

The next two chunks of code do the same thing for the remaining intervals:

```
elif distance > 33.3 and distance <= 66.7:
    distance = distance - 33.3
    PWM.set_duty_cycle(c_green,   100 - distance*3)
    PWM.set_duty_cycle(c_blue, distance * 3)
    PWM.set_duty_cycle(c_red, 0)
elif distance > 66.7:
    distance = distance - 66.7
    PWM.set_duty_cycle(c_blue,   100 - distance*3)
    PWM.set_duty_cycle(c_red, distance*3)
     PWM.set_duty_cycle(c_green, 0)
```

Note that you always shift the distance reading to a value of 0 to 33 (percent) — so that you are always working with the same values, making the code simpler — but you multiply it by 3 so that the PWM duty cycle that it sets is still 0 to 100 (percent).

Running the script for the enhanced version to fade an RGB LED with an IR distance sensor

Save and run the script, and experiment! Feel free to alter the code — namely, the duty cycles of the PWM — and save and run it again to see different results.

For fun, you could also try to change the RGB LED program to choose its color and/or brightness depending on the temperature readings.

Introducing UART

UART, which stands for *universal asynchronous receiver/transmitter,* is a well-known, commonly used way for different devices to communicate through serial. Many of UART's parameters, such as the data format and speed of transmission (*baud rate,* which is the same as bits per second), are configurable, which is why *universal* is part of its title.

Devices communicate through the use of RX (receive) and TX (transmit) pins. To make two devices send data to each other, you merely need to cross these pins: One device's RX connects to the other device's TX, and the first device's TX connects to the second's RX. The process is quite intuitive: You wire the pin that transmits the data of one device to the pin that receives data of the other device.

Wiring the BeagleBone to an UART device

The BeagleBone features five serial UARTs, although UART0 is reserved for communication with the computer (if you connect it through USB, that is). Also, UART3 features only a TX pin. People often say that the BeagleBone actually has 4.5 serial UARTs for this reason.

As stated in the preceding section, you want to cross the TX and RX pins of each device. Also, the device you're connecting to the BeagleBone needs to be powered, usually requiring a supply of 3.3V or 5V, and a GND pin that needs to be connected. So to use the BeagleBone's UART1, for example, you make the connections shown in Table 10-3.

Table 10-3   Connecting the BeagleBone's UART1 to a device

BeagleBone	Device
P9_24 (UART1_TX)	Device's RX pin
P9_26 (UART1_RX)	Device's TX pin
P9_7 or P9_8 (5V through USB) *or* P9_5 or P9_6 (external supply) for a 5V device. P9_3 or P9_4 for a 3.3V device.	Device's 5V or 3.3V power supply
P9_1, P9_2, P8_1, or P8_2	Device's GND pin

If you use a 5V device, be extremely careful with your wiring! Feeding 5V wires into the BeagleBone will severely damage it.

To work with and test UART communication on the BeagleBone, you'll be using two of its serial UARTs: UART1 and UART2. If you pretend that UART2 is another device altogether, you can easily use UART1 to write into it (see Figure 10-8). The wiring is as follows:

- Connect P9_24 (UART1_TX) to P9_22 (UART2_RX).
- Connect P9_26 (UART1_RX) to P9_21 (UART2_TX).

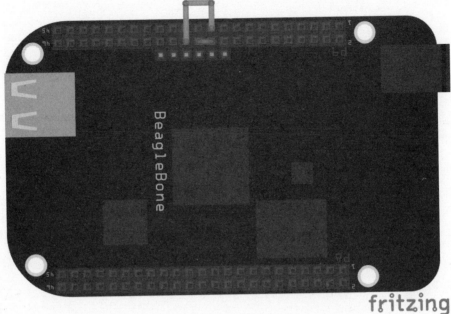

Figure 10-8:
UART com-
munication
established
on a
BeagleBone
Black.

Writing the code to test UART

To verify that communication is happening, you create two programs and run them at the same time. The programs are very similar; the difference is that one deals with UART1 and the other with UART2. We named our programs `UART1_test.py` and `UART2_test.py`.

Before you get into coding, make sure that you have the necessary Python library installed. Type the following code in the command line:

```
pip install pyserial
```

The code for `UART1_test.py` is the following:

```
import Adafruit_BBIO.UART as UART
import serial
import time

UART.setup("UART1")

ser1 = serial.Serial(port = "/dev/ttyO1", baudrate=9600)

ser1.close()
```

```
ser1.open()

while True:
    if ser1.isOpen():
        ser1.write("This is a message from UART1!\n")
        rxbuf = ser1.readline()
        print(rxbuf)
        time.sleep(0.05)
```

The code for `UART2_test.py` is very similar:

```
import Adafruit_BBIO.UART as UART
import serial
import time

UART.setup("UART2")

ser2 = serial.Serial(port = "/dev/ttyO2", baudrate=9600)

ser2.close()

ser2.open()

while True:
    if ser2.isOpen():
        ser2.write("This is a message from UART2!\n")
        rxbuf = ser2.readline()
        print(rxbuf)
        time.sleep(0.05)
```

As usual, the code starts with importing libraries. This time, you define an object named `UART` and initialize it with the serial UART that you'll be using (either 1 or 2):

```
UART.setup("UART1")
```

Next, you create a variable named `ser1` that actually serves as an *object* (a variable that contains multiple fields):

```
objectName.field1
objectName.field2
objectName.field3
```

That variable saves the value returned from a function:

```
ser1 = serial.Serial(port = "/dev/ttyO1", baudrate=9600)
```

The function takes the following parameters:

✔ **port:** The serial UART that you're using. After using `UART.setup` (`"UART#"`), you create a file in the `/dev` directory. This file is always `/dev/ttyO#`. Note that the filename contains the letter O, not the digit 0.

✔ **baudrate:** The speed at which you want to establish the communication. The BeagleBone supports the following baud rates:

- 9600
- 14440
- 19200
- 28800
- 38400
- 56000
- 57600
- 115200

If you have two devices operating at two different baud rates, the communication won't work! You can test this fact by giving different baud rates to UART1_ test.py and UART2_test.py. Most of the time, it's easier to alter the baud rate of the BeagleBone's UART than it is to change the device's baud rate.

If you have issues with communication, try lowering the baud rate.

Next, you close the serial port to reset it (in case it was used previously and data was still inside) and then reopen it:

```
ser1.close()

ser1.open()
```

Then comes the `while True:` loop, in which each UART writes a message to its TX pin and reads a message from its RX pin. This message is saved in the `rxbuf` variable. Finally, you print the message that was read from the RX pin.

In computer science, a *buffer* is often a block of memory used to save data temporarily, which is why we call the variable `rxbuf`.

Notice two important details in this last section of the code:

✔ **if ser1.isOpen():** If nothing wrong happened, `ser1.isOpen()` is the same as `True`, so that `if` will happen all the time. If something went wrong with accessing the serial port, however, `ser1.isOpen()` holds `False`, so it ensures that the program won't do anything.

✔ **ser1.write("This is a message from UART1!\n"):** The `\n` stands for *newline* — a special character that represents pressing the Enter key on your computer keyboard. Without this character, the program wouldn't work, because `rxbuf = ser1.readline()` reads data until it finds \n — that is, it reads an entire line. For this reason, the message you send requires \n. Without that character, all data would be sent on the same line, and this function would stay blocked forever because it would never find the \n.

Running the script to test UART

Select each script, and press F5 or click Run after saving. Nothing happens if you run just one script; it blocks at the readline() function, waiting for a message. When you run the two scripts, you see the messages being printed. This is a message from UART1! is printed in UART2's program (see Figure 10-9), and This is a message from UART2! is printed in UART1's program.

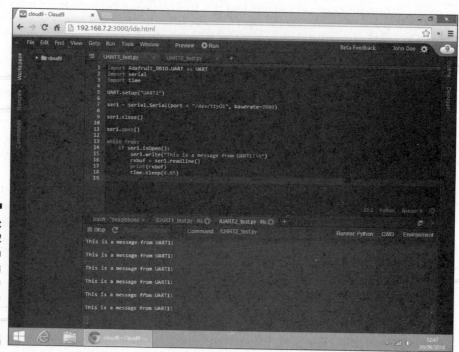

Figure 10-9: The UART2 program receiving a message from the UART1 program.

Feel free to experiment with other baud rates, although you won't notice the change immediately because the programs have the time.sleep(0.05) function slowing things down. If you increase the baud rate, data is transmitted faster.

Understanding UART's uses

Simply put, UART is awesome. It's simple and asynchronous, allowing for fast communications without much effort on your part.

Many devices communicate through UART. The BeagleBone, for example, communicates this way with your computer. Other examples include GPS modules, wireless modules (such as Bluetooth and Wi-Fi), and some sensors that are more complex than analog ones that simply relate data to a voltage level.

If you wired the BeagleBone to a GPS module, for example, you could easily read all the information it provided — normally, much more than merely longitude and latitude — with code very similar to the code in the "Writing the code to test UART" section. The only differences are that you want only to read from it, and you have to change the baud rate to make it the same as the GPS's:

```python
import Adafruit_BBIO.UART as UART
import serial
import time

UART.setup("UART1")

ser1 = serial.Serial(port = "/dev/ttyO1", baudrate=9600) #change according to
                the GPS's baudrate

ser1.close()

ser1.open()

while True:
    if ser1.isOpen():
        rxbuf = ser1.readline()
        print(rxbuf)
        time.sleep(0.05)
```

Chapter 11

Mastering the Art of Coding

*J*ust as Salvador Dali's artistic style was significantly different from Pablo Picasso's, every programmer has his or her own way of creating a program. Give two programmers the same task and their code will definitely look quite different. Although everyone has an individual style, some good practices are standard throughout the world of programming and can be quite useful.

Following standard programming guidelines isn't just about organization; it's also about making your code simple and straightforward so it's easy for you and others to read it and alter it. It's about making the program efficient. Most important, though, these practices greatly reduce your chance of getting bugs in your code and making debugging much easier when bugs do occur.

This chapter is about the art of good coding. Even though the information in this chapter may seem to consist of small tips and tricks, when your code starts to grow, these tidbits become extremely helpful. Trust us: Finding that one little bug in a huge script of code is one of the most frustrating endeavors of life. It's better to avoid bugs from the get-go.

General Programming Tips

This section explains some tricks you can use while programming in any language. They help you keeping your code organized, readable, and less prone to bugs. These tips also make it easier for you to detect bugs in your code.

Following a convention when writing code has the same effect as color-coding your circuit. It helps with readability, debugging, and teamwork.

Variables and function names

Very few programs work without variables, and those that do result in huge messes. We present several variables in earlier chapters of this book. Even though variable names are arbitrary, it helps greatly to use self-explanatory names such as the following:

- ✔ `led` to hold the name of the pin you're using to light an LED, such as `"USR3"` or `"P9_14"`
- ✔ `state` for a variable that holds `HIGH` or `LOW`
- ✔ `b` for a BoneScript module object
- ✔ `button` for an input pin to which a button is wired, such as `"P8_12"`
- ✔ `dutyCycle` for a variable that holds the duty-cycle value of a pulse-width modulation (PWM) output pin

Imagine opening your code two months after you wrote it or handing your code to someone else. Would you or the other person easily understand what each variable represents? Unless you have an exceptional memory, we greatly recommend that you employ this technique in your code.

Additionally, you can use several conventions for variable and function names. You should adopt one convention and use it in all your programs to avoid some pretty annoying bugs. It's quite common to declare a variable such as `dutycycle` and then write `duty_cycle` or `dutyCycle` somewhere else in your code. JavaScript and Python are case-sensitive languages, so this entry would be an error. Although this type of bug is easy to detect, correcting it is an unnecessary waste of time. Following are the two most widely used conventions for naming variables:

- ✔ **Camel case:** This convention is commonly used with the prebuilt functions of JavaScript, and we also prefer to use it when programming in BoneScript. All words after the first should have uppercase first letters. Using this convention, you'd enter **inputPin** rather than **inputpin**.
- ✔ **Underscores:** This convention is used in the prebuilt functions of many programming languages, including Python. The words that compose the variable names are separated by underscores, like so: `input_pin`.

Some people prefer the underscores convention, the reason usually being that an underscore makes the most sense as a replacement for a space and makes the variable more readable. On the other hand, some people prefer the camel case convention because it's faster to type (fewer keystrokes) and (in our opinion) looks more elegant. Follow the convention you prefer, or simply use the same one as the prebuilt functions of the language you're using.

Following are some other conventions for naming variables:

- ✔ `index` for a variable that indicates the index of an array or a list.
- ✔ `i` for loops, `j` for a loop inside a loop, and `k` for a loop inside a loop inside a loop. Additionally, these variables are often used as indexes of arrays or lists when the instructions regarding the array or list are inside loops.
- ✔ `aux`, `tmp`, and `temp` for *auxiliary* or *temporary* variables used to hold a value that will be placed in another variable later — you can't swap the value of two variables without using a third, for example.
- ✔ `n` and `count` for variables that count the number of times something happens.

We recommend that you keep variable names short, but don't shorten them so much that they become unreadable. Using `tmp` or `temp` for `temporary` is justifiable; using `iPin` rather than `inputPin` might lead to confusion.

Using names that somewhat explain the variable's or the function's task, as well as following conventions, makes changing parts of your code a faster process. You don't need to define a variable to deal with a pin's state; you could use `"P9_14"` all the time instead of defining `led = "P9_14"`. If you decide to change it to pin P8_12 for whatever reason — such as if you notice that P9_14 is already being used for another task — you have to change all the lines of your code instead of just one.

Constants

Constants are variables whose values never change throughout the program. They're great ways to ensure that altering your script is fast and simple. An example in Python may help you get the idea. The following example illustrates a (incomplete) snippet of code where the speed of several DC (direct current) motors — for an RC (remote control) car, for example — would be proportional to a constant value and the voltage read from some sensor.

```
motor1_speed = 5*voltage1
motor2_speed = 5*voltage2
motor3_speed = 5*voltage3
motor4_speed = 5*voltage4
```

When you test your remote-control car, find that you're not satisfied with the results, and want to change the constant 5, you have no choice but to change it everywhere. You could change it just once if you define a constant like this:

```
SPEED_CONSTANT = 5

motor1_speed = SPEED_CONSTANT*voltage1
motor2_speed = SPEED_CONSTANT*voltage2
motor3_speed = SPEED_CONSTANT*voltage3
motor4_speed = SPEED_CONSTANT*voltage4
```

When you define a constant, testing for different values becomes much less tedious.

Constants are regular variables like any others, but they're defined at the start and never changed through the program. To differentiate constants from other variables, type them in all caps.

You can also define a constant for a message that you'll be printing many times and don't want to type repeatedly, as in the following JavaScript script:

```
var SENSOR_MESSAGE = "The reading from your sensor is: "

(...)

console_output(SENSOR_MESSAGE + temperature_sensor)
console_output(SENSOR_MESSAGE + light_sensor)
console_output(SENSOR_MESSAGE + distance_sensor)
```

If you've programmed in languages such as C and C++ for example, you've probably dealt with constants in a similar fashion. From a computational point of view, those constants are quite different from what we did in the previous examples. For those languages, constants are their own data type; in fact, they're simply replaced with their values everywhere before the code actually runs. In Python and BoneScript, though, from a technical point of view they're regular variables like any others.

Comments, white space, and indentation

There's no such thing as a perfect method of programming. Advanced programmers usually develop their own style. There are definitely standards for writing better code, however. If you're working with a team, contributing to an open-source project, developing a program that will take several days or weeks to complete, or writing something that you may look at again a couple of months later, you should always do the following:

✔ **Comment your code.** Typing descriptive comments requires just a slight writing effort that can make an enormous difference in the long run. With proper comments, you never need to figure out what a snippet of code does. The explanation is right there!

✔ **Use white space.** Adding extra spaces between your variable names and functions, as well as lines between instructions, makes your code prettier and more readable. Most programming languages ignore extra white space, so there's absolutely no issue in using it to promote readability.

For example, you can use white space for organization in the form of extra lines between instructions to create blocks of similar code, as in this example:

```
import Adafruit_BBIO.PWM as PWM #import objects from libraries
import Adafruit_BBIO.ADC as ADC
import Adafruit_BBIO.UART as UART

import math #import libraries
import time
import serial

led = "P9_16" #define variables for pins
sensor = "P9_40"

PWM.start(led, 0) #initialize modules
ADC.setup()
UART.setup("UART1")
```

✔ **Indent your code.** Python forces you to use indentation, but many programming languages don't. Believe us when we say that being lazy in your programming and not caring about indentation may lead to a lot of frustration if a bug occurs. The bug may simply be a missing or extra closing brace (}), which is easy to detect if your code is indented — and a pain to find if it isn't.

The origin of the term *bug* comes from a literal bug in the system. The term was first used in computer science in 1946, when computer pioneer Grace Hooper revealed that the cause of a malfunction in an early electromechanical computer was a moth trapped in a relay.

Debugging

Quite often, your program might not work when you first run it. Sometimes, you come across runtime errors. These errors stop your program and print an error message on the terminal. In the following chunk of code, the closing parenthesis has been left out:

```
// Load BoneScript module
var b = require('bonescript; #bug is here
// Create a variable called led, which refers to the on-board USR3 LED
var led = "USR3";
```

That error results in this message:

```
/var/lib/cloud9/Projects/debug_example.js:9
var led = "USR3";
^^^
SyntaxError: Unexpected token var
    at Module._compile (module.js:439:25)
    at Object.Module._extensions..js (module.js:474:10)
    at Module.load (module.js:356:32)
    at Function.Module._load (module.js:312:12)
    at Function.Module.runMain (module.js:497:10)
    at startup (node.js:119:16)
    at node.js:902:3

[Process stopped]
```

The first line of the error message prints exactly where the trouble first arises: the ninth line of the debug_example.js file. The referenced line is always the first instruction after the line that was badly written, excluding blank and comment lines (because they aren't instructions). Thus, all you have to do is to check the instruction immediately before line 9.

These bugs are the best kinds of bug you can have. The interpreter notices that something is amiss and tries to help you figure out the issue.

Sometimes, though, you come across bugs that aren't really errors. Your program runs perfectly but doesn't do what it's supposed to do. These bugs are the tricky ones.

 A good analogy for this process is to think of the interpreter as a translator. You write the code in a language, and the interpreter translates it into something the computer can understand. Ultimately, the computer is a huge circuit that understands 1 and 0: HIGH and LOW. If the interpreter notices a grammatical error, it stops you and warns you about it. If you're spouting nonsense that's grammatically correct, however, the interpreter allows you to proceed. In the end, the interpreter warns that there's a problem with I is human because it's not grammatically correct, but it doesn't warn you about The BeagleBone is a microbanana.

The following script is the one used in Chapter 7 to blink an LED, with a very slight change. The change is almost unnoticeable, really, but it's enough to make the LED stay off rather than blinking. This is one of those bugs that the interpreter doesn't warn you about.

If you want to get a glimpse of how frustrating debugging can be, feel free to try to find the bug. Spoilers are after the code snippet.

```
/*
        Blink
        Turns an onboard LED on and off continuously,
        with intervals of 1 second.
*/
// Load BoneScript module
var b = require('bonescript');
// Create a variable called led, which refers to the onboard USR3 LED
var led = "USR3";
// Initialize the led as an OUTPUT
b.pinMode(led, b.OUTPUT);
// Create a variable called state, which stores the current state of the LED.
var state = b.LOW;
// Set the LED as LOW (off)
b.digitalWrite(led, state);
// Execute the toggle function every one second (1000 milliseconds)
setInterval(toggle, 1000);
// Function that turns the LED either HIGH (on) or LOW (off)
// depending on the parameter state.
function toggle() {
        if(state = b.LOW) state = b.HIGH; // if the LED is LOW (off), change
                the state to HIGH (on)
        else state = b.LOW; // otherwise, if the LED is HIGH (on), change
                the state to LOW (off)
        b.digitalWrite(led, state); // write the new state value to the led
                pin, turning the led on or off
}
```

The bug is in the following line of code:

```
if(state = b.LOW) state = b.HIGH; // if the LED is LOW
```

This mistake — using = instead of == when comparing two variables — is very common. Keep the following in mind:

- ✔ = is used to attribute a value to a variable.
- ✔ == is used to compare the value of two variables.

This is what happens inside that if statement:

1. state saves the value b.LOW (which is 0).
2. The condition inside the if is evaluated. This condition is merely the value of state, which is 0 (false).

3. The code inside that `if` — that is, `state = b.HIGH` — doesn't execute.

4. `state` always stays with the value `b.LOW`.

Had the code been written the other way around — that is, with `state = b.HIGH` — the `if` would always execute, and the `else` would never execute. The LED would just stay on.

Rather than scan the whole code with eagle eyes to find that one little mistake, you can detect which parts of the code are executing and which parts aren't, as well as finding the value of a variable by printing stuff everywhere. For example, in the following we add three instructions to print information on the terminal.

```
function toggle() {
        if(state = b.LOW){ // if the LED is LOW (off), change the state to
              HIGH (on)
                console.log("This happens 1.");
                state = b.HIGH;
        }
        else { // otherwise, if the LED is HIGH (on), change the state to
              LOW (off)
                console.log("This happens 2.");
                state = b.LOW;
        }
        b.digitalWrite(led, state); // write the new state value to the led
              pin, turning the led on or off
        console.log(state);
}
```

When you run the code with those changes, you see that only the code below `else` executes, and that the value of `state` is stuck on `0`. That shows you exactly where you have to look to find the problem with your program.

Another useful technique is to use comments for more than, well, comments. Whenever you want to remove a chunk of code but don't want to erase it (because you might use it later or because you're unsure whether removing it is the correct thing to do), you can simply wrap it up in comments: `/* code */` in BoneScript or `""" code """` in Python.

Despite being aware of several techniques to avoid bugs and to correct them when they do happen, naturally errors still happen frequently. It's true that searching for a bug is quite frustrating, but figuring it out and correcting it also provides great joy. Figure 11-1 shows the typical state of mind for a programmer over the course of time.

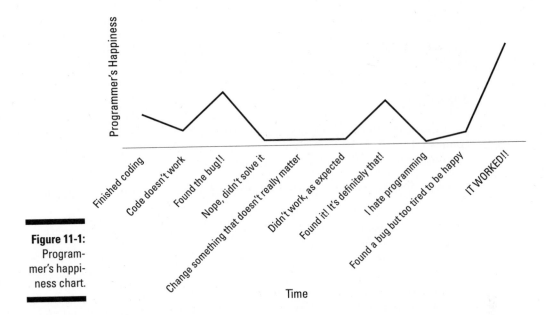

Figure 11-1:
Program-
mer's happi-
ness chart.

Diving into Binary and Data Storage

For simple applications, you don't need to know much about binary besides the fact that 1 is True/HIGH/on and 0 is False/LOW/off. A brief introduction to binary is important, however, for three reasons:

- ✔ In complex applications, especially (but not only) for mastering communication protocols such as UART, I2C, and SPI, having good knowledge of binary is very important.

- ✔ Binary is the foundation of all things regarding computers. Your variables are sets of ones and zeros. Your instructions are sets of ones and zeros. Everything you do on the computer is converted to a set of ones and zeros that command which parts of the computer's hardware go HIGH and which stay LOW.

- ✔ Knowing binary is awesome.

Have you ever wondered why copying things to a CD is often called *burning* the CD? Burning is what the CD recorder does. It has a laser that precisely burns some areas of the disc according to the data to be saved. The specific areas that the recorder burns and those that it doesn't are based on the data you're saving on the CD. The materials darkened by the laser are zeros; the ones left translucent are ones. The CD reader extracts the data by using another, much weaker laser to find all the ones and zeros on the disc. After that, the computer converts the binary code to user-readable data.

Binary

For those who don't understand it, binary often looks completely alien and complex. In reality, it's quite simple. It's like counting as though you had only two fingers in each hand. With ten fingers, here's what you do:

- ✔ 0, 1, 2, 3, 4, 5, 6, 7, 8, 9 and then add another number to the left, starting at 1.

- ✔ 10, 11, 12, 13, 14, (. . .), 19, 20, 21, 22 (. . .) and then add another number to the left, starting at 1.

- ✔ 100, 101, 102 (. . .), 110, 111, 112 (. . .).

In binary, though, you have only two fingers, so you proceed in the same way but you are limited to two numbers: 0 and 1 (hence, the name *binary)*. For example,

- ✔ 0, 1, and then add another number to the left, starting at 1.

- ✔ 10, 11, and then add another number to the left, starting at 1.

- ✔ 100, 101, 110, 111 and then add another number to the left, starting at 1.

- ✔ 1000, 1001, 1010, 1011, 1100, 1101, 1110, 1111, and then add another number to the left, starting at 1, and so on.

You read these numbers one by one. You read binary number 1001, for example, as "one zero zero one" (not "one thousand and one"). The same applies for hexadecimal (next section).

Converting from binary to decimal is quite straightforward. Look at the following example, which uses the binary code 1 0 1 0 0:

1	0	1	0	0
$1 \times 2^4 +$	$0 \times 2^3 +$	$1 \times 2^2 +$	$0 \times 2^1 +$	$0 \times 2^0 = 20$

Even though you may not realize it, the process is actually the same one you use for decimal numbers. Look at the decimal number 15634:

1	5	6	3	4
$1 \times 10^4 +$	$5 \times 10^3 +$	$6 \times 10^2 +$	$3 \times 10^1 +$	$4 \times 10^0 = 15634$

Hexadecimal

To avoid having hordes of ones and zeros filling computer screens, many applications use hexadecimal. For organization purposes, values are often displayed in hexadecimal rather than binary. Hexadecimal is another way to represent numbers, going from 0 to 15 in the following succession:

0, 1, 2, 3, 4, 5, 6, 7, 8, 9, A, B, C, D, F

In hexadecimal, you count up to 15 (hence the name **hexa**decimal), as if you had 16 fingers on each hand. The following example shows how to convert a hexadecimal number into a decimal number; it's a similar approach as the one in the previous section:

4	A	F	6	0
$4 \times 16^4 +$	$10 \times 16^3 +$	$15 \times 16^2 +$	$6 \times 16^1 +$	$0 \times 16^0 = 307040$

Data storage

Data on a computer is stored in bits (**bi**nary dig**its**). 0 is a bit. 01 is two bits. Nowadays, most computers are 32-bit or 64-bit, which means that the instructions, variables, and everything else that the computer works with are sets of 32 or 64 binary digits.

Characters on computers are often written based on the ASCII (American Standard Code for Information Interchange) table. This table defines a character for a set of 8 bits, which allows for a total of $2^8 = 256$ characters. The letter A (uppercase) is number 65 on the ASCII table, which is 0100 0001 in binary.

Signed integers require a bit (the first one is called the MSB, or most significant bit) to indicate whether a value is negative or positive. Thus, a signed integer on a 32-bit machine saves a value only up to 2^{31} rather than 2^{32}.

There's a lot more to talk about on the topic of how a computer uses binary to control everything that's going on inside it. For example, storing an integer value is completely different from storing a number with a decimal point, and negative values are also saved in a different way using a technique known as Two's complement (generally, as there are other techniques that can be employed). This book doesn't get into much detail on data storage, but if this section interests you, you should research it online.

Congratulations! You're now fully qualified to stamp Figure 11-2 on a T-shirt.

> There are 10 types
> of people in the world:
>
> those who understand binary
> and those who don't.

BoneScript-Specific Programming Tips

This section tells you a little about two concepts: looping and callbacks. These were briefly introduced in Chapter 7.

Looping, looping, and more looping

In Python, it's easy to make your code loop indefinitely. You simply use `while True:`, and the code runs forever until you manually stop it. Here's an example:

```python
#!/usr/bin/python

import Adafruit_BBIO.GPIO as GPIO
import time

led = "P9_14"
GPIO.setup(led, GPIO.OUT)

while True:
    GPIO.output(led, GPIO.HIGH)
    time.sleep(1)
    GPIO.output(led, GPIO.LOW)
    time.sleep(1)
```

BoneScript is a bit different, and you have a couple of ways to get it into looping. Chapters 7 and 8 cover some of these techniques, but we think that this topic deserves its own section.

Consider the following script to blink an LED:

```
var b = require('bonescript');
var led = "USR3";
b.pinMode(led, b.OUTPUT);
var state = b.LOW;
b.digitalWrite(led, state);
setInterval(toggle, 1000);

function toggle() {
        if(state == b.LOW) state = b.HIGH;
        else state = b.LOW;
        b.digitalWrite(led, state);
}
```

The preceding code makes your `toggle()` function run forever because the `setInverval()` function calls the `toggle()` function every second.

Alternatively, you can take advantage of the `setTimeout()` function to keep recalling your `loop()` function:

```
var b = require('bonescript');

var inputPin = "P9_36";
var outputPin = "P9_14";

b.pinMode(outputPin, b.ANALOG_OUTPUT);
loop();

function loop() {
    var value = b.analogRead(inputPin);
    b.analogWrite(outputPin, value);
    setTimeout(loop, 1);
}
```

The `loop()` function reads the analog `inputPin` and writes a value to the `outputPin` repeatedly until you stop your code. This simplicity is thanks to the `setTimeout()` function.

Understanding the importance of JavaScript callbacks

When you pass a function to another function as an argument, the process is called a *callback*. BoneScript projects in Chapters 7 and 8 use callbacks very often. Callbacks are extremely important in JavaScript, which is an asynchronous language, because they enable you to execute functions when an event occurs. In the preceding section, the `setInterval()` function has a loop as a callback; after 1 millisecond elapses, that function calls the `loop()` function.

The name *callback* refers to the fact that the callback is executed only upon completion of the main function.

If you consider that JavaScript was created for web interaction, it makes quite a lot of sense for it to be an asynchronous language. Most of the time, you don't want things to happen in succession. You want things to happen as responses to whatever the user does on the website.

Python-Specific Programming Tips

This section introduces some Python tips that can help you make your programs more organized, more efficient, and less subject to errors, while also introducing a few techniques for programming in Python.

Creating functions to clear up the mess

In BoneScript, creating functions is necessary because the code isn't read sequentially, so you need to use callbacks that refer to functions to make the code do what you want it to.

In Python, theoretically — and we place enormous emphasis on *theoretically* — functions aren't necessary. But writing a program that consists of several lines of code is extremely hard and frustrating if you don't resort to functions. The main part of a script should always feature little more than function calls.

Creating time-dependent code

When you work with projects that interact with the real world, managing the speed at which a program runs is important. Most of the Python code featured in Chapters 9 and 10 of this book have the `time.sleep()` function because you need to settle things down a bit when everything works at such high speeds. (The BeagleBone Black processes data every nanosecond!)

The `time.sleep()` function halts the program for a set amount of seconds. In some cases, that's not the kind of time control that you want. Imagine that you want part of your code to run for only a set amount of seconds instead of a set number of iterations. A good example would be a computer game in which the player has to accomplish a task in a limited amount of time. The code would use a new function, `time.time()`, in the following fashion:

```
#gets how many seconds have passed since the 1st of January of 1970
t0 = time.time()
t1 = time.time()
while t1 - t0 > 60: #runs this part for 60 seconds
        player_position = get_player_position()
        if (player_position > finish_line)
                    success = True
        else
                    success = False
        t1 = time.time()
```

The `time.time()` function returns how many seconds have elapsed since January 1, 1970 (midnight UTC/GMT), without counting leap seconds. This period is known as the *Unix epoch* and is basically Second Zero for Unix systems (such as Linux, Mac OS, iOS, and Android).

Most Unix systems store an epoch date as a signed 32-bit integer, which means that these systems can store only up to 2^{31} = 2147483648 seconds (see the "Data storage" section to better understand what a signed integer is). Problems may arise 2^{31} seconds after the Unix epoch on January 19, 2038. Think of this date as the Unix system's version of the Y2K problem. In fact, this event is often regarded as the Y2038 problem.

The code starts by defining two values that have the same value:

```
t0 = time.time()
t1 = time.time()
```

Thus, at the start of the program, $t1 - t0 = 0$.

Note that the `while` loop tests for $t1 - t0 > 60$. At the end of the loop, you determine the time again and save it as `t1`. You repeat this process over and over until 60 seconds have passed. `t0` stays the same throughout the entire `while` loop, whereas `t1` takes in the value of the time at every iteration. Eventually, the difference between these two variables will be greater than 60, which means that 60 seconds will have elapsed.

The `time` library has plenty of interesting functions. Feel free to check out its documentation at `https://docs.python.org/2/library/time.html`. You can also check its Python console manual by typing the following at the command line:

```
python
>>> import time as time
>>> help(time)
```

Part V
Turning Your BeagleBone into a Desktop Computer

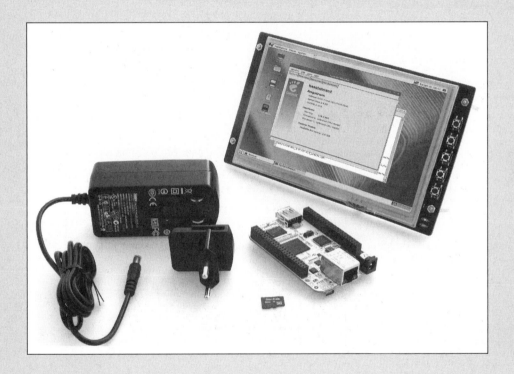

In this part . . .

✔ Gathering all the peripherals and turning your BeagleBone Black into a desktop computer

✔ Discovering the BeagleBone Black's desktop features

✔ Understanding how the World Wide Web works: HTML, CSS and JavaScript

✔ Creating your own website and publishing it for the world to see

Chapter 12

Using Your BeagleBone Black as a Desktop Computer

*Y*our BeagleBone Black definitely doesn't look like a regular computer. You might be wondering, "How can such a small device be compared to a laptop or a desktop computer?" Don't let that tiny board fool you. It's quite capable of doing tasks and projects that your computer can't do.

This chapter explains how you can connect a few peripherals to your BeagleBone Black and turn it into a desktop computer. It probably won't be as fast as your computer, but it still can be quite fun to play with.

Getting Started

The default graphical user interface (GUI) used for the BeagleBone Black is *LXDE,* which stands for *lightweight X11 desktop environment.* It's part of the Debian Wheezy distribution, and it's one of the best solutions for the BeagleBone Black because it's optimized for processor and memory use. It's a lightweight GUI.

Before you start connecting all your peripherals, keep in mind that this chapter is specifically about the BeagleBone Black. The Original BeagleBone doesn't support an HDMI output. If you purchase an LCD cape (such as the one shown in Figure 12-1) for your Original BeagleBone, however, you can still do the project in this chapter. You can also use the BeagleBone Black with it, if you prefer it that way. The LCD capes you can choose among have slightly different configurations, but they all come with documentation that explains exactly how to use them. When you get your BeagleBone with an LCD cape up and running, the desktop environment is exactly the same as we show you throughout this chapter, so you can easily follow along.

Figure 12-1:
Original
BeagleBone
with an LCD
cape.

Connecting the Peripherals and Booting Up

Most peripherals and cables required for this chapter are pretty standard. You may already have most of them, and those that you don't have are easy to acquire. You may need the following list of components:

- Micro HDMI cable
- USB hub

✔ Keyboard and mouse

✔ Ethernet cable

✔ Power adapter

Figure 12-2 shows where you connect each of the peripherals on the BeagleBone Black.

DC power   Ethernet

Figure 12-2:
BeagleBone
Black's
peripheral
connection
locations.

Micro HDMI

USB host

We assume that at this point, you've installed the latest image of the Debian operating system in your BeagleBone Black's eMMC memory or on a microSD card that's inserted into your BeagleBone. If that's not the case, see Chapter 2 for instructions.

Make sure that your BeagleBone Black is properly updated and upgraded. It's a good idea to connect to it through Secure Shell (SSH) and run the following on the command line:

```
sudo apt-get update && sudo apt-get upgrade
```

Connecting a Micro HDMI cable or DVI display

HDMI (High-Definition Multimedia Interface) displays have replaced DVI (Digital Visual Interface) displays. Although many DVI displays are still being used for many applications, the trend has been to shift to HDMI. The BeagleBone supports only Micro HDMI output, but if you have an adapter that can convert DVI to HDMI, you can repurpose an old DVI display. If you have an active HDMI converter, make sure that it has an external power source.

We recommend using a Micro HDMI cable with an HDMI display. Some DVI displays won't be compatible with your BeagleBone Black, and ultimately, a DVI display may not display anything in your screen. You could spend a lot of time trying to figure out the problem, only to realize that the screen you used isn't compatible with your BeagleBone Black.

Connecting a USB hub, keyboard, and mouse

Because the BeagleBone Black offers only one USB host slot, you must use a USB hub to plug in more than a single USB peripheral. You can get an inexpensive hub like the one shown in Figure 12-3 at most electronics or computer stores. To use the BeagleBone Black as a desktop computer, you need to connect a USB keyboard and mouse to it.

Figure 12-3:
A USB hub.

The virtual keyboard alternative

If you currently don't have a USB hub and/or a keyboard, but you want to use the BeagleBone as a desktop computer as soon as possible, you can plug the mouse into the USB port of the BeagleBone and download a virtual keyboard. This approach isn't optimal, but it's a good short-term solution. You download the keyboard by typing the following on the terminal:

```
sudo apt-get install Florence
```

This command installs a program named Florence that runs a virtual keyboard. You can install it via an SSH connection or by using the terminal on the Desktop environment, as shown in the section "Accessing the Terminal" later in this chapter.

Connecting to your router

Do you ever wonder whether it's still possible to use a computer without an Internet connection? We can't recall a time in the past few years that being on a computer without an Internet connection was an enjoyable experience. You can simply connect an Ethernet cable from your home router to the BeagleBone Black. After you've made that connection, you can easily install and update software or simply browse the web while using your BeagleBone Black as a desktop computer.

In Figure 12-4, you see an Ethernet cable connected to a BeagleBone Black.

Ethernet cable

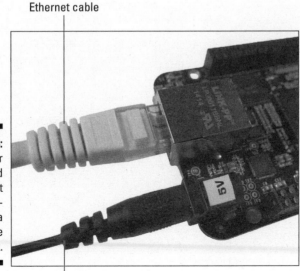

Figure 12-4: Power adapter and Ethernet cable connected to a BeagleBone Black.

Power adapter cable

Connecting the power

Connecting both a mouse and a keyboard to the BeagleBone Black — as you do in this chapter — can be quite power-consuming, so the power provided by an USB cable may not be sufficient for everything to work smoothly. If you connect your BeagleBone Black via USB to your desktop or laptop computer and everything lights up, great! The BeagleBone Black is getting power. Some functions may be slow or won't work properly, however. In the worst-case scenario, the peripherals may not even light up. To err on the side of caution, you should get a proper power adapter. That way, you can rest assured that your BeagleBone has all the energy necessary to run at its fullest speed and performance. In Figure 12-4, a 5V power source is connected to a BeagleBone Black.

Make sure your power adapter provides 5V — not more or less than that! Also, you need to ensure that the power adapter has the correct polarity on the jack: The center provides 5V, whereas the outer ring is ground (GND).

Booting up

As soon as you apply power to your BeagleBone Black, it automatically boots. After a few seconds, you should see the typical, awesome-looking beagle with its tongue sticking out as the background of the desktop (see Figure 12-5).

Figure 12-5:
First look at your BeagleBone Black's desktop environment.

If you don't see anything on the display, try disconnecting everything and then redoing the connections described in the preceding sections. Then reboot your board. Also, if you're using a TV set as your display, make sure that you change its source to HDMI.

If you can't see the full image shown in Figure 12-5, or if it's small in comparison with the screen, the problem has to do with your screen's adjustment. Try going into your screen's settings menu and adjusting the picture size until everything fits in a way that's pleasant to you.

Accessing the Terminal

When you have your BeagleBone Black set up like a desktop computer, you can do all the regular things that you do on a computer — such as creating files and folders or running applications — without using the terminal. If you have the knack of the terminal, however, and know how much faster things can be done that way, you can easily access it.

Even if you prefer doing everything in the desktop environment and using the terminal as little as possible, you still need to use it for some tasks, such as installing and updating software.

To access the terminal, click the icon in the bottom-left corner of your screen. Mouse over to Accessories and click LXTerminal, as shown in Figure 12-6.

You can read more about how to use the Linux terminal in Chapter 4.

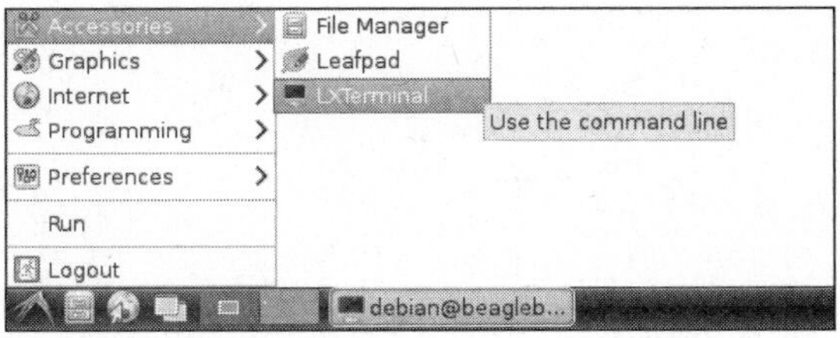

Figure 12-6:
Opening the
terminal.

Figure 12-7 shows an open terminal window. You can have several terminal windows and tabs open at the same time. Click File to generate a new terminal window or tab. You can also see the keyboard shortcuts that do the same things on the menu that appears when you click File.

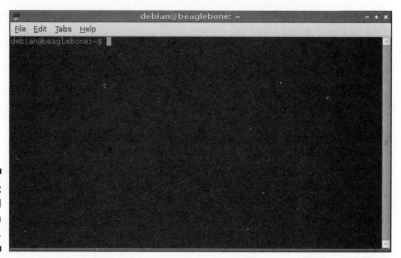

Figure 12-7:
The terminal
application
window.

During an LXDE session, you may need to resize or minimize your open windows, such as the terminal. You handle this task in much the same way as you would on a Mac or Windows computer.

In this terminal, you can do pretty much the same things you may have done in previous chapters, but here you're controlling the BeagleBone directly rather than controlling it remotely through the use of SSH. If you've created the `emailer.py` program from Chapter 10, for example, you can run it from the terminal. Start by logging in as `root` and then changing to the `Projects` folder:

```
sudo su
cd /var/lib/cloud9/Projects
python emailing.py
```

To run the Python script from the terminal, simply type

```
python emailing.py
```

Chapter 4 mentions the nano terminal text editor, which you can use to view and edit your text files. When you use your BeagleBone Black to create a desktop environment, you have other text-editor options, such as Leafpad. If you are in the Projects folder, type the following command in the terminal:

```
leafpad emailing.py
```

Note that after you issue the command line to start Leafpad, the terminal becomes stuck; you can't write anything in the terminal from that point on. (Well, you can, but it won't have any effect.) That's not a problem because you can have as many open terminal windows and tabs as you want, and only the one where you issued a command to run a program is stuck. Any other open tabs or terminal windows are still functional. When you want to terminate something that's being run in the terminal, for example Leafpad, simply press Ctrl+C with the terminal window that's running it open.

Ctrl+C is the Cancel command when you are operating the Terminal. If you need to copy something from the Terminal, the appropriate shortcut is Ctrl+Shift+C. You can use Ctrl+Shift+X for cutting and Ctrl+Shif+V for pasting.

If running the script failed, you probably don't have the necessary permissions. When you use the BeagleBone as a desktop computer, you're logged in as `debian`. Regardless, you can still run programs as `root`. Don't forget to log in as `root` or to precede your commands with `sudo`:

```
sudo python /var/lib/cloud9/emailing.py
```

Roaming the Desktop Environment

Before you start managing files or browsing the web, you need to know how to navigate the environment. This section explains the components of the interface.

Viewing the Applications menu

Click the leftmost icon (the Applications menu) in the bottom-left corner of your screen; it sort of looks like a bird. The Applications menu appears, as shown in Figure 12-6 earlier in this chapter.

The Applications menu is more or less the same as the Windows Start menu. After you've installed more programs, other categories should appear, such as Graphics for image-related programs and Programming for tools used to write code. Whenever you mouse over one of these categories, you see a list of applications associated with the category, and you can click a program's name to run it.

Using the task bar

At the bottom of the screen is a bar known as a panel. Most people, however, would call this the task bar. This bar provides both information and shortcuts for accessing your programs (see Figure 12-8).

Figure 12-8:
The task
bar.

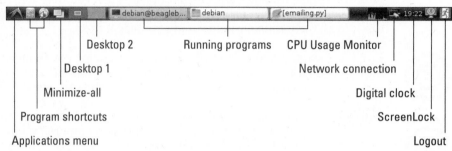

Desktop 2   Running programs   CPU Usage Monitor

Desktop 1   Network connection

Minimize-all   Digital clock

Program shortcuts   ScreenLock

Applications menu   Logout

From left to right, the task bar displays the following things by default:

- **Applications menu icon:** You can read more about this menu on the previous section.

- **Shortcut icons for programs:** By default, the two shortcuts are for the File Manager and the web browser, but you can add other shortcuts. This is shown later in this chapter in the "Adding application shortcuts" section.

- **Minimize-all button:** This button minimizes all the windows that are open on your LXDE session.

- **Buttons to change into different desktops:** By default, there are two of them. You can read about using multiple desktops in the "Working with multiple desktops" section later in this chapter.

- **All programs that you have currently running:** Programs that are currently minimized have their names enclosed in brackets. In Figure 12-8, for example, [emailing.py] is a minimized Leafpad window.

- **CPU Usage Monitor:** The green graph displays the toll that your CPU is taking at the moment. If the CPU is currently hard at work, the rectangle is filled with green. If you just started a processor-heavy program, several peaks show up at the rightmost side. Note that this graph runs from right to left, displaying the newest data on the right.

- **Information about network connection:** Mousing over this icon provides information regarding your network connection. You can double-click it to manage your available connections.

- **Digital clock:** The clock displays the current time. When you mouse over the time, the date and day of the week are displayed.

- **ScreenLock button:** At the time this book was written, that button was buggy and wouldn't work. When the bugs are fixed, clicking the icon locks the screen so that the screen saver displays and you have to type a password when you want to return to work.

- **Logout button:** When you click it, a new window opens so you can shut down, reboot, or log out of the current session.

Changing icon settings

Save for the CPU Usage Monitor, you can right-click all icons on the task bar to alter their settings, as you see in Figure 12-9.

Adding and removing plug-ins

In Figure 12-9 you also see an option to add and remove panel items. When you choose this option, the Panel Preferences dialog box opens (see Figure 12-10). Click the Add button in the Panel Preferences dialog box to see another window that features several plug-ins that you can add to the task bar. To add a plug-in, click the name of the plug-in and then click Add.

Figure 12-10:
Adding a
plug-in to
the task bar.

To remove a plug-in from the task bar, right-click it. You see the menu in Figure 12-9. Click Remove "*plug-in name*" (where *plug-in name* is the actual name of the plug-in) from Panel to remove the plug-in.

Adding application shortcuts

It's important to note that the previous section explains how to add plug-ins not shortcuts for applications. To add an application shortcut, you use the Application Launch Bar plug-in that's on the task bar by default; it's next to the Applications menu icon. Follow these steps to add a shortcut icon to the task bar:

1. **Right-click the Application Launch Bar plug-in icon, and choose Settings from the shortcut menu.**

   The Application Launch Bar dialog box opens (see Figure 12-11). On the left side, you see the applications for which you already have shortcuts.

2. **From the list on the right side of the Application Launch Bar dialog box, select the application for which you want to create a shortcut.**

   All applications you currently have on your BeagleBone are listed, separated by category.

3. **Click the Add button.**

Figure 12-11:
Adding a shortcut for an application on the task bar.

Adding task bars

You can add more task bars to your screen. Right-click anywhere on the current task bar and choose Create New Panel from the shortcut menu. A dialog box opens that enables you to choose the new task bar's position and size. You can also adjust its appearance and designate the plug-ins you want it to feature.

Working with multiple desktops

Linux systems in general allow you to use multiple desktops on the same monitor. Having multiple desktops open is handy for keeping things organized and doing tasks in parallel. There are several ways to change between desktops. For one, you can click the desktop buttons described in the preceding section (refer to Figure 12-8). The blue rectangle is the active desktop. To change to the other one, simply click the gray rectangle.

On the icons for the desktops, the smaller rectangle shows the windows that are open and where on the screen they are. In the case of Figure 12-8, all the windows are in the center of the screen, and the second desktop doesn't have any window open.

Even if you prefer using a single desktop, it's good to know about the desktop icons on the task bar. If you unknowingly change from the active desktop to the other desktop, and it looks as though all your work has disappeared in the blink of an eye, just click the other desktop icon to return to the desktop where you were working.

The two desktops are completely independent, so you can customize each one, with different icons on the desktop, different shortcuts, and different themes. You can also have a program running on one desktop but not on the other.

This feature can be really, really useful sometimes. For instance, you could use one desktop for work — featuring programming applications, documentation and a few folders with all your scripts — and another for play — featuring programs for media playing and/or some videogames. If you are working on something that requires both research and development, you could use Desktop 1 for all the websites, datasheets, and any kind of documentation necessary and Desktop 2 for writing the code.

To add a desktop, right-click the Desktop Pager plug-in — that's where the icons for choosing between each desktop are — and choose Desktop Pager Settings from the shortcut menu. A window opens, in which you can choose the number of desktops and assign them names.

To move a running program from one desktop to the other, simply right-click the application's title bar and choose Send to Desktop from the shortcut menu. You can choose which desktop you want the application to go to, and you can even send it to all desktops. If you drag the application window to either side of the screen, the application is sent to the next desktop.

You can have as many desktops as you want, but don't push the BeagleBone too hard. Even though it's quite powerful for its size, it's still a system with limited resources.

Customizing the BeagleBone

You use the Preferences tab of the Applications menu to set up the BeagleBone desktop environment in a way that's comfortable, good-looking, and easy to use.

Customizing the desktop appearance

To customize your desktop, choose Applications⇨Preferences⇨ Openbox Configuration Manager. After a second or two, you see the Openbox Configuration Manager, which includes many customization options (see Figure 12-12).

Figure 12-12:
The
Openbox
Configura-
tion
Manager.

With the configuration manager, you can change pretty much every single thing about the appearance of your desktop. Using the Theme tab, you can change the theme to one of the many predefined themes or installing themes that you fetch from the Internet. With the Appearance tab, you can change the font of all text that appears in your windows, such as the title, menu headers, and menu items.

You can also customize your windows, mouse, and the margins of the desktop. With the Desktops tab, you can change the names of your desktops to something that makes more sense.

These examples just scratch the surface of the customization you can do. Play around with the settings on the different tabs until you get the style that you prefer. Don't worry — it's impossible to break anything by merely changing its appearance.

Choosing a screen saver

On the Preferences tab, you can choose the Screensaver option to not only change your screen saver, but also define several parameters for it, such as the time it takes for the screen to lock and the time it takes for the screen-saver animation to restart.

You can choose among plenty of screen savers and modes. If you prefer not to use a screen saver, you can disable the feature or just have a blank screen.

Creating icons on the desktop

Apart from that awesome-looking beagle on the desktop, the screen looks kind of bland, doesn't it? To make your desktop look more like what you may be used to on a typical computer, you can add a few icons for applications, folders, and files that you use frequently.

First, you create shortcuts for applications on your desktop by following these steps:

1. Click the Applications menu icon for in the lower-left corner of your screen.

2. Mouse over to the application you want to have on the desktop and right-click it.

3. Select Add to Desktop as shown in Figure 12-13.

Figure 12-13:
Adding
shortcuts
for applica-
tions on the
desktop.

In several chapters of this book, you use the `Projects` folder quite a lot. If you've already created it when going through other chapters, then having it on the desktop would be convenient. Normally, you could add a folder to the desktop through standard drag-and-drop or copy-and-paste procedures (similar to what you'd do on a Windows or Mac computer).

Because the `Projects` folder isn't below `/home/debian`, however, you don't have the necessary permissions to move it around by standard means. Generally, any folder that isn't below `/home/debian` has only execute and read permission for users other than the administrator of the system, `root`, which means that although you can open the folder and see its contents, you can't edit or move the folder or its contents unless you're logged in as `root`. To move the `Projects` folder, use the following steps:

1. **Start the terminal and log in as** `root`, **as follows:**

```
sudo su
```

Keep in mind that you're logged in as `root` only in the terminal. Logging in as superuser doesn't give you `root` permissions in the desktop environment — only on the command line.

2. **Copy the** `Projects` **folder to the desktop.**

You have to do this recursively because other files are inside the `Projects` folder. Consequently, you use the `-r` option:

```
cp -r /var/lib/cloud9/Projects /home/debian/Desktop
```

The `Projects` folder should immediately show up on your desktop. You still don't have permission to see or change any of the files within it, though.

3. **Add read and write permission for all, doing so recursively to the entire folder by typing the following command:**

```
chmod -R a+rw Projects
```

Some commands use `-r` for the recursive option, whereas others use `-R`. The `cp` and `chmod` commands used in these steps are good examples. Using the wrong case is often a source of errors.

You should now be able to access and alter any files in your `Projects` folder within the desktop environment.

To change to the regular user again while you're in the terminal emulator, type **login <*username*>** and then enter a password. The default username is `debian`, and the default password is `temppwd`.

If you're unsure about the concepts of permissions, root and terminal commands, you should check Chapter 4. You can also read how to change the username and password of your BeagleBone's regular user in Chapter 4.

Changing the desktop background

You can search for backgrounds to download from the Internet. Alternatively, you can use a background from your usual computer by transferring it to the BeagleBone on a USB drive. The "Accessing external storage devices" section explains how to transfer a file from a USB drive. We challenge you to find a desktop background that looks cooler than that dog, though!

After you download or copy the background you want to use, follow these steps to change the background:

1. **Right-click any empty spot on the desktop, and choose Desktop Preferences from the shortcut menu.**

2. **Make your selections for customizing your desktop (see Figure 12-14).**

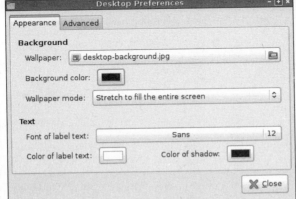

Figure 12-14: The Desktop Preferences dialog box.

Using the File Manager

The File Manager (see Figure 12-15) is the tool you use to manage your files. (Whew, didn't see that one coming!) Chapter 4 explains how to create directories, rename and copy files, and so on by using command-line options while controlling the BeagleBone remotely through SSH, but you can do those things with a more familiar approach by using the File Manager. If you prefer, you can still use the command line, naturally.

The File Manager bears many striking resemblances to Windows's File Explorer. You do things such as selecting and copying files in the exact same way. Additionally, most of the keyboard shortcuts available in Windows and Mac OS X are supported by LXDE. The widely known Ctrl+C and Ctrl+V shortcuts are available for copying and pasting files and folders, for example.

Even though using the terminal may seem alien and difficult at first, after you get the gist of it, it greatly speeds the process of managing files. Being a Linux Shell ninja is not about style alone. The terminal really does have several advantages; it just takes a while to get used to it.

Previous Folder

Next Folder

Folder History

Up to Parent's Folder

Home

Current path

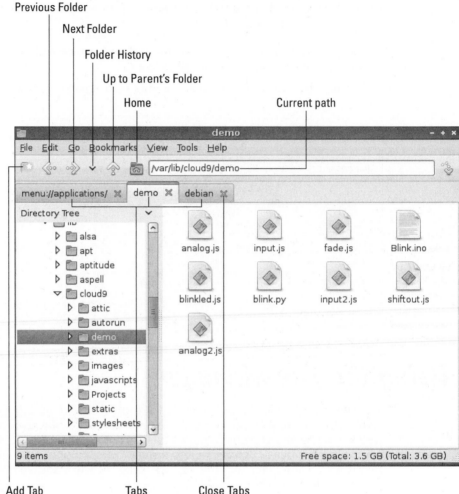

Figure 12-15:
The
LXDE File
Manager
on the
BeagleBone.

Add Tab   Tabs   Close Tabs

 You start the File Manager by choosing Applications⇨Accessories or clicking its button in the bottom-left corner of the screen.

Navigating the File Manager

On the right side of Figure 12-15, shown earlier in this chapter, you see all files and folders within the open folder. You open folders and files by double-clicking them. Files open in the default application for that type of file. If Leafpad is your default text editor, for example, a .txt file would open in it.

In some cases, you may want to open a file with a different application. Take an `.html` file, for example. You would want to open it with a text editor to edit its contents and with your web browser so you can see the actual page. (This type of thing happens a lot in Chapter 15, which introduces HTML.) To open a file with an application other than the default, follow these steps:

1. **Right-click the file, and choose Open With from the shortcut menu.**

   The Choose an Application dialog box opens, enabling you to choose the application you want to use to open the file (see Figure 12-16).

2. **Click the application you want to use.**

3. **If you want this application to be the default application for that type of file, select the Set Selected Application as Default Action of This File Type box at the bottom of the dialog box.**

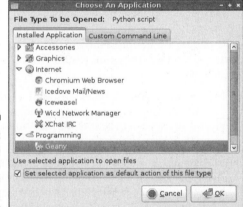

Figure 12-16:
Choosing an application to open a file.

On the left side of the File Manager window (refer to Figure 12-15) is the directory tree, which shows the parent folder of the current folder and all the folders above that. The `root` directory is also shown.

Geany

In Figure 12-16, the default application for opening Python scripts is set to be Geany. Geany is a helpful yet simple integrated development environment (IDE) for programming. Unlike Leafpad, but like Cloud9, it highlights different parts of code in different colors and provides several other useful tools, such as a terminal window in the IDE itself, akin to Cloud9. You can install it by typing the following command:

```
sudo apt-get install geany
```

Immediately above those directories, you can change what you want to be displayed. Instead of having the directory tree showing, for example, you could have Places showing. You can select between one or the other by pressing the arrow next to Directory Tree/Places (see Figure 12-15, earlier in this chapter). Figure 12-17 shows what you see when you have the Places displaying.

Figure 12-17:
Displaying
Places.

Places are special types of folders, and at least four are always available:

- ✔ debian is what could be called the main directory. Because you're logged in as debian, this place is the only one where you have permission to create and edit files.

- ✔ Desktop, a folder inside debian, holds the files and folders that you can see on the desktop of your BeagleBone. It should be filled with documents and programs that you use frequently and want to have easy access to.

- ✔ Trash holds your deleted files and folders. Whenever you delete something (by selecting it and then pressing the Delete key), it's not erased from your BeagleBone; it goes to the Trash folder. This is a good thing. If you change your mind about deleting something, you can just go to the Trash folder, right-click a file, and restore it from the shortcut menu. On the other hand, if you want to erase the files in the trash from your computer, just right-click the Trash icon and choose Empty Trash from the shortcut menu.

  There's no turning back after you choose the Empty Trash command! Your files are gone.

- ✔ Applications has all the applications on your BeagleBone, sorted by categories. Save for the Run and Logout buttons, it shows virtually the same things as the Applications menu.

Additionally, any mounted devices show up as places. When we captured Figure 12-17, for example, we had a LEXAR USB stick plugged into the USB hub. Bookmarked folders also appear as places.

Note that the File Manager has a similar design to that of a web browser. It features several familiar buttons, such as Home, Add Tab, and Bookmarks. You can also check your folder history and access a folder directly by typing the full path to a folder in the Path bar (labeled as Current Path in Figure 12-15), the same as you would do with a website's address.

Creating blank files

To create a blank file, choose File⇨Create New⇨Blank File. You see a dialog box that prompts you to enter a name for the new file. If you change your mind about creating the file, you can click the Cancel button. Alternatively, you can right-click any empty space in the desired folder and choose Create New from the shortcut menu.

A cool thing about Linux systems is that they let you turn a blank file into pretty much anything. That blank file could easily be a program in Python, C, or JavaScript; an HTML file; or a shell script. It could also merely be a text file, which is the default. The extension you assign when you save the file is what defines its application.

Creating new folders

Folders are great ways to keep your files organized. You can have all the programs, files, and folders structured in a way that feels comfortable for you.

Creating a new folder is much like creating a blank file. Choose File⇨Create New⇨Folder, or right-click an empty space and choose Create New from the shortcut menu. In the dialog box that opens, type the name you want to use for the folder you're creating.

You don't have the necessary permission to create files and folders in other folders except those that are inside the `debian` directory unless you go through the terminal and are logged in as `root`.

Opening a folder in the terminal

A very useful option on the Tools menu is the Open Current Folder in Terminal option, which does exactly what its name suggests. This command enables you to use the Linux commands to make changes in the current folder. (Read Chapter 4 for more information about the Linux commands you can use.)

There are several advantages to using a terminal window:

✔ You can run scripts that you have in that folder by using the terminal.

✔ If you've mastered using the command line, you can do things much faster than you can by using the File Manager.

✔ Even though you're not logged in as root in your session, you can issue root commands through the terminal. Simply precede each command with sudo.

The Tools menu also includes an Open Current Folder as Root command. Sometimes, though, this command doesn't work properly until you add some extra features that aren't enabled in the BeagleBone by default. In addition, being logged in as root is often somewhat dangerous, especially if you're connected to a network. We think that anything that you want to do as root, you can achieve more easily and safely by using the terminal.

Accessing external storage devices

Any external USB storage device (such as an external hard drive or USB stick) that you plug in is automatically recognized by the BeagleBone. After you've plugged in a device, you see the window shown in Figure 12-18. Afterward, the device appears in Places (see LEXAR in Figure 12-17 earlier in this chapter).

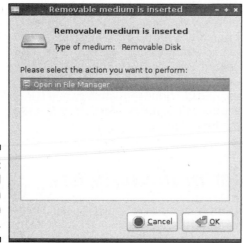

Figure 12-18:
An external medium has been inserted.

Using the Task Manager

The CPU Usage Monitor on the task bar displays the heavy lifting that the BeagleBone's processor is doing. If the graph shows many green peaks or just a flat bar, the processor is hard at work, and the BeagleBone may be slow for the time being. Maybe it's still loading a program, or maybe you're running way too many programs.

The CPU Usage Monitor scrolls from right to left, which means that the green peaks on the right display the most recent data.

You can press Ctrl+Alt+Del to start the Task Manager, which shows which programs are currently running (see Figure 12-19). You can also open it through the Applications menu, under the category System Tools.

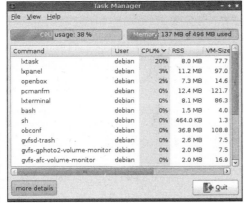

Figure 12-19: The Task Manager.

LXDE's Task Manager may not come installed by default, in which case, pressing Ctrl+Alt+Del won't work. But this is Linux, which means that installing software is a breeze. With an Internet connection, you install the Task Manager, by typing the following in the terminal:

```
sudo apt-get install lxtask
```

The Task Manager shows all the processes that are currently running on the BeagleBone, as well as the CPU and memory use. If a program isn't responding, you can terminate it from the Task Manager, by right-clicking the program name and choosing Term from the shortcut menu. With this command you are politely asking the program to close, allowing it to shut down safely and closing all files and programs that depend on it. If the process is being stubborn, you can also use the rough method, which is to kill it. When you right-click a process and choose Kill from the shortcut menu, the program is terminated immediately, and some data may be lost.

Many processes shown in the Task Manager are probably alien to you, and some are necessary to run the board itself. Don't play around with processes that you don't recognize: You may crash the BeagleBone and corrupt some data. Additionally, be patient. Programs usually don't crash; they just take a while to initiate. You should use the Task Manager to terminate or kill programs only as a last resort.

Browsing the Web

To browse the web, you need to start a web browser. Although several options do exist, the only one that comes installed by default on the BeagleBone is the Chromium web browser. To start it, you have two options:

- ✔ Click the task bar icon for the web browser in the bottom-left corner of the screen.

- ✔ Choose Applications➪Internet➪Chromium Web Browser.

Don't forget to have your BeagleBone connected to the Internet before you launch the web browser. The "Connecting to your router" section explains how to have your BeagleBone connected to the Internet.

Figure 12-20 shows the Chromium web browser. It includes a toolbar with some useful buttons, as well as an address bar. Naturally, most of the web browser's space is allocated for the web page itself.

Chromium is the open-source web browser that provides the source code for the widely known Google Chrome browser. If you normally use Google Chrome, you'll feel just at home using Chromium.

Using the Customization menu

Figure 12-21 shows Chromium's Customization menu, which lets you open new tabs, new windows, and Incognito windows, which are windows that don't save the web pages that you visit in your history.

From the Customization menu, you can also access your bookmarks, check your recent tabs, and zoom the page. Several tools are available, such as Find and Print, and you can check your history and your recent downloads by choosing their commands.

Previous Page

Next Page

Reload Page   Tabs

Add New tab

Close tab

Address bar

Bookmark Page

Next Match

Previous Match

Find bar

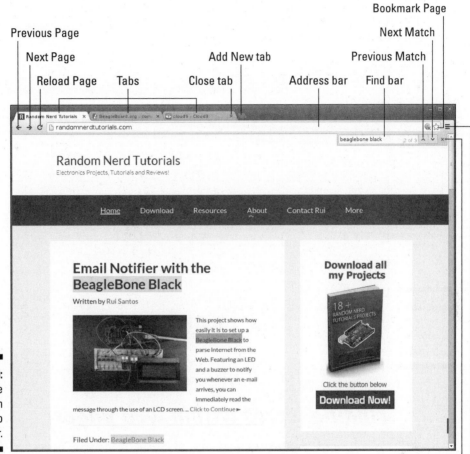

Figure 12-20:
The
Chromium
web
browser.

Close Find bar

Customization menu

Searching for web pages

Chromium's default search engine is Google, which should meet most of your needs as far as search engines are concerned. To search for something on the Internet, you can simply type what you're looking for in the address bar. If you type something other than a web-page address, the browser treats the text as a Google search.

If you prefer another search engine, you can change it by choosing Customization➪Settings and changing the default search engine in the Search section of the resulting dialog box.

Figure 12-21: Chromium's Customization menu.

Finding words within web pages

To find words on the web page you're currently visiting, press Ctrl+F. The Find bar appears (refer to Figure 12-20). When it does, type the word or group of words that you want to search for. Found instances of the search item are highlighted on the web page, and you can use the up and down arrows on the Find bar to move to the next or previous match.

The Find tool of Chromium's web browser is not case-sensitive.

When your search item includes more than one word, Find tries to locate a phrase that looks exactly the way you typed it.

Using tabbed browsing

Figure 12-20 shows three open tabs: Rui's website, beagleboard.org, and our reliable Cloud9 IDE. Having multiple tabs open enables you to change between open web pages quickly and easily.

To add a new tab, click the New Tab button, choose Customization⇨New Tab, or you press Ctrl+T. The page that opens includes links to some of your most-visited web pages, as well as a Google search bar. Additionally, if you want to open a web page by clicking a hyperlink, but you want it to be opened on a new tab, you can click the hyperlink while pressing and holding the Ctrl key.

To move among the different tabs, click the one you want to go to. To close a tab, click the X button next to its name. If you close a tab by mistake and want to reopen it, choose Customization⇨Recent Tabs. You see a list of the tabs you've had open recently; click one to reopen it.

You have several useful keyboard shortcuts for navigating tabs:

- ✔ Ctrl+Tab cycles through the tabs in order from left to right.
- ✔ Ctrl+Shift+Tab cycles through the tabs from right to left.
- ✔ Ctrl+*number* takes you to a specific tab. If you have more than nine tabs open, Ctrl+9 always takes you to the last tab.

Be careful about having too many tabs open! The BeagleBone's CPU may not be able to handle that much data.

Adding and using bookmarks

Adding bookmarks is a great way to open your favorite web pages easily. When you click the star next to the address bar (refer to Figure 12-20), the Bookmark dialog box pops up (see Figure 12-22). You can change the name of the bookmark and designate the folder in which the bookmark will be stored.

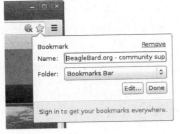

Figure 12-22: Adding a bookmark.

If you have a Google account, you can sign in to it to have your bookmarks shared across all your computers.

To see your bookmarks, choose Customization⇨Bookmarks. You can also check the Show Bookmarks Bar box that appears in the Bookmarks menu to have all your bookmarks appear below the address bar in the Chromium web browser.

Changing settings

Naturally, several settings are defined by default in Chromium, such as the search engine. You can change these settings by choosing Customization⇨Settings.

You can set your preferences for how a new page opens in Chromium. Choose Customization⇨Settings. Under On startup (see Figure 12-23), you have the following options to specify what should happen when you start Chromium:

- **Open the New Tab Page:** This option starts Chromium with blank page featuring a Google search bar and links to your most frequented websites. This is the default setting.

- **Continue Where I Left Off:** the page restores to where you left off the last time you used the browser. The tabs you had open previously reopen.

- **Open a Specific Page or Set of Pages:** You can define a set of pages automatically open when you start Chromium. For example, you might choose to have your email service, Facebook page, and favorite newspaper open.

You can choose a theme for Chromium. In the Appearance section (see Figure 12-23), you can choose to show the Home button, which appears next to the Reload button and takes you back to your home page. When you check that box, you have the option to define a home page.

When you click the Show Advanced Settings link, even more options show up. In the advanced settings, there are three different sections that deserve special attention.

- With the Privacy section you activate services that protect you while you're on the Internet.

- With the Web Content section you choose the zoom of your web pages and the size of the text on the pages.

- With the Languages section you choose which language(s) your spell-checker should check for errors when you are writing something on the browser. Additionally, you can check a box to have the browser offer the possibility to translate a page whenever a page isn't on its default language.

There are plenty of settings for you to explore; feel free to nose around until Chromium is customized in a way you feel comfortable with.

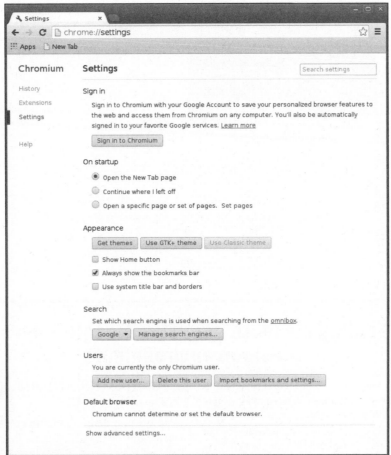

Shutting Down, Rebooting, and Logging Off

In an LXDE session, you can shut down your BeagleBone, reboot it, or temporarily log off so that no one messes around with the computer while you're away. To do so, you have to click the green guy running out of a door. Somehow, he manages to be in two places at the same time, and as such you have two ways to access the logout option:

- Choose Applications⇨Logout.
- Click the Logout icon in the bottom-right corner of the screen.

You see the window shown in Figure 12-24.

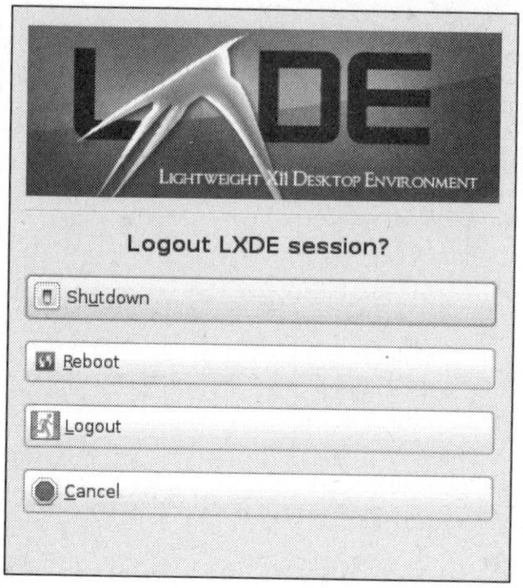

Figure 12-24:
Terminating
an LXDE
session.

Finding out more about the BeagleBone's desktop environment

The best way to find out how to use the BeagleBone's desktop environment is simply to explore. If you want to get some more specific instruction, try doing an Internet search. In your search, you should include the specific thing you are looking for and one of the following keywords:

- ✔ BeagleBone, which is the computer you're using

- ✔ Debian/Debian Wheezy, which is the Linux distribution that's running on the BeagleBone

- ✔ LXDE, which is the GUI you're using

- ✔ Openbox, which is the window manager of your desktop environment

- ✔ PCManFM, which is the standard file manager program for LXDE

If you want to find out how to customize the digital clock on the task bar, for example, you could try searching for *LXDE digital clock.*

Naturally, you can also search for useful and interesting software packages that you can use on your BeagleBone. Many people have posted lists on the Internet of software packages that they consider to be useful, fun, or even essential. At www.dummies.com/go/beaglebone/webextras you can also find a list of some software packages.

You can choose to shut down the BeagleBone completely, reboot it, or merely log out. If you log out, you're prompted to enter your username and password when you return to the computer.

The username is debian, and the default password is temppwd.

Sometimes, the reboot option doesn't work due to lack of authorization to use that command.

You can also shut down and reboot from the command line by using sudo shutdown -h now and sudo reboot.

Chapter 13

Building Your Website

*N*ot so long ago, only a few people could have the luxury of having a website. Coding for a website was an obscure skill that not many people had the chance to develop. Now the game has changed, and people regularly build their own websites. Even though building your own website may seem like a daunting feat, this chapter shows you how to do it.

This chapter walks you through building a two-page website, with practical examples that you can follow along and test in real time. The examples involve a website featuring electronics projects with the BeagleBone; nevertheless, if you have a personal interest such as photography, painting, gaming, writing, or pretty much anything that you want to share with the Internet, this is the perfect chance for you to do so.

Chapter 15 is all about building a web server hosted with the BeagleBone, which you can use to control electronic devices through the web. Prior knowledge of HTML (which is what this chapter is about) is required to complete the project in Chapter 15.

Introducing HTML, CSS, and JavaScript

A good web page requires three things:

> ✔ **HTML (Hypertext Markup Language)** is a markup language used to create web pages. Web browsers were created to read HTML files. A web browser uses the HTML tags to interpret where the content goes on the page.

HTML is a markup language, not a programming language. A markup language turns your text into an image, a link, or a list.

✔ **CSS (Cascading Style Sheets)** describe the appearance of your HTML documents.

Cascading Style Sheets can format all elements or just one element when more than one style is applied (hence, the name *Cascading*).

✔ **JavaScript** is a programming language that's most commonly used on websites. If you've ever visited a website that does really cool things through interactive buttons, slideshow animations, alert messages, or pop-up windows, some sort of JavaScript was certainly working on the back end. JavaScript is used in web browsers and allows interactions with clients without talking to the server.

Lately, the trend has been to use JavaScript in many applications other than web design, such as BoneScript introduced in Chapter 7.

Getting Started

You can use two launch pads to get started in web design with your BeagleBone. You can either use your BeagleBone Black as a desktop computer or control your BeagleBone remotely through secure shell (SSH).

Using a BeagleBone Black as a desktop computer

One way to work through this chapter is to turn your BeagleBone Black into a desktop computer, complete with peripherals, and use Leafpad (the default text editor) or any other text editor to write HTML or CSS code. Chapter 12 explains how to turn your BeagleBone Black into a desktop computer.

You can get to Leafpad by using Applications menu⇨Application⇨Leafpad.

After you write your HTML files, you can open them with the Chromium web browser, which is installed by default on the BeagleBone Black. Choose Applications menu⇨Internet⇨Chromium.

Controlling the BeagleBone remotely through SSH

If you don't want to set up your BeagleBone Black as a desktop computer, or if you have an Original BeagleBone, you can use the Cloud9 integrated development environment (IDE) to code your web pages. (Read Chapter 7 for more about the Cloud9 IDE.) Cloud9 is one of the best ways to write code for your BeagleBone in any language, including HTML and CSS.

Your website will be locally hosted, which means that it will be a file on your computer, not something you can access through the Internet. When you're working through SSH, the .html file you create is saved on your BeagleBone's file system. Because you aren't working in in a graphical environment, you can't promptly see the fruits of your labor. Fortunately, Cloud9 IDE offers a solution: Simply right-click your .html file and choose Preview from the shortcut menu.

Creating Your First Website

In this section, you create your first website. The example website is about electronics and programming; naturally, you can make your website about whatever you want.

The book's website at www.dummies.com/go/beaglebone includes downloads for the two web pages, the style-sheet file, and the images that are the final result of this chapter.

Organizing your files

When you're working, it's always a good idea to keep everything well organized, especially if you have several files for the same project. Start by creating a new folder on your desktop or from the cloud9 IDE, and name it myWebsite. Inside the myWebsite folder, create another folder called images (see Figure 13-1).

Opening a new file

Open a new file in a text editor such as Leafpad or in the Cloud9 IDE. Choose File⇨Save, and save the new file as index.html.

Your new file's name should end with the `.html` extension. Otherwise, your web browser won't recognize the file, and it won't open properly.

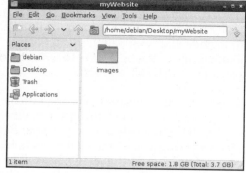

Figure 13-1: The myWebsite folder on a BeagleBone Black.

Writing the first line

The first line of any HTML document is always the following:

```
<!DOCTYPE html>
```

!DOCTYPE isn't an HTML-specific tag. It's simply an instruction that tells your web browser that it's reading an HTML file and which version of HTML you're using.

Even though !DOCTYPE isn't case sensitive, most IDEs — such as Cloud9 — will only give a special color to it if you type it in capital letters.

Structuring an HTML document

The overall structure of an HTML document looks like the following snippet of code. Start by typing the following code in your text editor:

```
<!DOCTYPE html>
<html>
        <head>
        </head>
        <body>
        </body>
</html>
```

The HTML that defines the structure of your page goes between the `<html>` and `</html>` tags.

Because most web pages require the preceding snippet of code, you can use that template every time you start writing a new web page.

An HTML document is divided into two main parts:

- ✔ **Header:** The `<head>` and `</head>` tags mark the start and end of the header. You insert the title of the web page into the `<head>` tag.
- ✔ **Body:** The `<body>` and `</body>` tags mark the start and end of the body. Everything that goes inside those tags is the visible page content.

HTML tags aren't case sensitive, but we recommend that you use lowercase.

Formatting Your HTML Content

This chapter highlights the most important HTML tags. Don't worry; you don't need to memorize them. You can always use this book as a reference when you're creating a website.

Adding a title

The title goes inside the `<head>` and `</head>` tags. The title is exactly what it sounds like: the title of your document, which shows up in your web browser's title bar.

Here's how you can add the `<title>` tag to your code. The result is shown in Figure 13-2.

Chromium's title bar

Figure 13-2:
Chromium web browser displaying the web page's title on the tab.

```
<!DOCTYPE html>
<html>
<head>
      <title> Electronics Projects with BeagleBone</title>
</head>
<body>
</body>
</html>
```

Indentation! Indentation! Indentation! Web design uses a lot of tags that go inside tags that go inside tags. Even though using indentation is not strictly necessary, it's extremely easy to get lost if you don't use this technique.

Adding headings

Now you can start adding visible content to the web page, starting with a heading. Different levels of HTML headings are defined with the <h1> through <h6> tags (h1 stands for heading number one), and the heading tags always go inside the <body> tags. Type the following code:

```
<!DOCTYPE html>
<html>
<head>
      <title>Electronics Projects with BeagleBone</title>
</head>
<body>
      <h1>Electronics Projects</h1>
      <h2>Home</h2>
</body>
</html>
```

Most web browsers help you by going through your errors and trying to fill in some blanks. For example, a closing tag such as </h1> could be considered optional, and if you try the following example, your web page works as expected. At some point, however, you may run into a web browser that doesn't fill in the blanks, so you should always use end tags to prevent unexpected errors (and to keep yourself organized, too).

```
<!DOCTYPE html>
<html>
<body>
      <h1>This is a heading 1
      <h2>This is a heading 2
</body>
</html>
```

The purpose of heading tags is to structure your document with the relevant headings so search engines can index your website and find relevant content with those headings. Even though you can adjust the font size of your text with the heading tags, that's not what you should use them for. You should use CSS to make your website pretty, as described later in this chapter in the "Changing text appearance" section.

Inserting paragraphs

To mark text as a paragraph, you use the `<p>` tag. Most of your readable content goes inside a paragraph tag. Add a paragraph tag to your `index.html` file like so:

```
<!DOCTYPE html>
<html>
<head>
        <title>Electronics Projects with BeagleBone</title>
</head>
<body>
        <h1>Electronics Projects</h1>
        <h2>Home</h2>
        <p>My first web page.</p>
</body>
</html>
```

Viewing your web page

Save your `index.html` file; then right-click it and choose Preview from the shortcut menu, or open it in Chromium. You see something similar to Figure 13-3.

Figure 13-3: First glance at your web page.

You can start experimenting with your web page by adding some of the HTML tags that you already know. Feel free to add new headings and paragraphs; then open your web browser to see the result. HTML doesn't do much besides add raw text, though, so the page won't look very pretty. Later in the "Styling your HTML content with CSS" section you find out how to dress it up with CSS.

Save your file every time you make changes. Refresh the web browser after saving, and all changes should be updated immediately.

Inserting links

Most websites contain multiple pages. To make it possible for your visitors to navigate through the pages of your website, you have to insert hyperlinks to the other web pages with the <a> tag:

```
<a href="about.html">About this website</a>
```

The reader sees the words About this website, which is called the anchor text. If he or she clicks the anchor text, the about.html web page opens. The code for that page has to be inside your myWebsite folder.

The <a> tag introduces attributes, which are represented in this case by href="". HTML elements have attributes that usually add functionalities or provide additional information to an HTML element.

You can also insert links that go to any web page on the Internet if you type the following:

```
<a href="http://beagleboard.org">Visit BeagleBoard website</a>
```

The user sees the message Visit BeagleBoard website. If he or she clicks the hyperlink, the official BeagleBone website opens.

Even though most web browsers don't display http:// at the start of the domain name, you need to type that prefix in your href="" attributes; otherwise, the website may not open.

You can also include in your About page a link with the following attribute:

```
<a href="mailto:name@example.com">Contact me here.</a>
```

When your reader clicks the Contact me here link, his or her default email application opens, ready to shoot you an email. Simply replace name@example.com with the email address of your choice.

Keep in mind that posting your address online may attract a lot of spambots that will send you unsolicited emails.

Adding images

Images are great ways to capture the attention of your website's visitors. You insert an image by using the `<img>` tag.

You need to have an image to work with in your `images` folder, so copy an image there. The image in the example is called `beagleboneblack.jpg`. Add the following tag to your code, but replace `images/beagleboneblack.jpg` with the path to your image file:

```
<img src="images/beagleboneblack.jpg">
```

Did you notice that the `<img>` doesn't have a closing tag? Some HTML tags don't have a closing tag because everything they need to do their task is actually placed inside the opening tag — not between an opening and a closing tag.

If the image is a bit bigger than you needed, you can change its size by inserting a couple of attributes to manipulate the width and height of your image. Here are some of the attributes that you can use with the `<img>` tag:

- ✔ **src (source):** Specifies where your image is located. You can insert an URL or the path to your image location.
- ✔ **width:** Changes the width of your image, measured in pixels.
- ✔ **height:** Changes the height of your image, measured in pixels.
- ✔ **alt:** Stands for *alternative text*. If a browser can't display your image for some reason, it displays your alternative text instead of the image.

If you want to change the width of your image to 290 pixels and the height to 350, type the following:

```
<img src="images/beagleboneblack.jpg" width="290" height="350">
```

Figure 13-4 shows the web page with the photo.

You can also use two tags together. If you want to make your image clickable so that another page opens when the user clicks the image, you insert the `<img>` tag between the `<a>` and `</a>` tags, as follows:

```
<a href="http://beagleboard.org">
     <img src="images/beagleboneblack.jpg">
</a>
```

Figure 13-4:
Your web
page with a
BeagleBone
Black photo.

Creating lists

Lists help you organize your content. There are two types of lists:

✔ **Ordered lists:** You designate an ordered list with the <ol> and </ol> tags when the order of your items is important, as in step-by-step instructions. Each item in the list starts with a number or a letter (see Figure 13-5).

```
<ol>
        <li>Follow step number one</li>
        <li>This is step number two</li>
        <li>That's the final step</li>
</ol>
```

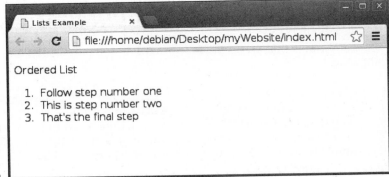

Figure 13-5:
Ordered list.

✔ **Unordered lists:** You use the `<ul>` and `</ul>` tags when the items can be presented in any order, as shown in Figure 13-6.

```
<ul>
        <li>One tip</li>
        <li>Another tip</li>
        <li>Last tip</li>
</ul>
```

Figure 13-6:
Unordered
list.

You can also use an unordered list to create a navigation bar on your website. Into each list item, simply insert an `<a>` tag that links to your other web pages.

```
<ul>
        <li><a href="index.html">Home</a></li>
        <li><a href="about.html">About</a></li>
</ul>
```

Right now, the result of the preceding code doesn't look anything like a navigation bar. The formatting is done with CSS in the "Customizing your logo and navigation bar" section.

Formatting Your HTML Document

Many other tags that are useful for formatting web pages, including the following:

- **`<strong>`:** Put text inside the `<strong>` and `</strong>` tags to mark the text as important. In a web browser, the text appears in bold but keep in mind that HTML is used to mark things, not to make them pretty; the primary use of this tag is to mark your text as important. If you simply want to make your text bold, you should use CSS.

- **`<em>`:** Put text inside the `<em>` and `</em>` tags to emphasize it. The web browser displays this text in italic.

- **`<hr>`:** Use the `<hr>` tag to add a horizontal line to separate portions of content. If you're describing your project, for example, you could separate the parts list and the circuit schematic with a `<hr>` tag.

- **`<!--insert comment-->`:** Keep your code organized with this tag. Comments don't appear on your web page, so you can use them to remember why you wrote some of the HTML tags when you revisit that code sometime later.

You can use lots of other tags to mark your text, but we don't cover them because they're not relevant to the remainder of this book.

Styling Your HTML Content with CSS

At the moment, your web page is basic, with no color or customization (see Figure 13-7). It merely contains the text marked with HTML. Ew. Using CSS, you can add some colors and change the layout to make it look better. Who said programmers can't be artistic?

Embedding a style sheet

All your style instructions are stored in a separate text file. Open a new file in your text editor, name it `stylesheet.css`, and save it in your `myWebsite` folder.

Your filename should have the `.css` extension; otherwise, the file won't work properly.

Figure 13-7:
How your
web page
looks so far.

To embed a style sheet into your HTML document, type the following in your header tag:

```
<link rel="stylesheet" href="stylesheet.css" type="text/css">
```

At this point, you should have all this code in your header tag of your HTML document:

```
<head>
        <title>Electronics Projects with BeagleBone</title>
        <link rel="stylesheet" href="stylesheet.css" type="text/css">
</head>
```

Now you have your style sheet connected to your HTML document. This process saves you a ton of time because you can embed the same style sheet in all your other web pages. Also, when you edit that single file, it applies the changes to all your other web pages at the same time, which makes it easy to give all your web pages the same colors, fonts, and overall organization.

Knowing the basics of CSS

Each CSS instruction requires three things: a selector, a property and a value, as shown here:

```
selector { property: value; }
```

`selector` is the HTML element you want to change. After that, you insert all the instructions inside the brackets. The property you want to alter is followed by a colon and the value. All instructions end with a semicolon.

For example, copy this code snippet into your `stylesheet.css` file:

```
h1 { color: navy; }
```

Then save your file, and refresh your web browser. Now all your elements that use the `<h1>` tag are navy blue.

You can have more than one instruction for the same `selector`, as follows:

```
selector {
        property: value;
        property: value;
}
```

 CSS ignores extra spaces, so nothing stops you from, say, having all your instructions on the same line. However, we suggest that you organize your code as in the preceding example to keep your code cleaner and more user-friendly. It's also the standard way of writing CSS.

You can select more than one HTML element at the same time. The following example changes the color to navy for all elements that use the `<h1>` or `<h2>` tags:

```
h1, h2 { color: navy; }
```

Experimenting with colors

When you visit a website, you usually notice a main color. The navigation bar, headings, and hyperlinks may be the same color or similar colors. This color scheme makes the website more memorable and more pleasant to navigate. The examples in this chapter use mainly blues for your website, but you can use any color you desire.

In the preceding section, you change all your headings to navy blue. You can also change the color of your background with the following instruction:

```
body { background: #E6E6E6; }
```

What do those numbers and letters mean? That's hardly the name of a color. They're *hexadecimal numbers,* used in this case to specify combinations of red, green, and blue (RGB). Hexadecimal values range from 0 to 9 and from A to F. The lowest value for a hexadecimal number is 0, and the highest is F. From 0 to F, there are a total of 16 values for each hexadecimal digit. All web browsers support 140 color names, which means that each color name has a hexadecimal color value. Following are some of the most basic values:

- **Black:** #000000
- **Red:** #FF0000
- **Green:** #00FF00
- **Blue:** #0000FF
- **White:** #FFFFFF

To find the right color, you don't need to keep trying combinations of numbers and letters. You can use any color picker online, such as the one at www. w3schools.com/tags/ref_colorpicker.asp. You simply select the color you want and then copy the hexadecimal number to your CSS code.

Changing text appearance

When you're working with HTML, you can customize your text to look exactly as you want. HTML is like a word processor with all the options you're already familiar with: font family, font size, text position, and so on. Instead of using a graphical user interface (GUI), however, you need to write code instructions in your style sheet. Here are the most important properties you can modify:

- **text-align:** Sets where your text is aligned horizontally. You can set your text left, center, right, or justified.
- **text-decoration:** Removes or sets text decorations. You can use any of four values: none, underline, overline, and line-through.
- **font-family:** Changes the default font for the text.
- **font-style:** Changes the style of the text to italic, bold, or normal.
- **font-size:** Increases or decreases the sizes of letters.
- **font-weight:** Specifies the weight of a font. The options are normal, bold, bolder, and lighter.

You can also change the indentation, change capitalization, and make plenty of other text customizations. If you want to know how to do something specific, simply search for it online.

Usually, when using `font-family`, you should specify more than one font, because you want to make sure that each visitor's web browser has at least one of those fonts:

```
body { font-family: Verdana, Geneva, sans-serif; }
```

You define a priority in the preceding example. Geneva is the font only if the web browser doesn't have Verdana, and so on.

Next, you customize hyperlinks to make them look better. First, you define your hyperlinks as navy and remove the underline by changing `text-decoration` to `none`:

```
a {
        color: navy;
        text-decoration: none;
}
```

To give your visitors some interaction, you want your hyperlinks to be underlined when visitors move a mouse pointer over them. Add the following snippet to your CSS file:

```
a:hover, a:active { text-decoration: underline; }
```

Understanding the box model

In discussions of CSS, you frequently hear the term *box model*. This important subject is one that a lot of people don't fully understand.

Because the layout determines the look and feel of your web page, controlling the position of your HTML elements is important, and that's done with CSS. You can think of each HTML element as being a box that holds your content. The CSS box model contains a few properties that help you position your HTML elements where you want them:

- ✔ `content`: Sets where your text, hyperlinks, or images appear
- ✔ `width`: Sets the width in pixels
- ✔ `height`: Sets the height in pixels

✔ **padding:** Adds a layer of transparent space around your content box

✔ **border:** Adds a border around your padding

✔ **margin:** Adds a layer of transparent space around your border

Figure 13-8 depicts all these properties.

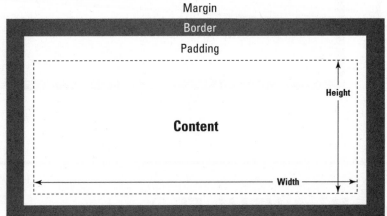

Figure 13-8:
The CSS box
model.

To see the box model in action, you can create a new HTML document called boxModel.html with the same tags as shown in the "Structuring an HTML document" section and insert the following code into the <body> tags:

```
<div>
      <p>Your content goes here!</p>
</div>
```

Then add this code to your style sheet:

```
div {
      width: 100px;
      padding: 15px;
      border: 10px solid blue;
      margin 25px;}
}
```

Now save all your files and refresh your web browser to see the final result (shown in Figure 13-9). The spaces around your content show all the CSS properties being applied to it.

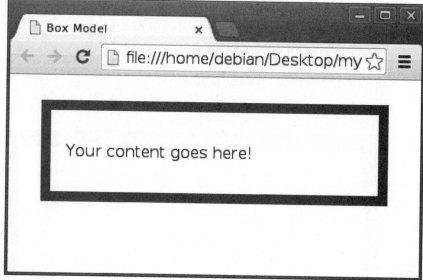

Figure 13-9:
Demon-
strating the
box model
with CSS.

Styling Your HTML Elements

Imagine a website on which each heading is a different color, size, and font. Some artist from Pablo Picasso's age probably would love it, but that's not really what you're aiming for.

On the other hand, sometimes it's useful to change things individually. You may want to set the navigation bar's hyperlinks to a different color, for example. The ease with which you can select all or just a single HTML element shows how powerful CSS can be with just the slightest effort.

You can select an ID from an HTML element and customize that HTML element. You can add a footer to your web page index.html by creating a <div> tag with an id called footer and then add the paragraph with all your content. The id could have a name other than footer, if you prefer, as shown here:

```
<div id="footer">
       <p>Created by <a href="about.html">Name</a></p>
</div>
```

Add the following code to your style sheet:

```
#footer p {
       text-align: center;
}
```

When you refresh your web browser, you see your footer paragraph, and only your footer paragraph, centered on the page.

Wrapping up your content

Changing the margins of your page isn't necessary, but it makes your website look better. Imagine that someone opens your website on a very wide screen. Your content will be stretched and hard to read. To accommodate such a screen, insert your HTML elements between the `<div>` tags.:

```
<body>
<div id="wrapper">
       <!--Insert all your HMTL elements here-->
</div>
</body>
```

The ID name given to `<div>` tags used in this fashion is usually `wrapper`, but it could be any other name. You should always try to give intuitive names to your IDs.

In your CSS file, change the margin of your wrapper with the following code:

```
#wrapper { margin: 20px 70px; }
```

Dividing your web page

You still need to divide a few elements of your web page. You have to separate your logo and your navigation in two different `<div>` tags. Add the following `<div>` with the ID `logo` to your HTML document:

```
<div id="logo">
       <h1><a href="index.html">Electronics
          Projects</a></h1>
</div>
```

Insert the `<ul>` and `<li>` tags you created in the "Creating lists" section in a `<div>` with the ID `nav`:

```
<div id="nav">
       <ul>
             <li><a href="index.html">Home</a></li>
             <li><a href="about.html">About</a></li>
       </ul>
</div>
```

Customizing your logo and navigation bar

To make your logo stay on the navigation bar and on the left side of your web page, add this snippet of code to your style sheet:

```
#logo {
        display: inline-block;
        float: left;
}
```

Now change the appearance of the unordered list to make it look like a real navigation bar. Copy the following code to your `stylesheet.css` file and save it. This change moves your navigation bar to the right side of your web page inline with the logo; it also makes the background navy blue and makes a few other adjustments.

```
#nav {
        float: right;
        background: navy;
        height: 40px;
        line-height: 30px;
        margin-bottom: 20px;
        display: inline-block;
        text-align: center;
        font-weight: bold;
        width: 250px;
        border-radius: 10px;
}

#nav ul {
        list-style: none;
        margin: 0 auto;
}
#nav li {
        float: left;
        display: inline;
        margin: 0;
}
```

The following code makes your hyperlinks for the navigation white and keeps them in place:

```
#nav ul li a {
        display: inline-block;
        height: 30px;
        padding: 5px 20px;
        color: white;
}
```

Your web page with the logo and navigation bar should look similar to Figure 13-10.

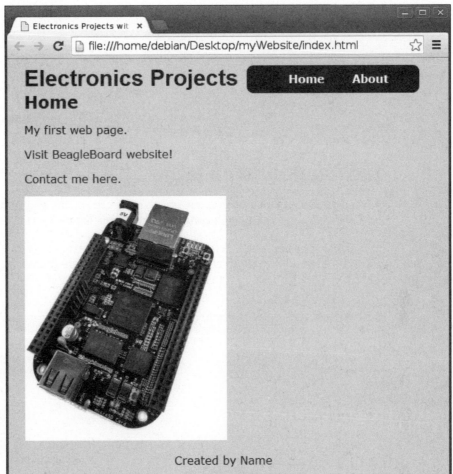

Figure 13-10:
Logo and
navigation
bar.

Customizing your container

At this point your background is grayish, which makes it hard for visitors to read your content. Create a new `<div>` tag with the `container` ID so that you have a place to insert all your readable content with a white background. Insert the following between `<div>` tags:

```
<div id="container">
      <h2>Home</h2>
      <p>This is my first web page!</p>
      (...)
</div>
```

Next, with the help of CSS, make your background white and make the proper spacing adjustments:

```
#container {
     padding: 40px;
     clear: both;
     background: white;
     border-radius: 10px;
}
```

Testing your web page

Save all your files, open or preview your `index.html` file, and refresh your web browser. Does the page look as expected (see Figure 13-11)? Cool!

If your page doesn't look like the one in the figure, go to `www.dummies.com/beaglebone` and download all the source files. Compare them with the code you wrote and try to figure out what's missing.

Figure 13-11: The final result.

Start navigating through your website and check whether all the hyperlinks go where they should and all your images load fine.

The beauty of a website is that after it's published, you can update your code any time, so fear not! This is just your starting template; the goal is to inspire you to build upon this website. Update it with some of the projects elsewhere in this book. Take pictures. Show it to your friends and customize it any way you want.

Publishing Your First Website

Hosting your website on a reliable hosting service isn't free; you have to pay a certain amount per month to get your own domain and a hosting plan. Companies such as Bluehost (`www.bluehost.com`), HostGator (`www.hostgator.com`), and GoDaddy (`https://www.godaddy.com`) offer starter plans that are relatively cheap and are more than enough to host a personal website.

Part VI
Playing with the BeagleBone

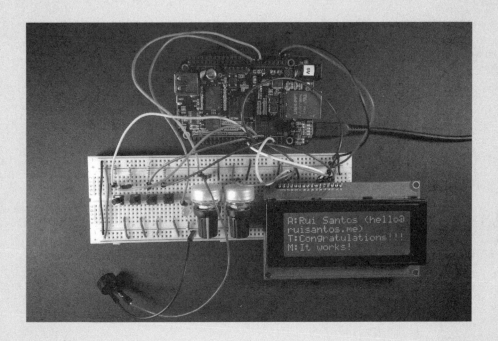

Visit www.dummies.com/go/beaglebone for additional Dummies content related to the BeagleBone.

In this part . . .

✔ Having some fun with the BeagleBone by taking on more advanced projects

✔ Analyzing your email with Python and read messages on an LCD screen

✔ Discovering how to use the BeagleBone as a tool for home automation projects

✔ Using a home automation web server to interact with your BeagleBone

Chapter 14

Building Your First Project

In This Chapter

▶ Preparing to build a complete, functional, and useful apparatus

▶ Dividing and conquering to build the project incrementally

▶ Wiring up an LCD and programming an email reader

▶ Building a device that reads and displays your emails

*T*his chapter shows you how to build a lasting, complete, and useful project.

In the completed project, your BeagleBone functions as a small, energy-efficient apparatus that notifies you when you receive an email, and allows you to use buttons and an LCD screen to go through your entire mailbox and read any message.

Getting Started

Before you get to work, you need to assemble your supplies. Here's the shopping list:

- ✔ A breadboard

- ✔ Many jumper wires

- ✔ A 3.3V liquid crystal display (LCD) screen, preferably one that's 20 character by 4 line and is compatible with the Hitachi HD44780 LCD controller

- ✔ Four pushbuttons

- ✔ Four 10K Ω resistors

- ✔ A light-emitting diode (LED)

- ✔ A 470 Ω or 220 Ω resistor

- ✔ An Ethernet cable and a stable connection to the web

✔ Two potentiometers, preferably 5K Ω and 10K Ω

✔ A buzzer

So that you know what your objective is for this project, Figure 14-1 shows the completed email notifier and reader.

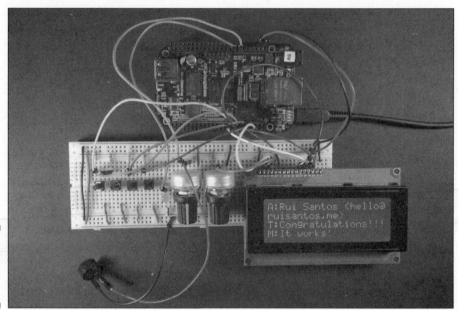

Figure 14-1:
LCD email
notifier and
reader.

The best way to build a project that integrates various pieces of hardware and software is to divide and conquer. You work incrementally, because building and testing one part before moving on to the next usually yields the best results. If instead you wire up everything, write all the code, and turn on the device without having tested the parts, you'll most likely get unexpected results, and debugging the whole thing is much harder and tedious than testing and debugging each part individually.

Here's the attack strategy for this chapter:

1. Create a program that can print a simple message on the LCD.

2. Create a program that reads your email and prints the important details on the terminal.

3. Integrate this program into the main one, while adding buttons to select the email and scroll the message.

4. Add an LED and a buzzer to notify you when a new email arrives.

Wiring Up the LCD

In this section, you wire up the LCD and create a script to print a simple message on it. You do this by creating a function that drives the screen; when that's done, all you have to do is have the function receive the message from the web as a parameter rather than as a message written by you.

Figure 14-2 shows a standard 20x4 LCD Hitachi HD44780 LCD, which is the type we recommend for this project.

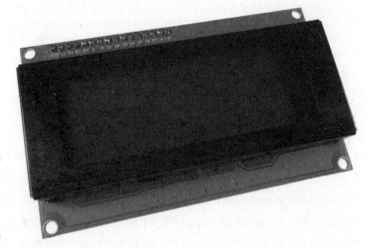

Figure 14-2:
A standard
HD44780
LCD.

 If you use a different LCD from the one we recommend, you may have to add wiring. Hitachi's LCDs feature built-in resistors for the backlight LEDs, but some other LCDs may not, which means that you have to integrate them yourself. Be sure to read the important parts of the datasheet with care! If you're still unsure, you can always add an 1K Ω resistor between 3.3V and the LCD's pin 15. We strongly recommend, however, that you get an LCD as similar as possible to the one we used. In any case, all lines of code that depend on the LCD you use have a comment that says so.

 There are several LCDs that require 5V to operate. We strongly recommend that you stay away from those and use a 3.3V LCD because this project is a complex one that involves lots of wiring. If you mistakenly plug 5V into the BeagleBone, you may blow up its processor.

Wiring the LCD

Follow these steps to wire up the LCD (and check Figure 14-3 for reference):

1. **Connect 3.3V to the power rails of the breadboard.**

   You can get the voltage from the BeagleBone's pins P9_3 and P9_4.

2. **Connect ground (GND) to another rail of the breadboard.**

   Pins P9_1, P9_2, P8_1 and P8_2 of the BeagleBone all provide ground.

3. **Power the LCD.**

   Use jumper wires to connect the 3.3V to LCD pin 2 (VDD) and LCD pin 15 (LED+). If your LCD doesn't feature built-in resistors for the backlight LEDs, place a resistor between pin 15 and the 3.3V. To set your ground, connect GND to LCD pin 1 (VSS) and LCD pin 5 (R/W).

4. **Add a potentiometer to control the contrast.**

   Connect one of the outer leads to 3.3V and another outer lead to GND; the middle lead connects to LCD pin 3 (VO/contrast).

5. **Connect the BeagleBone's pin P8_8 to LCD pin 4 (RS).**

6. **Connect the BeagleBone's pin P8_10 to LCD pin 6 (E/clock enable).**

7. **Connect the BeagleBone's pin P8_18 to LCD pin 11 (DB4).**

8. **Connect the BeagleBone's pin P8_16 to LCD pin 12 (DB5).**

9. **Connect the BeagleBone's pin P8_14 to LCD pin 13 (DB6).**

10. **Connect the BeagleBone's pin P8_12 to LCD pin 14 (DB7).**

11. **Connect 3.3V to LCD pin 15 (A/+backlight).**

12. **Connect GND to LCD pin 16 (K/-backlight).**

If your circuit doesn't work, you might need to troubleshoot it with a multimeter. Check www.dummies.com/go/beaglebone to see how to do so.

Writing the code for the LCD

Before you get into any actual coding, you need to install Adafruit's Python library, which features plenty of functions that you can use with the LCD.

We encourage you to visit www.dummies.com/go/beaglebone to download all the code for this chapter. Sometimes, typing the code yourself or copying and pasting can lead to unexpected errors that can be quite time-consuming to figure out. Downloading the code ensures that you don't have any snippet of code missing.

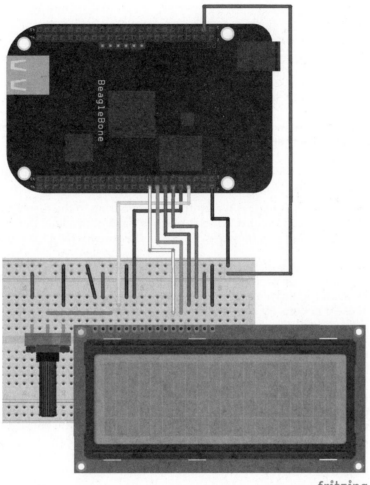

Figure 14-3:
LCD wired to
BeagleBone
Black.

fritzing

Start by installing some necessary dependencies. Most likely, you already
have these dependencies installed, but just to make sure, enter the following
commands:

```
sudo apt-get update
sudo apt-get install build-essential python-dev python-smbus python-pip git
sudo pip install Adafruit_BBIO
```

Create a dedicated folder for this project. We created ours on `/var/lib/`
`cloud9` and called it `email_notifier`. Change to the directory where you
created the folder, and type the following on the command line:

```
cd /var/lib/cloud9/email_notifier
git clone https://github.com/adafruit/Adafruit_Python_CharLCD.git
cd Adafruit_Python_CharLCD
sudo python setup.py install
```

`git clone` is a useful command that clones entire repositories from GitHub. In this case, you clone the necessary source code to install the LCD library.

Before you see the code that runs the script, here's an introduction to the LCD functions that you use for your program:

- ✔ `clear()`: Clears the LCD, erasing any message that was printed on it previously.

- ✔ `message(string)`: Writes the desired string to the display. Note that the LCD can't realize when it reaches the end of a line; thus, messages must include \n (newline) to use all the rows of the LCD.

You can use many other functions with the LCD. Even though they're not necessary for this project, they're interesting and can be useful for plenty of tasks (or even for improvements on this project). You can get a complete rundown of these functions by typing the following on the command line:

```
python
>>>import Adafruit_CharLCD as LCD
>>>help(LCD.Adafruit_CharLCD)
```

The `backlight()` function won't work due to the fact that you connected the backlight pin directly to 3.3V and not a GPIO; thus, you have no control over it. We opted to do this for simplicity because controlling the backlight isn't really important for this project.

To start writing the code, create a file named `LCD.py`, and type the following:

```
#!/usr/bin/python
import math
import time

import Adafruit_CharLCD as LCD

lcd_rs        = 'P8_8'
lcd_en        = 'P8_10'
lcd_d4        = 'P8_18'
lcd_d5        = 'P8_16'
lcd_d6        = 'P8_14'
lcd_d7        = 'P8_12'
lcd_backlight = 'P8_7'
```

```
# Define LCD column and row size for 20x4 LCD.
# Change depending on your LCD
# We use these a lot so we define them as constants
LCD_COLUMNS = 20
LCD_ROWS    = 4

# Initialize the LCD using the pins above.
lcd = LCD.Adafruit_CharLCD(lcd_rs, lcd_en, lcd_d4, lcd_d5, lcd_d6, lcd_d7,
              LCD_COLUMNS, LCD_ROWS, lcd_backlight)

message = "Hello\nWorld!"
lcd.clear()
lcd.message(message)
time.sleep(10)
lcd.clear()
```

This script does the following things:

1. Imports libraries.

2. Creates variables referring to the pins of the LCD that are connected to the BeagleBone. These variables are necessary to initialize the LCD.

3. Defines constants referring to the number of columns and rows that the LCD features. These two values are important when you want to display bigger messages.

4. Initializes the LCD.

5. Creates a string to hold the message you want to print.

6. Clears the LCD's previous message and displays the new message.

7. Waits 10 seconds and then clears the LCD message.

Running the script for the LCD

After saving, you can press F5 to see a result similar to Figure 14-4. Feel free to play around. Send other messages, experiment with other functions to, for example, scroll messages sideways and change the contrast. Get a feel for how to work with an LCD, because this skill is both useful and fun.

If you don't see anything, you may not have enough contrast. If everything was wired correctly, the contrast is defined by the potentiometer; rotate it to see whether rotation solves the problem. If not, recheck the code and the wiring.

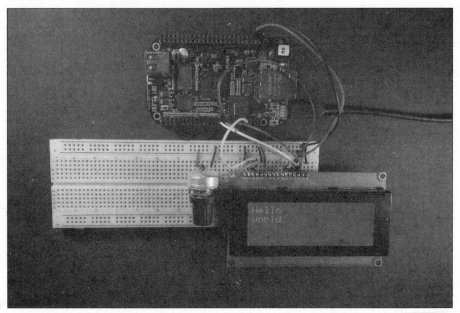

Figure 14-4:
Hello world!

Programming the Email Reader

This part of this chapter shows you how you can use Python code to access your email and print details about the most recently received messages on the console terminal. When that's done, you merely have to adapt this program and the one you created earlier in this chapter to display the message on your LCD.

To check your email with Python, you use what's known as the *Universal Feed Parser.* feedparser is a Python library that analyzes feeds in all known formats of web standards.

This project uses Gmail as an example for the following reasons:

✔ It's the most popular email provider worldwide.

✔ Gmail is very developer-friendly, so accessing its feed is easy and straightforward.

Explaining how to access the feed of every email provider is beyond the scope of this book, so we strongly recommend that you use a Gmail account to get through the remainder of this chapter and find out how to parse a feed. With some Internet research, you should be able to adapt the feed parser for this specific application for a different email provider or any other web-based application — provided that the provider or website allows you to access its feed. Later in this section, you can see some more information on how to do so.

Parsing web feeds

Web feeds allow programmers to create software that checks for updates published on a website. For programmers to do this, though the site owner needs to use specialized software to publish a feed of content in standard format that the computer can interpret. Then this feed can be read by programs such as the one you create in this section.

Website owners use different standards to publish their feeds. Atom, RSS, and RDF are probably the most popular standards. Things change somewhat from standard to standard.

One last thing before you start coding. You need to install the following libraries:

```
sudo apt-get install python-pip python2.7-dev
sudo pip install feedparser
sudo easy_install -U distribute
```

Enter the following code:

```python
#!/usr/bin/python

import feedparser
import time

USERNAME = "YOUR_USERNAME"     # just the part before the @ sign, add yours here
PASSWORD = "YOUR_PASSWORD"

MAIL_CHECK_FREQ = 10      # check mail every 10 seconds

while True:
            d = feedparser.parse("https://" + USERNAME + ":" + PASSWORD
            "@gmail.google.com/gmail/feed/atom")
            print(d.entries[0].published)  #prints email's date
            print(d.entries[0].title) #prints email's title
            print(d.entries[0].author) #prints email's author
            print(d.entries[0].description) #prints email message
            time.sleep(MAIL_CHECK_FREQ)
```

This code shouldn't be too hard to understand. After the libraries are imported, three constants are declared: two strings to hold your username and password, and an integer to define the frequency at which this program runs. The MAIL_CHECK_FREQ constant is used with a time.sleep() function at the end of the while True: loop. Without including the time.sleep()

function, your program would run at the CPU frequency (1 GHz), which is 1 nanosecond per instruction (on a BeagleBone Black). It's safe to assume that you don't receive that many emails in such a short period of time.

What's important for you to understand here is the part where the feed parser functions are used. First, you create an object that you name d; this object holds the feed after it has been parsed (analyzed) by the function `feedparser.parse()`. Afterward, you can access each entry of the email by using `d.entries`; the index 0 stands for the most recent email. You can check whichever email you want by using another index up to 20 entries.

You can find more about Python's feedparser at `https://pythonhosted.org/feedparser`. You should go to Common RSS Elements for matters specific to what you're doing in this section. If you want to try getting your own email or some other website running with the feedparser, you should read more on the previously mentioned website, as well as do an Internet search on your website/email provider's feed.

When you run the script, information about the latest email you received should print on the console output. This information is updated every `CHECK_MAIL_FREQ` seconds. The next section shows how to make the output print on an LCD.

Putting It All Together

This project uses two pushbuttons to swap messages in succession. One pushbutton selects the previous message, and the other selects the next message.

What makes this program somewhat complex is the fact that you need to implement some way to scroll down for messages that have more total characters than the LCD can display at any time — that is, rows × columns. For this purpose, you use another two pushbuttons that scroll the message up or down.

Wiring the pushbuttons

The opposite leads of a pushbutton are disconnected, and when a user presses the button, the leads establish a connection. You can quickly test that feature by using a multimeter in continuity mode. Follow these steps or refer to Figure 14-5 to add each of the pushbuttons to your circuit:

1. **Attach one of the pusbhutton leads to the 3.3V breadboard rail.**

2. **Attach a 10K Ω resistor to the opposite lead of the pushbutton.**

3. **Connect the other lead of the resistor to the ground rail.**

4. **Repeat the same process for all four pushbuttons.**

5. **Insert a jumper wire between the pushbutton and the resistor into the BeagleBone's pin for that pushbutton.**

The left pushbutton, which scrolls up, is attached to P8_15. The next pushbutton scrolls down and is attached to P8_13. The third pushbutton selects the previous email and is connected to P8_11. The last pushbutton selects the next email and is connected to P8_9.

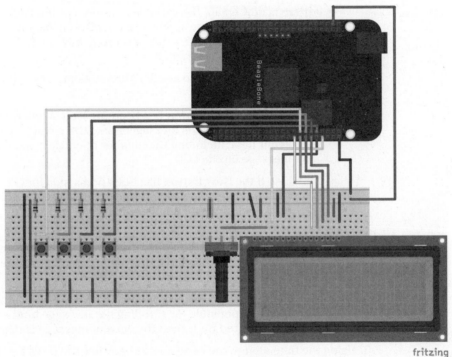

Figure 14-5: LCD and four pushbuttons wired to the BeagleBone Black.

fritzing

Understanding the concept

This section provides a short summary of how the algorithm is done without getting into any specifics of the code. The following sections explain each part minutely.

After importing libraries and initializing modules, you set up some important variables. You use functions to do the following things:

- ✔ Get the date of the latest email received

- ✔ Parse the latest email, saving all the relevant data, including the number of entries

✔ Display the first four lines of the most recent email, which consists of title, author, and the first two lines of the message

✔ Create a time stamp so that you can create conditions that depend on the elapsed time

When that's done, you move on to the `while True:` loop, which does the following things:

1. It checks for new email.

   • If there is new email, the variables — one that holds the number of the current message and one that's responsible for scrolling the message on the LCD — are reset to `0`, and the LCD screen is updated with the latest email.

   • If not, a check is done to see whether any of the buttons has been pressed.

     • If the Previous button has been pressed, a function runs to select the previous message; parse the email to save the relevant data, including the number of entries; and display the message on the LCD.

     • Else if the Next button has been pressed, a function runs to select the next message; parse the email to save the relevant data, including the number of entries; and display the message on the LCD.

     • Else if the Scroll Up button has been pressed, the code decrements by 1 the variable that's responsible for scrolling the message on the LCD; then the current message is displayed.

     • Else if the Scroll Down button has been pressed, the variable that's responsible for scrolling the message on the LCD is incremented by 1; then the current message is displayed.

2. Using the time stamp, the code checks whether the program has been running for longer than 60 seconds. If so, the email is checked again for any new messages, and the time stamp is reset.

3. The program is halted for 5 seconds at every iteration of the `while True:` loop.

The following sections cover specifics.

Writing the code

As always, the first thing to do is import libraries, as follows:

```
#!/usr/bin/python
# Email Notifier
# Importing libraries
import math
import time
import feedparser
import Adafruit_CharLCD as LCD
import Adafruit_BBIO.GPIO as GPIO
```

Next, you define variables for the BeagleBone pins that you'll use as pushbuttons:

```
# Defining variables
button_scroll_up = "P8_15"
button_scroll_down = "P8_13"
button_previous = "P8_11"
button_next = "P8_9"
```

Then you initialize all the inputs:

```
# Initializing all the inputs
GPIO.setup(button_scroll_up, GPIO.IN)
GPIO.setup(button_scroll_down, GPIO.IN)
GPIO.setup(button_previous, GPIO.IN)
GPIO.setup(button_next, GPIO.IN)
```

Following that, you add events to detect the button presses:

```
# Setting buttons to detect rising edge events
GPIO.add_event_detect(button_scroll_up, GPIO.RISING)
GPIO.add_event_detect(button_scroll_down, GPIO.RISING)
GPIO.add_event_detect(button_previous, GPIO.RISING)
GPIO.add_event_detect(button_next, GPIO.RISING)
```

Using events to work with buttons is a nonblocking technique. The program continues running even if no button is pressed; it doesn't wait. You can read more about events in Chapter 9.

Next, you initialize some important variables and constants:

```
USERNAME = "YOUR_USERNAME"      # Just the part before the @ sign, add yours here
PASSWORD = "YOUR_PASSWORD"      # Replace with your password
LOOP_FREQ = 5                   # Check buttons every 5 seconds
CHECK_LATEST_MAIL = 60          # Check for a new email every 60 seconds

current_message = 0             # Store position of our current message selected
scroll = 0                      # Store how much you want to scroll down or up
            your mail
```

The variable `current_message` has a value that changes depending on the presses of the Previous and Next buttons. The `scroll` variable changes depending on the presses of the Scroll Up and Scroll Down pushbuttons.

Next, you set up the LCD by configuring it according to the BeagleBone pins that are connected to it, defining constants for the number of rows and columns you have (you'll be using these constants a lot), and finally initializing the LCD by using the characteristics you defined. You also clear the screen to get rid of any messages that could have been there before you started running the program.

```
# BeagleBone LCD configuration
lcd_rs        = 'P8_8'
lcd_en        = 'P8_10'
lcd_d4        = 'P8_18'
lcd_d5        = 'P8_16'
lcd_d6        = 'P8_14'
lcd_d7        = 'P8_12'
lcd_backlight = 'P8_7'


# Define LCD column and row size for 20x4 LCD
# You can change the columns and rows size to any LCD size. For example 16x2
LCD_COLUMNS = 20
LCD_ROWS    = 4


# Initialize the LCD using the pins above
lcd = LCD.Adafruit_CharLCD(lcd_rs, lcd_en, lcd_d4, lcd_d5, lcd_d6, lcd_d7,
             lcd_columns, lcd_rows, lcd_backlight)
# Clear LCD screen
lcd.clear()
```

After that come the function definitions. Those functions are the real brains of the program, and each one of them deserves special attention.

Select previous mail

This function gets as a parameter the `current_message` variable, which holds a value from `0` to `19` that decides which entry of the feed parser (in other words, which email in your inbox) you want to display. The main part of the code calls this function whenever the Previous button is pressed and returns `current_message – 1` to indicate that you want to display the previous message. Note that the program returns `0` if you attempt to go beyond that.

```
# Select previous mail
def select_previous_message(current_message):
    current_message -= 1
    if current_message < 0: # can't go further than this
        current_message = 0
    return current_message
```

Select next mail

This function works in a similar fashion to the preceding one, except that it happens when the Next button is pressed, and it returns current_message + 1 to indicate that you want to display the next message.

```
# Select next mail
def select_next_message(current_message, number_entries):
    if current_message < (number_entries-1): # can't go further than this
        current_message += 1
    return current_message
```

Note that this function also receives the parameter number_entries, which holds the number of emails inside your mailbox (up to a maximum of 20). You can increase the variable only if it hasn't surpassed the number of entries — hence, that if. Also note that current_message is used as an *index,* and indexes start at 0, which is why you compare current_message with number_entries - 1 rather than simply number_entries.

Return date of latest mail

This function runs every CHECK_LATEST_MAIL seconds and parses the email in the same fashion described in the preceding sections. After saving all the data from the email at the variable m, you simply return the date of the most recent email. If there are no emails in the mailbox, you return an empty string.

```
# Return date of latest mail
def latest_mail_date():
    m = ""   # Clear m list
    # Save all mail date in list called m
    m = feedparser.parse("https://" + USERNAME + ":" + PASSWORD +
            "@gmail.google.com/gmail/feed/atom")
    # Check if m list is empty
    if len(m.entries) == 0:
        date = ""
    else:
        # Save our latest mail date in variable date
        date = m.entries[0].published
    return date
```

Read and save current mail

This function does all the heavy-lifting. The function takes the entry that you want to read (0 if no buttons were pressed) and does the following things sequentially:

1. The function clears the previous list of parsed email data and saves the data from the current email in an object called m:

```
m = ""    # Clear m list
    # Save all mail date in list called m
m = feedparser.parse("https://" + USERNAME + ":" + PASSWORD +
        "@gmail.google.com/gmail/feed/atom")
```

2. The function checks the length of m to know the number of emails in your mailbox and saves the value in number_entries. This variable is returned at the end of the function call. Afterward, the function checks whether the mailbox is empty and saves mail_data as an empty list if that's the case. This variable is also returned at the end of the function.

```
# Store the number of unread mails in number_entries variable
    number_entries = len(m.entries)
    # If no emails in inbox, returns mail_data empty
    if number_entries == 0:
        mail_data = []
```

If the mailbox isn't empty, the function saves the email's author, title, and message in three variables and creates a temporary variable to hold all that data, with the fields separated by \n, separating each field line by line. Additionally, a special null character, \0, is added at the end of the message to detect in a simple way when the end of the message has been reached.

Keep in mind that the feed parser can fetch only the first 100 characters of an email's feed.

```
author = m.entries[current_message].author # Save author name
title = m.entries[current_message].title   # Save mail title
message = m.entries[current_message].description  # Save first 100
        characters of our mail
# Create a string with all the data in a temporary variable
tmp_mail_data = "A:" + author + "\n" + "T:" + title + "\n" + "M:" +
        message + "\0"
```

4. After clearing the variables i, tmp_data, and mail_data, the program goes through each character of the tmp_mail_data string to find the relevant information and saves it, ready to be sent to the LCD, in tmp_data.

Before you go any further, it's important that you understand the task of four variables within this function:

- tmp_mail_data saves all the data that you want from the parser, separated by \n characters.

- tmp_data is a variable that saves the data in a format ready to be displayed on the LCD, which means placing \n every 20 or 16 characters (depending on your LCD).

- `mail_data` is the main string to be sent to be displayed on the LCD.

- `i` is just a counter that lets you know when you've copied a number of characters equal to `LCD_COLUMNS`. When that happens, it's time to display the message on the LCD in a new line.

Thus, you have a `for` loop that goes through each character in `tmp_mail_data` and does the following things:

a. Adds the character to `tmp_data`.

b. Checks for the end of a line (`LCD_COLUMNS`) or `\n`. If the code reaches the end of a line without finding `\n`, it adds `\n`. Then the code appends the data to the `mail_data` list, using the `append()` function. When this `if` happens, the code fetches the next line to be displayed on the LCD, which means resetting the `tmp_data` and `i` variables.

c. Otherwise, if the code detects `\0`, the end of the message has been reached. It appends this last part of the message to `mail_data`, also using the `rstrip()` function. The `rstrip()` function removes a character from a string. You want to remove `\0` because it's merely there to help you figure out when you reach the end; you don't want it to be part of the message.

d. Increments `i` at every iteration of the `for` loop.

e. Returns `mail_data` and `number_entries`.

```python
for character in tmp_mail_data:
        tmp_data += character # Concatenate each character in our
        variable tmp_data
        # Check if you reached the max number of characters per row
        # or if it is time to do newline
        if i == lcd_columns or character == '\n':
            # Add a newline to the end of string, if it doesn't have
        one yet
            if character != '\n':
                tmp_data += "\n"
            # Appends the data to our list
            mail_data.append(tmp_data)
            # Reset variables
            tmp_data = ""
            i=0
        # If we reached the last character, it appends the last data
        in our mail_data list
        elif character == '\0':
            mail_data.append(tmp_data.rstrip('\0'))
        i += 1   # Increment variable i by 1
return  mail_data, number_entries
```

Here's the complete code:

```
# Read and save current mail
def read_save_mail(current_message):
    m = ""    # Clear m list
    # Save all mail date in list called m
    m = feedparser.parse("https://" + USERNAME + ":" + PASSWORD +
            "@gmail.google.com/gmail/feed/atom")
    # Store the number of unread mails in number_entries variable
    number_entries = len(m.entries)
    # If no emails in inbox, returns mail_data empty
    if number_entries == 0:
        mail_data = []
    else:
        author = m.entries[current_message].author # Save author name
        title = m.entries[current_message].title   # Save mail title
        message = m.entries[current_message].description  # Save first 100
            characters of our mail
        # Create a string with all the data in a temporary variable
        tmp_mail_data = "A:" + author + "\n" + "T:" + title + "\n" + "M:" +
            message + "\0"
        # Clear variables i, tmp_data and mail_data
        i = 0
        tmp_data = ""
        mail_data = []
        # Go through each character of tmp_mail_data string
        for character in tmp_mail_data:
            tmp_data += character # Concatenate each character in our variable
                tmp_data
            # Check if you reached the max number of characters per row
            # or if it is time to do newline
            if i == lcd_columns or character == '\n':
                # Add a newline to the end of string, if it doesn't have one
                yet if character != '\n':
                    tmp_data += "\n"
                # Appends the data to our list
                mail_data.append(tmp_data)
                # Reset variables
                tmp_data = ""
                i=0
            # If we reached the last character, it appends the last data in our
                mail_data list
            elif character == '\0':
                mail_data.append(tmp_data.rstrip('\0'))
            i += 1   # Increment variable i by 1
    return  mail_data, number_entries
```

Display selected mail in the LCD screen

This last function displays the email on the LCD, using all the variables you've created so far. It takes `mail_data` and `number_entries` from the preceding function as parameters, as well as `current_message`, which depended on the Previous and Next button presses. Another parameter is the `scroll` variable, which should be a value (minimum 0) indicating whether you want to scroll the message up or down, depending on which button (Scroll Up or Scroll Down) has been pressed.

The function clears the LCD screen and checks for the number of entries as follows:

✔ If the number of entries is bigger than `0`, the mailbox isn't empty, and the function has work to do. After resetting the variables `i` and `tmp_data`, the code goes through each row of the LCD in a `while` loop.

In this `while` loop, that runs while `i` is less than `lcd_rows`, the code prepares the message to be displayed line by line. The `tmp_data` variable saves the part of the `mail_data` variable that you want to display, depending on the current line as well as the use of the Scroll Up and Scroll Down buttons.

After this loop, the message is ready to be displayed inside the `tmp_data` string. When sending the message to the LCD through `lcd.message()`, though, the code strips it of the final `\n`.

✔ Otherwise, if the number of entries is 0, display a message saying that there are no emails in your mailbox.

```
# Display selected mail in the LCD screen
# Each time the button_scroll_down is pressed, it scrolls down our mail by
            one line
def display_message(mail_data, number_entries, current_message, scroll):
    lcd.clear()     # Clear LCD screen
    # Check if there is a mail to display
    if number_entries > 0:
        # Reset variables before while loop
        i = 0
        tmp_data = ""
        # Goes through each row of our LCD
        while i < lcd_rows:
            # Prepare message to be displayed in LCD screen
            tmp_data += mail_data[scroll+i]
            i += 1   # Increment variable i by 1
        # Display final message in LCD screen
        lcd.message(tmp_data.rstrip('\n'))
    else:
        # Display following message in your LCD, if there are no new mails
        lcd.message("No new emails in\n your inbox...")
```

Setup

The next part of the code is straightforward. It simply uses the functions you created to define initial conditions, and it creates a `time_stamp` to see when exactly the program started running.

```
# Initial setup
# Updates variables and LCD screen with the latest mail
recent_date = latest_mail_date()
date = recent_date
mail_data, number_entries = read_save_mail(current_message)
display_message(mail_data, number_entries, current_message, scroll)
time_stamp = time.time()
```

The `time_time()` function checks the current time in seconds since the January 1, 1970. By saving that value into a variable, you create a time stamp. You can then use the `time_time()` function again and compare the value it returns to your time stamp to see how many seconds have passed since the last call of the `time_time()` function. Chapter 11 talks a little bit more about time stamps and the time library.

The while True: loop

The `while True:` loop deals with detecting events on the buttons, calling all the required functions to display the email that you want, as well as the part that you desired (scrolled up or scrolled down). It's important to note that at the end of the loop, the `time.time()` function determines whether `CHECK_LATEST_MAIL` has elapsed so your program accesses your email only every `CHECK_LATEST_MAIL` seconds.

```
while True:
    # check if we have a new mail
    if date != recent_date:
        # Reset our variables
        current_message = 0
        scroll = 0
        # Update our variables and LCD screen with the latest mail
        mail_data, number_entries = read_save_mail(current_message)
        display_message(mail_data, number_entries, current_message, scroll)
        recent_date = latest_mail_date()
    else:
        # Detect if we have pressed button previous
        if GPIO.event_detected(button_previous):
            scroll = 0      # Reset scroll variable
            # Update our variables and LCD screen with the latest mail
            current_message = select_previous_message(current_message)
            mail_data, number_entries = read_save_mail(current_message)
            display_message(mail_data, number_entries, current_message, scroll)
        # Detect if we have pressed the button next
```

```
        elif GPIO.event_detected(button_next):
            scroll = 0      # Reset scroll variable
            # Update our variables and LCD screen with the latest mail
            current_message = select_next_message(current_message, number_
                entries)
            mail_data, number_entries = read_save_mail(current_message)
            display_message(mail_data, number_entries, current_message, scroll)
        # Detect if we have pressed the button scroll up
        elif GPIO.event_detected(button_scroll_up):
            if scroll > 0:
                scroll -= 1     # Decrements our variable 1 position
                # Scrolls down one line of text in our message
                display_message(mail_data, number_entries, current_message,
                    scroll)
        # Detect if we have pressed the button scroll down
        elif GPIO.event_detected(button_scroll_down):
            if (scroll+lcd_rows) < len(mail_data):
                scroll += 1     # Increments our variable 1 position
                # Scrolls down one line of text in our message
                display_message(mail_data, number_entries, current_message,
                    scroll)
    # 60 second timer, to check if we have received a new mail
    if time.time() - time_stamp > CHECK_LATEST_MAIL:
        date = latest_mail_date() # Update variable date with the most recent
            mail date
        time_stamp = time.time()  # Resets our timer
    # Wait 5 seconds
    time.sleep(LOOP_FREQ)
```

Adding the LED and Buzzer

No advanced electronics project is complete without an LED. Also, if this program is supposed to notify you whenever you receive an email, having a buzzer outputting sound whenever a new mail arrives would be fun. This section adds a cherry on the top of your project.

In our experience, some buzzers that are simply connected to a voltage without anything in between output a deafening, ridiculously sharp sound that will probably give you nightmares. Given that fact, this project includes a potentiometer that enables you to reduce the intensity of the buzzer, or even mute it, by limiting the current that goes into the buzzer. We suggest that you double-check your wiring and your code before you run this script. Buzzers are fun, but if you happen to have a bug that makes it stay on forever, you may want to throw your BeagleBone out the window. If that happens, remember that you can turn off the buzzer quickly by pulling the wire that connects it to GND or 3.3V. It's generally inadvisable to pull wires on powered-on circuits, but a non-stopping buzzer is almost a national emergency.

Wiring the LED and buzzer

Follow these steps or check Figure 14-6 to wire up these new additions:

1. **Connect the positive leg (longer lead) of an LED to P9_16 by using a jumper.**

2. **Connect a 220 Ω or 470 Ω resistor between the LED and GND.**

3. **Connect one of the outer legs of the potentiometer to P9_14.**

   You could use the buzzer alone, but this project uses a potentiometer in series with the buzzer so that you can limit its output or even mute it.

4. **Connect the other outer leg of the potentiometer to GND.**

5. **Connect the middle leg of the potentiometer to the positive wire — the red one — of the buzzer.**

6. **Connect the buzzer's negative wire — the black one — to GND.**

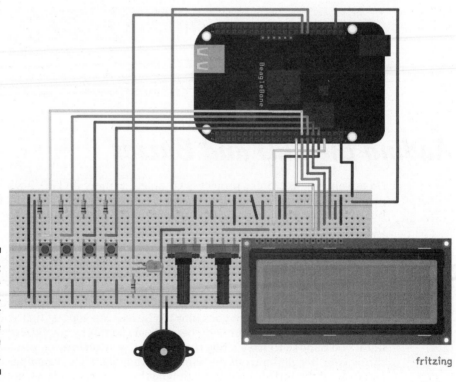

Figure 14-6: LCD, buttons, LED, and buzzer wired to the BeagleBone Black.

fritzing

Writing the code for the LED and buzzer

To add functionality for the LED and the buzzer to your code, follow these steps:

1. **Initialize two more variables.**

```
buzzer = "P9_14"
led = "P9_16"
```

2. **Set up two general purpose input/output (GPIO) outputs.**

```
GPIO.setup(buzzer, GPIO.OUT)
GPIO.setup(led, GPIO.OUT)
```

3. **Change the code of the first `if` of the `while True:` loop, which checks for new email.**

```
# check if we have a new mail
    if date != recent_date:
            # New stuff starts here
            # If we have a new mail, it turns our buzzer ON for 2 seconds and
                the LED for 10 seconds.
            GPIO.output(buzzer, GPIO.HIGH)
            GPIO.output(led, GPIO.HIGH)
            time.sleep(2)
            GPIO.output(buzzer, GPIO.LOW)
            time.sleep(8)
            GPIO.output(led, GPIO.LOW)
            # New stuff ends here
            # Reset our variables
            current_message = 0
            scroll = 0
            # Update our variables and LCD screen with the latest mail
            mail_data, number_entries = read_save_mail(current_message)
            display_message(mail_data, number_entries, current_message, scroll)
            recent_date = latest_mail_date()
```

Running the script of the complete project

It's time to try the script! Save the latest file — the one that contains the code for the complete project — and run it. Set those `LOOP_FREQ` and `CHECK_LATEST_MAIL` constants to values that you feel comfortable with. Send yourself tons of emails (you can do this automatically with the script in Chapter 10 in the section "Sending an Email with Python") to see whether everything is working properly.

All the code for this project is available at `www.dummies.com/go/beaglebone`.

Chapter 15

Running Your Home Automation Web Server

*T*he BeagleBone is an outstanding platform for integrating computation with electronics, which allows you to create awe-inspiring projects featuring the best of both worlds. In this chapter, you build your very own home automaton web server — a web page that interacts with the physical world. The objective of this chapter is to help you build a canvas to which you can add more features as you desire.

Exploring What You Can Do

This section explores the possibilities of this project and explains the limitations of creating a web server.

The BeagleBone is quite a powerful tool when it comes to home automation. Because it provides easy access to the web and lots of general purpose input/ outputs (GPIOs), you can do several neat things with it. All the projects from the other chapters — and more! — can be controlled remotely through the web server that you build with this chapter. You can control everything from LEDs to your toaster to your air conditioner. Isn't that exciting?

Limitations exist, however. The main limitation of this project is the fact that accessing your BeagleBone from anywhere in the world (through a hosted website) isn't as straightforward as you might hope. You're limited to accessing the

BeagleBone through any device — laptop or desktop computer, smartphone, tablet or even another BeagleBone — that's connected to your router.

If you really want to control your web server from locations outside your workplace or home, you can overcome this limitation through a technique known as *router port forwarding*. In router port forwarding, a computer — the BeagleBone, in this case — on your network is made accessible by any computer on the Internet. Explaining this technique is beyond the scope of this book, but plenty of tutorials are available on the web. If you port-forward your router and put your website on the Internet, nothing will stop you from using the web server from anywhere in the world.

Examining the Framework

To complete this project, you should know the basics of BoneScript, HTML, and CSS. If you need more information, read Chapters 7 and Chapter 13.

When you're done with the project in this chapter, your BeagleBone will be hosting a web server, establishing a communication between your device's web browser and your BeagleBone GPIOs. Your web server is created with some `Node.js` code, and when you access IP address `192.168.7.2:8888`, your web browser requests two files — `index.html` and `stylesheet.css` — that are stored on your BeagleBone (see Figure 15-1). Those files are displayed like regular web pages in your web browser so you see a nice graphical user interface (GUI).

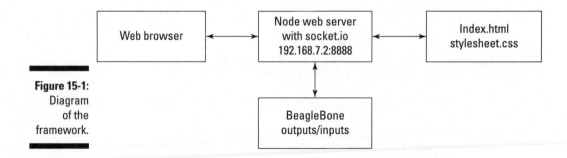

Figure 15-1: Diagram of the framework.

`192.168.7.2` is the local USB address of your BeagleBone; `8888` is the port that you'll be using. A *port* is an application-specific software construct that acts as the endpoint on a computer's operating system. Theoretically, you can use any number from `0` to `65535` as the port, but some numbers won't work because they're reserved — for example, 3000 is reserved for the Cloud9 IDE. You can try whichever port you want, but rest assured that `8888` works just fine.

When you click one of the buttons on your web page, an event triggers and talks with your Node.js code, which has the package socket.io listening for an event to occur. Based on that event message, your Node.js code can either read from or write in your BeagleBone's pins.

The following sections get into the specifics.

Installing socket.io

Your BeagleBone comes with most Node.js packages that you need, but for this project, you have to install an additional package called socket.io. Type the following commands in a terminal:

```
sudo npm install update
sudo npm install -g socket.io
```

The first command updates the list of all available packages to the latest version, and the second one installs socket.io globally. This package allows real-time communication between your web-browser events and your BeagleBone. In other words, as soon as you click a button on your web page, your Node.js code that was listening acts immediately according to the message sent in that event.

You must ensure that your BeagleBone has an Internet connection before you update and install the socket.io package.

Keeping your files organized

We encourage you to use the Cloud9 IDE as often as possible to program your BeagleBone. For this chapter particularly, Cloud9 is perfect for running and debugging projects in Node.js.

Keeping your files organized is a must. Follow these steps to get organized:

1. **Create a new folder called controllingOutputs.**

   This folder is where you're going to store all the other files.

2. **Create the following files in the controllingOutputs folder:**

   • A JavaScript file named server.js

   • An HTML file named index.html

   • A CSS file named stylesheet.css

Repurposing your previous HTML and CSS

Chapter 13 explains how to build a website. If you've already worked through that chapter, you can start by copying the website files to your new files `index.html` and `stylesheet.css`.

We don't describe the changes that we made in our `stylesheet.css` file because they're really minor and not relevant to this chapter. If you've read Chapter 13, you should be able to make these changes easily, or customize your web page to look as you prefer. You can also download those files at `www.dummies.com/go/beaglebone`.

Wiring Your Circuit

For the circuit, you need a breadboard, a light-emitting diode (LED), a 220Ω or 470Ω resistor, and two jumper wires. The LED must be connected to pin P9_14 of your BeagleBone. For details on how to wire this circuit, read Chapter 7.

This project isn't about the LED; it's about getting the communication between your web server and the BeagleBone running. Normally, lighting up an LED is the first thing you do when employing a new technique. In this case, the new technique is working with the web server. In fact, every electronics enthusiast rejoices whenever they are able to light up an LED with a different technology. But here's the most important thing: If you can control an LED, you can control any electronic device — such as your toaster, your desktop light, or your air conditioner — through a neat web page that you can access with your smartphone or tablet from the comfort of your sofa. How cool is that?

Writing Your Web Page

You can download all the code used throughout this chapter at `www.dummies.com/go/beaglebone`.

At first, your `index.html` file will be very similar to the web-page file in Chapter 13. It simply has a few basic tags: `<html>`, `<head>`, and `<body>`. You give a title to your web page and link it to your `stylesheet.css` file. Finally, you insert a wrapper, a logo, a footer, and some `<div>` tags to organize your content in a centered container. Nothing new here.

```
<!DOCTYPE html>
<html>
<head>
        <title>Home Automation Web Server with BeagleBone</title>
        <link rel="stylesheet" href="stylesheet.css" type="text/css" />
</head>
<body>
<div id="wrapper">
        <div id="logo"><h1>Home Automation Web Server</h1></div>
        <div id="container" align="center">
        </div>
        <div id="footer"><p>Powered by BeagleBone</p></div>
</div>
</body>
</html>
```

Creating your GUI

The best thing about this project is that it makes building your own GUI easy. You don't need a terminal window to input data in or read your data from. Inside the container `<div>`, type the following code, which displays in your web page the word LED with a heading number two:

```
<h2>LED</h2>
```

Below your heading number two, you should have a paragraph tag (`<p>`) that's updated when you click the buttons and that also gives you feedback on the LED's status (on or off):

```
<p id="outputStatus">Status</p>
```

In the next snippet of code, you create two buttons that appear on your web page. When you click these buttons, the `changeState()` function is triggered. This function takes only one parameter: `state`, which can be 1 or 0.

```
<div id="buttons"><ul>
        <li><a onclick="changeState(1);">ON</a></li>
        <li><a onclick="changeState(0);">OFF</a></li>
</ul></div>
```

Adding JavaScript to your web page

Inserting scripts into your web page makes the page interactive. Any scripts that you want to add to your web page always go inside the `<head>` tag. Type the following line of code:

```
<script src = "/socket.io/socket.io.js" ></script>
```

That snippet of code imports the `socket.io` library, which is required for establishing a communication between your web page and your server.

Next, you add JavaScript to your web page by adding `<script>` tags:

```
<script>
// Your JavaScript code goes here
</script>
```

Explaining your main JavaScript

All the code in this section goes inside the `<script>` tags. First, you have to establish communication with your server with the `io.connect()` function:

```
// Establishing connection with server
var socket = io.connect();
```

The `changeState(state)` function is triggered every time you click a button in the interface. This function takes a `state` parameter. If `state` is equal to `1`, it emits a `changeState` event that tells your BeagleBone that it has to turn on the LED. It also updates the paragraph with the ID `outputStatus` to "Status: ON".

```
// Changes the led state
function changeState(state){
        if (state==1){
                // Emit message changing the state to 1
                socket.emit('changeState', '{"state":1}');
                // Change led status on web page to ON
                document.getElementById("outputStatus").innerHTML = "Status: ON";
        }
        else if (state==0){
                // Emit message changing the state to 0
                socket.emit('changeState', '{"state":0}');
                // Change led status on web page to OFF
                document.getElementById("outputStatus").innerHTML = "Status: OFF";
        }
}
```

The following paragraphs break down the new functions.

The `emit()` function takes two parameters:

```
socket.emit(<event name>, <event message>)
```

  ✔ **event name** is a string with the event name that your `server.js` file is listening to.

  ✔ **event name** is an object with one value called `state`, which is `1` or `0`.

The getElementById() function searches for an HTML tag with the ID outputStatus and changes the HTML content of that tag to "Status: ON", as shown in the following snippet of code:

```
document.getElementById("outputStatus").innerHTML = "Status: ON";
```

 Describing the whole communication process in such detail makes it look as though it will take forever for an LED to turn on or off, but as soon as you start experimenting with this project, you see that this occurrence happens immediately.

Running Your Web Server

This section describes how to create and run a web server. You use some new JavaScript functions and modules for real-time communications. This section is where you see and understand the code you have to run in the Cloud9 IDE to serve your index.html and stylesheet.css files.

Loading modules and initializing a variable

First, you load all the modules required by server.js, such as the following:

- ✔ **http:** This module offers an easy way to interface with the HTTP protocol.
- ✔ **fs (file system):** This module allows you to access your file system.
- ✔ **path:** This module has utilities to handle and transform file paths.
- ✔ **bonescript:** This module makes interactions with your BeagleBone's GPIOs as easy as possible.

```
//Loading modules
var http = require('http');
var fs = require('fs');
var path = require('path');
var b = require('bonescript');
```

Next, you create a new variable called led, which refers to pin P9_14 on your BeagleBone, and initialize that pin as an OUTPUT:

```
// Create a variable called led, which refers to P9_14
var led = "P9_14";
// Initialize the led as an OUTPUT
b.pinMode(led, b.OUTPUT);
```

Creating your web server

This part of the code is the trickiest part. The following snippet creates your web server on port 8888. This code is executed only when you access the web page through your web browser. It starts by opening your index.html file; then it checks whether you have a .css file. If it finds one, it styles your web page. If you don't have your files in the same folder as your server.js file, the web page will be blank, displaying a 404 (page not found) error message.

```
// Initialize the server on port 8888
var server = http.createServer(function (req, res) {
    // requesting files
    var file = '.'+((req.url=='/')?'/index.html':req.url);
    var fileExtension = path.extname(file);
    var contentType = 'text/html';
    if(fileExtension == '.css'){
        contentType = 'text/css';
    }
    fs.exists(file, function(exists){
        if(exists){
            fs.readFile(file, function(error, content){
                if(!error){
                    // Page found, write content
                    res.writeHead(200,{'content-type':contentType});
                    res.end(content);
                }
            })
        }
        else{
            // Page not found
            res.writeHead(404);
            res.end('Page not found');
        }
    })
}).listen(8888);
```

Establishing socket communication

The code in this section is dedicated to establishing the socket communication. First, you have to load socket.io module.

```
// Loading socket io module
var io = require('socket.io').listen(server);
```

Sockets are methods for establishing communication between a client program and a server. Normally, a server runs on a specific computer — in this case, the BeagleBone — and features a socket that stays listening. While listening, the server is waiting for a client to make a connection request. A socket is the endpoint of a two-way communication. Simply put, a socket is like your house's mailbox: It's the place you go to fetch the data that arrives.

When communication is established, the code waits for an `emit` with the `'changeState'` event name. As soon as that event is triggered, the `handleChangeState()` function executes.

```
// When communication is established
io.on('connection', function (socket) {
    socket.on('changeState', handleChangeState);
});
```

The `handleChangeState(data)` function takes a parameter called `data`, which contains a string that shows the current state of your LED. Then the code gets the data by using the `JSON.parse()` method. Next is the `digitalWrite()` function, which is the code that actually turns your LED on or off.

```
// Change led state when a button is pressed
function handleChangeState(data) {
    var newData = JSON.parse(data);
    console.log("LED = " + newData.state);
    b.digitalWrite(led, newData.state);
}
```

If all goes well, a few seconds after you click Run in the Cloud9 IDE, you see a message in the output window saying that the server is running and waiting for a client (your web browser) to make a connection request:

```
// Displaying a console message for user feedback
server.listen(console.log("Server Running ..."));
```

Launching your web server

Launching your web server is easy. You simply save all three files. Click Run in the Cloud9 IDE, and you should see a message in your output window that says Server Running....

That's it! Your web server is up and running, ready to be accessed. Open a tab in your web browser, and type **192.178.7.2:8888**. You see a page similar to Figure 15-2.

This code works only if your computer is connected directly to the BeagleBone by USB. If that's not the case, read the next section to see how to access the BeagleBone through a device connected in your workspace network.

Figure 15-2:
Project
controlling
outputs run-
ning on the
BeagleBone
Black.

Accessing Your BeagleBone with Another Device

With the setup described in the preceding section, you can access your BeagleBone only with devices that are connected directly to your BeagleBone via USB, such as your laptop. The reason is that 192.178.7.2 is the board's local USB IP address. Perhaps it would be cooler to access the BeagleBone through its Ethernet IP — that is, the address it occupies on your home or office network.

Start by connecting your BeagleBone to your router with an Ethernet cable. In a terminal window — either in the Cloud9 IDE or at a terminal connected via secure shell (SSH) — type the following command:

```
ifconfig
```

You should see something similar to Figure 15-3. The ifconfig command displays various information about your Linux computer's network accessibilities. You see, for example, that usb0 has the address 192.168.7.2, as expected.

What you're interested in is the Ethernet IP address, which appears immediately after eth0 and is called out in Figure 15-3. That address is the BeagleBone's IP address in our home network, so it should be a different address for you. Instead of typing **192.168.7.2:8888** in the web browser, you can type your address instead, followed by the port, which is 8888. You can do this on any device — such as a tablet or smartphone — that's connected to the same router as the BeagleBone, allowing you to access the web page and, ultimately, the BeagleBone's GPIOs.

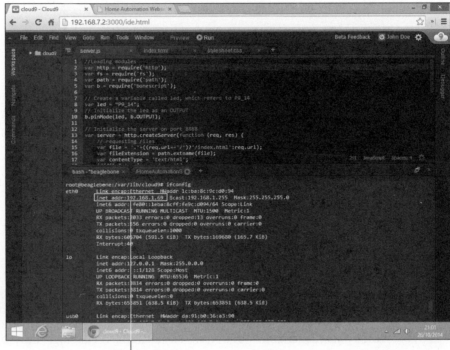

Figure 15-3:
Entering
the ifconfig
command.

Ethernet IP
address

Dropping Your LED and Controlling an Appliance

We hope you're happy about seeing that LED light up! We know that it's just an LED, but socket communication isn't a very trivial thing, and it's an extremely useful concept.

Controlling some house appliances may be more exciting than lighting up an LED. You can easily and immediately replace the LED with a new component that allows you to control any device that connects directly to the sockets on the wall.

The easiest route is to get yourself a PowerSwitch Tail II (www.powerswitch tail.com), which provides a safe way of dealing with high-voltage devices (see Figure 15-4).

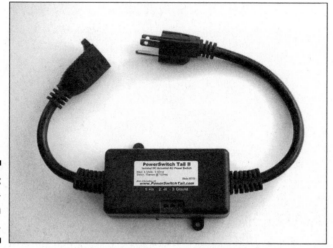

Photo courtesy of Adafruit Industries

Figure 15-4:
Power-
Switch
Tail II.

The way this bulky component works is quite straightforward. Rather than connecting a house appliance directly to the wall, you connect it to the PowerSwitch Tail II which plugs into the wall. The PowerSwitch Tail II has three pins that enable it to behave like a simple digital logic device. You connect the device to an output pin of the BeagleBone and GND. Your output pin will send a signal that's either HIGH or LOW. Whenever the signal is HIGH, there's a connection to the wall socket; when it's LOW, the connection is broken, as though the device were unplugged. Table 15-1 shows the pinout according to the code given earlier in the "Running your web server" section, in which P9_14 is the pin that provides the signal.

Table 15-1	Pinout of PowerSwitch Tail II	
Pin Number	*Signal Name*	*BeagleBone Pins*
1	+in (3.3V)	P9_14
2	-in	GND
3	GND	Not used

Search for the PowerSwitch Tail II's instruction sheet for more details on how to wire it up.

There's another way to have your BeagleBone control a house appliance, but that method is more complicated, requires a bit of extra knowledge and wariness because you're dealing with alternating current, and involves relay modules. Also, it's not directly related to the BeagleBone itself. This book doesn't explain the trick, but plenty of tutorials are available on the Internet.

Adjusting Outputs with PWM

All the projects featured in this book with BoneScript and Python can be modified to work with a custom interface like the one you've been building in this chapter. (Read Chapters 7 to 11 for details on BoneScript and Python.) For this project, you need the following supplies:

- ✔ A servo motor
- ✔ A 1K Ω resistor
- ✔ Four jumper wires

Use the circuit diagram in Figure 15-5 as a reference.

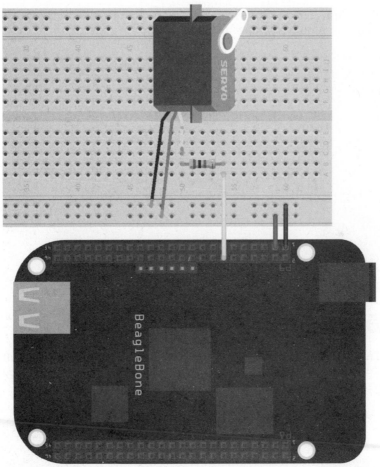

Figure 15-5:
A servo wired to a BeagleBone Black.

fritzing

Keeping all your files organized is the key to preventing many annoying bugs and complications. Set up your folder and files as described in these steps:

1. **Create a new folder called `adjustingPWM`.**

   That folder is where you're going to store all the other files.

2. **In the `adjustingPWM` folder, create the following files:**

   - A JavaScript file named `server.js`

   - An HTML file named `index.html`

   - A CSS file named `stylesheet.css`

This `stylesheet.css` file is exactly like in the examples earlier in this chapter. Keep in mind that the `index.html` file also starts from the same place in all examples.

The following code shows the part of the `index.html` file that should be the same for all the examples in this chapter:

```html
<!DOCTYPE html>
<html>
<head>
        <title>Home Automation Web server with BeagleBone</title>
        <link rel="stylesheet" href="stylesheet.css" type="text/css" />
        <script src = "/socket.io/socket.io.js" ></script>
</head>
<body>
        <div id="wrapper">
                <div id="logo"><h1>Home Automation Web server</h1></div>
                        <div id="container" align="center">
                        </div>
                <div id="footer"><p>Powered by BeagleBone</p></div>
        </div>
</body>
</html>
<!--All the code up until this point will always be the same.-->
```

Designing the GUI

This project is quite fun to experiment with! You have a slider that you can drag to adjust the pulse-width modulation (PWM) output. Start by creating a heading 2 that tells what your project is all about:

```html
<h2>Servo Position</h2>
```

Next, you use the HTML `<input>` tag:

```
<input type="range" min="0" max="1" step="0.1" onchange="changePosition(this.
          value)">
```

This tag has five attributes:

- ✔ **type:** Displays a range element on your web page
- ✔ **min:** Sets the minimum value for an input (in this case, 0)
- ✔ **max:** Sets the maximum value for an input (in this case, 1)
- ✔ **step:** Sets the interval between values (in this case, 0.1)
- ✔ **onchange:** Executes the `changePosition(this.value)` function every time you drag the slider

If you start dragging your slider a few steps to the left, and then suddenly stop and release the slider, the last value is sent to your server to update its current servo position.

As soon as you can move a servo, you can adjust the brightness of an LED or the intensity of a buzzer, to name a few examples. This example is just an idea to spark your creativity, displaying how PWM can be controlled through your web server.

Writing your main script

All the following code goes inside `<script>` tags. First, you have to establish a communication with your server with the `io.connect()` function:

```
// Establishing connection with server
var socket = io.connect();
```

Next, you create a new function called `changePosition(value)`, which takes only one parameter value that refers to the last value read from the slider.

The `emit()` function triggers a `changePosition` event that goes with a message telling your server the last position of the slider:

```
// Changes the servo position
function changePosition(value){
// Emit message changing the servo position to a value from 0 to 1
socket.emit("changePosition", '{"position":"' + value +'"}');
}
```

Creating your web server

The next bit of code is quite similar to the preceding ones. In fact, parts are exactly the same, so we explain only the newest parts, which are highlighted with bold.

```
//Loading modules
var http = require('http');
var fs = require('fs');
var path = require('path');
var b = require('bonescript');


// Create a variable called servo, which refers to P9_14
var servo = "P9_14";

// Initialize the server on port 8888
var server = http.createServer(function (req, res) {
    // requesting files
    var file = '.'+((req.url=='/')?'/index.html':req.url);
    var fileExtension = path.extname(file);
    var contentType = 'text/html';
    if(fileExtension == '.css'){
        contentType = 'text/css';
    }
    fs.exists(file, function(exists){
        if(exists){
            fs.readFile(file, function(error, content){
                if(!error){
                    // Page found, write content
                    res.writeHead(200,{'content-type':contentType});
                    res.end(content);
                }
            })
        }
        else{
            // Page not found
            res.writeHead(404);
            res.end('Page not found');
        }
    })
}).listen(8888);

// Loading socket io module
var io = require('socket.io').listen(server);

// When communication is established
io.on('connection', function (socket) {
    socket.on('changePosition', handleChangePosition);
});
```

```
// Change servo position according to the slider value
function handleChangePosition(data) {
    var newData = JSON.parse(data);
    b.analogWrite(servo, newData.position, 60,
        console.log("Servo Position = " + newData.position));
}
// Displaying a console message for user feedback
server.listen(console.log("Server Running ..."));
```

The hardest and most complicated part of this code is the part that deals with running and communicating with the web server itself. Listening to commands from a web browser doesn't involve any changes. What changes is what you want to do. In this case, you want to control a servo, not set an LED on or off. You start by creating a new variable:

```
// Create a variable called servo, which refers to P9_14
var servo = "P9_14";
```

Next, you need to handle what comes through your socket. Specifically, as soon as the web browser establishes a connection, you're interested in the sliding bar's current position, which is returned when the changePosition event is triggered, and you want the handleChangePosition() function to be called.

```
// When communication is established
io.on('connection', function (socket) {
    socket.on('changePosition', handleChangePosition);
});
```

This function features code that you're already used to if you've completed the "Establishing socket communication" section. The JSON.parse() method extracts the data from the socket communication; then it writes the PWM value into the pin of the servo and prints a message about the servo's position.

```
// Change servo position according to the slider value
function handleChangePosition(data) {
    var newData = JSON.parse(data);
    b.analogWrite(servo, newData.position, 60,
        console.log("Servo Position = " + newData.position));
}
```

Launching the web server to control a PWM output

To launch your web server, you save all three files and click Run in your Cloud9 IDE. When you open your web server, you see a page similar to the one shown in Figure 15-6.

Drag the slider left and right. Enjoy watching your servo move according to your slider bar's position!

Figure 15-6:
Project
adjusting
PWM run-
ning on a
BeagleBone
Black.

Connecting a temperature sensor

The preceding sections showed how to control outputs through a web server, but it's also helpful to know how to read and treat inputs. You can create your own weather station that tells you the room temperature, humidity, and brightness level. You can have a passive infrared (PIR) sensor displaying on your web page when someone enters your room. You can even have a wind-speed sensor in your window. There are lots of possibilities.

To add a temperature sensor, you need the following items:

- A breadboard
- Three jumper wires
- A temperature sensor TMP36, which has three pins wired as shown in Figure 15-7

You can use any temperature sensor if you can extract the important details of its datasheet and make the appropriate changes in the code.

The BeagleBone's Analog-to-Digital Converter (ADC) input pins can only handle input voltages up to 1.8V. If you feed one of them with more than that, things might get nasty. The TMP36 temperature sensor that we suggest you to use surpasses 1.8V only for 266 degrees F (130 degrees C), so it should be safe to wire it directly to the BeagleBone. If you use another sensor, one that surpasses 1.8V at a much lower temperature — or if you're afraid that the TMP36 will read more than 266 degrees F — you need to use a voltage divider and slightly adapt the code. You can read more about this in Chapter 10.

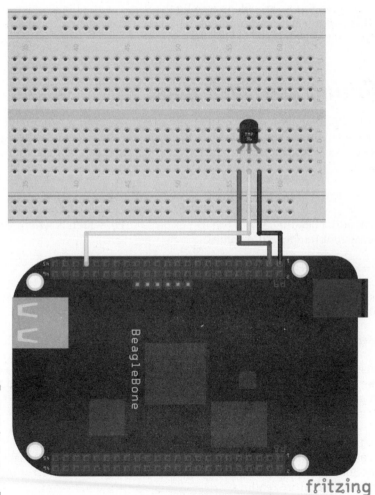

Figure 15-7:
Temperature sensor wired to a BeagleBone Black.

As usual, keeping all your files organized is the key to preventing many annoying bugs and complications, so we suggest that you follow these steps:

1. **Create a new folder called `readingInputs`.**

   That folder is where you're going to store all the other files.

2. **In the `readingInputs` folder, create the following files:**

   - A JavaScript file named `server.js`
   - An HTML file named `index.html`
   - A CSS file named `stylesheet.css`

The `stylesheet.css` file is exactly the same as the file discussed earlier in this chapter. The beginning of the `index.html` page, which affects the design of the web page, is also the same.

Writing your web page

For this project, you don't really have a GUI. You aren't prompted to click or change anything. You just look at the page to read information about your sensor. As before, start by displaying on your web page what your project is about:

```
<h2>Temperature</h2>
```

Next, add a heading 3 with the ID `temperature`, which is where you output the current temperature values:

```
<h3 id="temperature"></h3>
```

Inside your main `<script>` tags, you have to establish a communication with your server with the `io.connect()` function:

```
var socket = io.connect();
```

This time, you don't want to emit data to your server. Instead, you wait for your server to send a new temperature value. When the `sensorsUpdate` event is triggered, you receive a new input reading that's extracted with the `JSON.parse()` method.

Next, you do some math with the voltage that you received to calculate temperature in Celsius and Fahrenheit. Finally, by using the `getElementById()` function, you update the HTML tag with the `temperature` ID showing the latest temperature reading.

```
socket.on('sensorsUpdate', function (data) {
            // store new data on reading variable
            var reading = JSON.parse(data);
            // calculate the temperature according to our voltage
            var voltage = reading.temperature * 3.3;
            var temperatureC = (voltage-0.5) * 100;
            var temperatureF = (temperatureC * 9/5) + 32;
            // Displaying temperature in C and F in the web page
            document.getElementById("temperature").innerHTML = " " +
            Math.round(temperatureC)
            + "&deg;C    " + Math.round(temperatureF) +
            "&deg;F";
});
```

Creating your web server

The following script is quite similar to the preceding ones, so this section explains only the newest snippets of code, which are highlighted with bold:

```
// Loading modules
var http = require('http');
var fs = require('fs');
var path = require('path');
var b = require('bonescript');

// Create variables
var temperature = 'P9_39';
var s;

// Initialize the server on port 8888
var server = http.createServer(function (req, res) {
    // requesting files
    var file = '.'+((req.url=='/')?'/index.html':req.url);
    var fileExtension = path.extname(file);
    var contentType = 'text/html';
    if(fileExtension == '.css'){
        contentType = 'text/css';
    }
    fs.exists(file, function(exists){
        if(exists){
            fs.readFile(file, function(error, content){
                if(!error){
                    // Page found, write content
                    res.writeHead(200,{'content-type':contentType});
                    res.end(content);
                }
            })
        }
```

```
        else{
            // Page not found
            res.writeHead(404);
            res.end('Page not found');
        }
    })
}).listen(8888);

// Loading socket io module
var io = require('socket.io').listen(server);

// When communication is established
io.on('connection', function (socket) {
    s = socket;
    // Execute updateSensors function every one second
    setInterval(updateSensors, 1000);
});

// Update the new temperature value
function updateSensors(){
    temperatureReading = b.analogRead(temperature);
    s.emit("sensorsUpdate", '{"temperature":"' +
    temperatureReading + '"}');
    console.log("Updating Sensor");
}
// Displaying a console message for user feedback
server.listen(console.log("Server Running ..."));
```

The following code creates a new variable called `temperature` to refer to your pin P9_39. You also need a variable to store your socket object; we call it `s`.

```
// Create variables
var temperature = 'P9_39';
var s;
```

When communication is established, this code is executed. As you see, the `setInterval()` function executes the `updateSensors()` function every second for as long as your web server is running.

```
// When communication is established
io.on('connection', function (socket) {
    s = socket;
    // Execute updateSensors function every one second
    setInterval(updateSensors, 1000);
});
```

As its name implies, `updateSensors()` reads the current value of the temperature value and uses the `emit()` function to send that reading to your web page, which is listening for the `sensorsUpdate` event to occur.

```
// Update the new temperature value
function updateSensors(){
    temperatureReading = b.analogRead(temperature);
    s.emit("sensorsUpdate", '{"temperature":"' + temperatureReading +
        '"}');
    console.log("Updating Sensor");
}
```

Launching the web server for your temperature monitoring

Simply save all three files and click Run in your Cloud9 IDE. Open your web server. A page similar to the one shown in Figure 15-8 should appear.

Figure 15-8: Project reading inputs running on a BeagleBone Black.

See whether the temperature is correct according to your common sense. We don't expect you to be able to pinpoint the temperature, but if the temperature reading is off, it'll be really, really off. You should be able to notice that.

Taking this project further

We don't think it's necessary to elaborate on more outputs and sensors that you could connect to the BeagleBone. This chapter explains the three most important things for interacting with the physical world: digital outputs and analog (PWM) outputs and inputs. Whatever ideas you have next are within your reach.

You could incorporate a PIR motion sensor (described in Chapter 8) and create a simple surveillance system for your home. A message could appear on your web page, saying An individual entered your room # seconds ago!, and a buzzer could sound. In the same fashion, you could have a PIR sensor counting the number of people who go in and out of your room, store, or office in a day. That's interesting data.

The coolest thing about home automation is that you can keep adding new things forever. You could end up with a web page that provides loads of data about what's going on your house, or you could have the BeagleBone turn on several appliances, such as an air conditioner or a sound system, from anywhere in your house. This chapter is meant to be used as your canvas; from this point, you should be fully capable of throwing some ink into the painting.

Part VII
The Part of Tens

the
part of
tens

Visit www.dummies.com/go/beaglebone to be introduced to ten software packages to install in your BeagleBone.

In this part . . .

- ✔ Ten amazing projects for the BeagleBone
- ✔ Ten resources to give you a pleasant experience with the BeagleBone

Chapter 16

Ten Amazing Projects for the BeagleBone

In This Chapter

▶ Discovering some extremely cool projects featuring the BeagleBone

▶ Replicating some amazing projects

▶ Getting the motivation you need to take on projects of your own

*T*he BeagleBone is an outstanding tool for so many programs because . . . well, it has pretty much everything. It operates at a very high frequency; it features all the most popular communications ports; it can be set to consume very little energy; it can be programmed in a wide array of programming languages. It isn't an overstatement to say that the BeagleBone offers boundless possibilities in many areas, from fast-reacting systems and processing-heavy programs to low-consumption vehicles.

This book explores the virtually unlimited possibilities that the BeagleBone has to offer. The BeagleBone is truly an outstanding device, capable of significantly narrowing the gap between having an idea and actually building an apparatus.

This chapter is here to stir your imagination. It suggests ten amazing projects for you to consider. Each description includes a link where you can find information about these projects. In some cases, the links provide instructions so you can replicate the projects.

Underwater Exploration Robot

As its name suggests, OpenROV is a tiny yet awesome-looking (just look at Figure 16-1!) underwater exploration robot. The OpenROV website is very well organized and provides a great deal of information, such as where to buy an OpenROV and how to assemble one yourself. All the code and instructions for building the robot are provided, and the company welcomes anyone (including you!) to join its mission to explore the ocean.

Figure 16-1:
OpenROV,
the under-
water explo-
ration robot.

On the website's Documentation page is an extremely detailed guide to making your own OpenROV, including how to assemble the chassis and how to mount the motors, the camera, an Ethernet adapter, and all other necessary electronics. You can download all the software from the same page and add your own twist to the code. Visit www.openrov.com to find out more. This project is also featured on the BeagleBoard website at http://beagleboard.org/project/openrov.

Autonomous Sailboat to Tame the Seas

FASt (see Figure 16-2) stands for *FEUP Autonomous Sailboat* — an 8.2-foot (2.5-meter) unmanned and fully autonomous sailing boat created by a group that Luís was part of at the Faculty of Engineering of the University of Porto.

The sea is a harsh and unstable environment for operating robotic boats. Even though sailing boats typically are slow vehicles, the data acquired from the navigation sensors has to be read and processed quickly to actuate the outputs so that the boat sails where it's supposed to. At the same time, the boat has to be able to make the appropriate maneuvers and choose the best route to the destination. FASt automatically adjusts its sail and rudders by reading data from sensors that measure the wind, water speed, orientation, GPS satellites, and other sensors. A BeagleBone Black is the main brain of the whole operation, running all the software that handles the sensors and actuators, and making the navigation decisions in a clever way.

Figure 16-2:
FASt, the
autonomous
sailboat.

The great thing about sailing robots is that they're full green devices; they don't require motors that eat up huge amounts of energy. Because its computer is powered by solar cells and its electronic system is designed to consume as little energy as possible, FASt can theoretically stay in the sea forever, taking on many missions, from performing ocean sampling or surveillance to tracking sea mammals. Interested? Take a look at the website at www.roboticsailing.pt.

Autonomous Robot for BeagleBone Black

Jon Hoffman decided to start playing around with the BeagleBone Black and ended up creating a robotic rover. It's a very interesting ongoing project. Hoffman's blog includes step-by-step instructions that cover everything from assembling the rover to coding it. The goal is to control the rover remotely, as well as have it drive itself to a destination autonomously.

For such a task, the rover features five rangefinder sonars placed all around it that precisely and quickly detect its position relative to the objects around it. The rover also includes a Bluetooth adapter so that it can be controlled remotely.

This project is interesting and fun, and has many degrees of complexity. The best part is that you can implement the basics — just having the rover drive around a little bit can spark a great feeling of realization — and then add to the project incrementally. Hoffman decided to add the sonars, and he still keeps working to improve the rover with every blog post.

Check out this project at the BeagleBoard website at `http://beagleboard.org/project/FirstRobot`. You can also visit Jon Hoffman's blog at `http://myroboticadventure.blogspot.de`.

BoneScript

When programming the BeagleBone, it's quite probable that you use BoneScript extensively. It allows you to use many useful capabilities to write some interesting programs. By providing many intuitive, simple-to-use functions, BoneScript makes it possible for even the newest programmers to control complex components. We thought it would be interesting to let you in on the BoneScript project itself so you can understand how Jason Kridner created a language that brings simplicity to digital electronics.

BoneScript is an interesting — and ongoing — project that provides an excellent platform for input/output programming. Because all its functions are asynchronous, BoneScript is an excellent library in which to create applications that rely on fast responses to events. In addition, BoneScript provides great support for applications that interact with the physical world and the web at the same time.

To find out more about what's happening behind the scenes for this programming language, visit Kridner's GitHub page at `https://github.com/jadonk/bonescript`. This project is also featured on the BeagleBoard website at `http://beagleboard.org/project/bonescript`.

Multimedia Center with Kodi

Kodi, formally named as XBMC, is a full-featured, award-winning multimedia center that's capable of running on several platforms and in several operating systems. It's an open-source entertainment hub that you could install on your BeagleBone.

When you connect the BeagleBone to the television set through HDMI, watching videos alone or with your family becomes the easiest thing ever. Just sit comfortably on the couch, and use Kodi's remote-controlled user interface.

(You can even use a smartphone as the remote control!) You can use Kodi to play and view most videos, music, podcasts, and digital media in general from local and network storage, as well as from the Internet.

The wiki and forums are full of helpful material to make sure you have an enjoyable experience using Kodi, whether you want to develop for it or simply use it. The website provides everything you need to get Kodi up and running and to get the most out of it; if you'd like to get involved with the project, you can see how at their website. Visit `http://kodi.tv` to find out more. This project is also featured on the BeagleBoard website at `http://beagleboard.org/project/XBMC`.

Kodi is quite a heavy application for the BeagleBone. Make sure that you have very few other programs running to have a smooth experience.

BeagleBone Gaming Console

Max Thrun decided to bring together many existing open-source BeagleBone capes to create GamingCape (see Figure 16-3), a handheld game console that features a BeagleBone Black and is reminiscent of the classic Nintendo Game Boy.

Figure 16-3:
BeagleBone
GamingCape.

Photo courtesy of Max Thrun

GamingCape is truly a marvelous piece of work. Electronics, software, and a little bit of materials knowledge have been brought together to create a hand-held emulator that features several classic games for NES, Sega, and Game Boy systems. It can even run the good old Doom because it has all the necessary components: a color LCD, a joystick, and two thumb buttons, as well as plugs for headphones and a microphone. Max Thrun, the creator of the GamingCape, says, "Just drop in 4 AAA batteries and you'll be playing your favorite games ~~discretely at work~~ in no time".

Visit Thrun's blog at `http://bear24rw.blogspot.pt/2013/07/beagle bone-gamingcape.html` to find out more about this project.

BeagleBone As Super Nintendo

A guy named Andrew Henderson thought that it would be a good idea to turn his BeagleBone into a Super Nintendo — and we couldn't agree more. With the BeagleBone Black, you have a chance to take a trip down Memory Lane by creating your own game system.

The so-called BeagleSNES project is an entire Linux file-system image that turns the board into a stand-alone console, enabling you to play game titles for Super Nintendo by using an emulator and an HDMI port or an LCD3 cape.

Naturally, a Super Nintendo console and the BeagleBone Black have quite different hardware. The BeagleBone Black runs at 1 GHz, for example, whereas the SNES runs at 3.58 MHz, which is much, much slower. This difference in the frequency at which they run allows each hardware instruction that would take place on the SNES to be emulated in the software of the BeagleBone Black, even if the BeagleBone Black requires many instructions to translate just one instruction from the SNES. Because the BeagleBone Black is much faster, it has plenty of time to run the extra instructions.

The BeagleSNES website features some very neat trailers as well as complete documentation and links to download all the source code. Whether you want to hack the code to make your own thing or you just want to play some of the old games you remember from years gone by, everything you need is at `http://beaglesnes.sourceforge.net/`. This project is also featured on the BeagleBoard website at `http://beagleboard.org/project/ beaglesnes`.

BeagleBone Cape for Drones

Ron and Traci Battles started their website as a simple hobbyist blog. Now the site is a full-fledged business. The couple love to create products that extend the capabilities of open-source platforms such as the BeagleBone.

One project, the BeagleDrone, is an autopilot project that uses a BeagleBone and an Inertial Measurement Unit (IMU) cape. The IMU cape provides a three-axis magnetometer, accelerometer, gyroscope, and barometer — everything necessary for you to know the exact position of a device along a three-axis referential.

Additionally, two of the BeagleBone's UARTs (Universal Asynchronous Receiver/Transmitter) have connectors for external modules such as GPS and telemetry. The BeagleDrone also features a voltage regulator, which makes it possible for power to come from a Reverse Capacity (RC) battery, keeping the voltage at 5V DC. Consequently, you can power the BeagleBone, the communication modules, and any servo motors. All this hardware makes the BeagleDrone a perfect device for any flying project in which you want to invest your time and creativity.

The BeagleBone's powerful 32-bit microcontroller and Linux's extensive libraries provide the foundation for this project and have very few limitations, allowing your imagination to soar as high as your project (lame pun?).

You can check out this project at http://andicelabs.com/beagledrone. The project is also featured on the BeagleBoard website at http://beagle board.org/project/BeagleDrone.

 You should drop by the Battles' website — http://andicelabs.com — to see more interesting stuff!

Desktop Five-Axis CNC Mill

A CNC (computer numerical control) mill is a machine that's used to create pretty much everything. It operates by cutting a piece of material to the desired shape. CNC mills have been around for industrial purposes for a long while, but over the past decade, there has been remarkable growth in people's desire to build things themselves. This growth has created a new market for personal CNC mills that can sit on a desktop.

Normally, these machines cut material in the three translational axes of motion: X, Y, and Z. Matt Hertel and his crew decided to go one step further by creating Pocket NC (see Figure 16-4), a desktop five-axis CNC mill that allows for the manufacture of complex parts. Among desktop CNC mills, five-axis capability is quite an innovation.

Figure 16-4:
Desktop
CNC mill.

Photo courtesy of Pocket NC

A BeagleBone Black handles the computational prowess of motion control, running extremely precise software that decides how the Pocket NC operates to cut the material to the desired shape. For the electronics part, Hertel's team designed a custom-made cape for the BeagleBone. The board runs a Linux distribution specially created for this kind of job: LinuxCNC. Head over to www.pocketnc.com if you want to find out more. This project is also featured on the BeagleBoard website at http://beagleboard.org/project/pocketnc.

BeagleBone 3D Printer

Elias Bakken, Tom Andersson, and Øyvind Dahl at Intelligent Agent AS came up with the phenomenal idea of creating a 3D printer featuring either the BeagleBone or the BeagleBone Black. They named their printer Replicape.

Replicape is an open-source 3D printer cape for the BeagleBone. It's extremely fast; its source code can be altered for customization; and it provides access to the Internet.

The Replicape website provides a lot of documentation, including a wiki, and many interesting videos. We suggest that you watch the short video at www.thing-printer.com/product/replicape not only to hear about this project from Bakken himself, but also to watch it in action. This project is featured on the BeagleBoard website at http://beagleboard.org/project/Replicape.

Chapter 17

Ten Resources and Tips for BeagleBone Users

*T*his chapter introduces you to ten useful resources that can help you get the most out of your BeagleBone.

The first part of the chapter focuses on tips on getting started with digital electronics — where to buy the required tools and components, for example. Later in the chapter, we provide some guidance on how you can continue learning and improving your skills as a BeagleBone programmer. This chapter is the last chapter of *BeagleBone For Dummies,* but it shouldn't be your last experience with the BeagleBone. Your experience is just starting!

Finding Components and Parts

You can get electronic components for your projects in quite a few places. We encourage you to purchase your components from local stores. Components such as resistors, light-emitting diodes (LEDs), potentiometers, and motors are quite standard, and any electronics store should have them.

As your projects grow and you require more specific components, however, you may find it easier to locate them online. A simple online search can help you find electronics stores that sell the exact component that you require. Don't forget that shipping costs and taxes affect the final price of your components when you purchase them online. To save on shipping costs, it's a good idea to get them from somewhere close by when you can.

When you do have to order from a store in a remote location, it isn't a big deal. Electrical components usually are very small; thus, shipping costs typically aren't very high. Whatever component you need, there's a good chance that these sites have it:

- **Sparkfun:** www.sparkfun.com
- **Farnell:** http://farnell.com
- **Radio Shack:** www.radioshack.com
- **Adafruit:** www.adafruit.com
- **Tigal:** https://www.tigal.com
- **Logic Supply:** www.logicsupply.com

Acquiring Electronics Starter Kits

In many electronics stores, such as those mentioned in the preceding section, you can find plenty of starter kits for electronics newcomers. Starter kits are really great ideas because they save you the time and effort of sorting out everything you need to get started with digital electronics. These kits come in different varieties and prices, and the one that's right for you depends on how broad you want it to be. A good starter kit includes the following items:

- LEDs
- Resistors
- Potentiometers
- Jumpers
- Needle-nose pliers
- Servo motors
- Buzzers

Naturally, you can go for starter kits that feature many other useful tools and components, such as wire-cutting and wire-stripping pliers; equipment wires; and a soldering iron, stand, and glasses. The type of starter kit you get depends on how far you want to go on your electronics trip.

You can also find BeagleBone Black starter kits. These kits feature a BeagleBone Black and some useful components and capes to go with it. You can get BeagleBone Black starter kits from Adafruit (www.adafruit.com/product/703) and Logic Supply (www.logicsupply.com/components/beaglebone/boards-cases-kits/bblk-kit).

Protecting Your BeagleBone with a Case

A good way to keep your BeagleBone safe is to enclose it in a plastic case specifically designed for the board (see Figure 17-1). Aside from protecting the board from harmful things that can happen, such as a fall, a case also helps prevent unconnected wires from creating a short circuit. (Short circuits are quite hazardous to the board.)

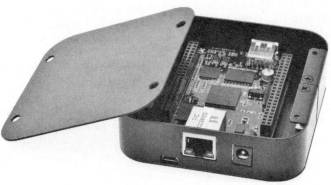

Figure 17-1: BeagleBone Black case from Tigal.

Photo courtesy of Tigal

A case features slots that let you access both headers as well as the USB ports, power jack, Ethernet jack, power buttons, Micro HDMI jack, and microSD card. All the USR (user) LEDs are visible with your BeagleBone inside it.

Covers feature feet for mounting the board in slide-in wall slots and vents for keeping the board cool. Also, a nice cover looks pretty neat, and most covers are relatively inexpensive.

Attending Events and Workshops

Be on the lookout for nearby events and workshops, which cover all kinds of topics: robotics, sensor networks, mobile communications, home automation, and pretty much anything else you can imagine. Getting together with other electronics enthusiasts gives you a chance to have fun and get some knowledge from others. You can see some really cool projects or even go ahead and present your own (and there's also the possibility of free food and coffee).

Universities and schools often hold such events, and there are many independent events, such as the popular Maker Faire and the events held by Hackaday. If you ever have the opportunity to attend a Maker Faire or

Hackaday event, we highly recommend the experience! Find a location near you at `http://makerfaire.com` or `https://hackaday.io/events`.

Joining the BeagleBoard Community

The BeagleBoard community is a welcoming, active, and open group of people with a common interest. The site includes a blog, a live chat, forums, and videos featuring all kinds of tinkering, hacking, and developing. You can jump right into this environment by visiting `http://beagleboard.org/Community`.

The community page of BeagleBoard.org offers many ways for you to get involved in the BeagleBoard community, including

- Finding solutions for problems you're having with your board and helping others come up with solutions to their problems
- Checking out interesting ideas from other people
- Showing off your own project

Interacting with the Community

The BeagleBoard community loves helping new users, but before asking something, there are a few good practices that you should follow.

Asking the same questions over and over again, especially if you can find answers with just a couple of clicks or an online search, is considered rude. You should always try to get answers on your own before posting online. Rooting out a problem without relying on others helps you gain more insight into digital electronics and the BeagleBone. Plus, if you have a simple problem that could have been solved by a few minutes of troubleshooting or an online search, the community may consider it rude that you posted the question to the group.

You can visit `http://beagleboard.org/support/faq` for a collection of some of the most frequently asked questions.

Here are some tips for getting help on two of the most common types of questions:

- **Hardware:** Try posting a figure with your circuit diagram so others can see exactly how you're wiring your project. Posting links to datasheets when you mention particular components is also a good practice so that the community members don't have to search it by themselves.

✔ **Software bugs:** When you have a bug, don't copy and paste your whole code to a forum thread. Instead, use websites created specifically for code sharing — such as the free `http://pastebin.com/` — where you can copy your code, select the code syntax according to the programming language, and get a unique URL. Posting that link to the forum thread makes it much easier for others to read your code and help you with your problem.

Sharing Your BeagleBone Projects with Others

If you believe that your project is pretty neat, there are bound to be other people who think the same thing about it. You can find those people by posting your project online.

The Internet is a great asset for us electronics and computing enthusiasts. There are plenty of websites that can help you to share your project. When you post your project, you can provide step-by-step instructions and images so that others can try it. You'll receive comments — both good and bad — and some people will ask questions or offer suggestions. Sharing a project isn't just about letting others see it. It's also about getting advice from other people and improving it with the help of everyone.

The following three websites are great places to post the details of your project:

✔ **Beagleboard.org:** `http://beagleboard.org/Project`

✔ **Instructables:** `www.instructables.com`

✔ **Hackaday:** `http://hackaday.io`

Improving by Failing

Electricity works at an atomic level. Many things are happening inside your circuits that you just can't see and can hardly visualize. Sure, you have knowledge to back you up, but an LED can burn out just because you forget to put a resistor in series with it. Your BeagleBone might even be severely damaged by a short circuit caused by two random wires that you didn't even notice were 5V and GND.

Failing is often annoying, especially when you can't figure out why something didn't work. But the good thing about failing is that if you can root out the issue, you have gained more knowledge than you would have if you'd succeeded on your first try. Failing enables you to gain insight into how the electrical world works.

Failing means that you tried. Nowadays, access to most components is easy, straightforward, and relatively cheap. Whenever you fail, don't just throw the project away and start over: try to understand the problem, find a solution, and come up with an explanation based on what you observed. Search online if need be. Sooner than you'd guess, you'll be spouting loads of electrical knowledge to your friends and family.

Looking for Project Ideas

Chapter 16 suggests some projects that we think are quite interesting, but they're far from being the only ones out there that should spark your interest. After all, we chose them based on our tastes, which may be different from yours.

You can check some more projects featuring a BeagleBone at these websites:

- **Beagleboard.org:** http://beagleboard.org/Project
- **Instructables:** www.instructables.com/howto/beaglebone
- **Hackaday:** http://hackaday.com

You should try out the projects that interest you most. These can also spark your imagination to create something of your own. If you have an idea, don't be afraid to follow through with it.

Finding Out More about BeagleBone

This book only scratches the surface of electronics stuff that you can play around with. Many functions are available other than those that we cover in the example projects. You may even want to figure out how to program the BeagleBone by using programming languages other than BoneScript and Python.

The following four websites are great resources to help you continue your journey:

- **Embedded Linux:** http://elinux.org/BeagleBoard
- **BeagleBoard:** http://beagleboard.org/Support/bone101
- **Adafruit:** https://learn.adafruit.com/category/beaglebone
- **Derek Molloy:** http://derekmolloy.ie/tag/beaglebone-2/

Appendix A
Troubleshooting

· ·

One frustrating thing about electronics and computation is that quite often, things don't work as they should. You find yourself angrily asking "Why?!", and you may even blame the BeagleBone for not doing what you asked it to.

Then you find the source of the issue, and you bring your palm to your face when you realize how simple the mistake was. You may even apologize to your computer for having unjustly accused it of causing the problem.

This appendix describes some common issues and explains how to solve them, and it provides a few tips and tricks on how to tackle problems that aren't included in these pages. We hope there won't be many!

Common Sources of Errors

This section presents a few typical mistakes that even the most experienced programmers and electronics enthusiasts often experience.

Issue:

The BeagleBone doesn't power on. Its built-in light-emitting diodes (LEDs) aren't lighting up.

Possible causes:

✔ Not enough power or faulty USB cable/USB port. This may happen if you have too many peripherals connected to the BeagleBone and you're feeding it through a USB cable.

✔ You have a short circuit somewhere in your external wiring. A short circuit causes the board to shut down to prevent any further damage — but a short circuit always does some harm.

Solutions:

✔ Disconnect some peripherals; try a different USB cable or a different USB port. If these remedies fail, connect an external DC power source that can provide more current than a USB cable can.

✔ The problem might also be in your external DC power source, so if you have another one, try it.

✔ Double-check your circuit to ensure that everything's wired up correctly. If your board went off immediately after establishing a connection, dismantle that connection, and wire it correctly. If not, grab a multimeter, and check the continuity. If there's a short circuit, you hear the "beep" of a connection where it shouldn't be.

You can read all about how to use a multimeter at www.dummies.com/go/beaglebone/webextras.

✔ If none of the aforementioned solutions works, do a full power cycle. Press your BeagleBone's power button for about 10 seconds. It should shut down and start over. This process isn't the same as rebooting.

If all these attempts fail, perhaps contacting BeagleBoard.org support is the way to go. The board may be damaged, and you may have to fill out an RMA (Return Merchandise Application) form. This page should help you: http://beagleboard.org/support.

Issue:

The BeagleBone is on, but you aren't able to log in via Secure Shell (SSH).

Possible causes:

✔ Faulty USB/Ethernet cable.

✔ Your USB cable is power-only; it doesn't feature pins for data transmission. In this case, the user LEDs of your BeagleBone light up as normal.

✔ The default IP to connect through Ethernet has changed, so you can't log in by typing **beaglebone**.

Solutions:

✔ To address the first two causes, attempt to establish the connection by using other cables. Try to connect your Mini USB cable to other devices to see whether it can establish a communication.

✔ If you can't connect through an Ethernet cable, find the BeagleBone's IP address and type it in the terminal window or PuTTY.

There are several ways to list all the IP addresses in the network that your computer is connected to:

- For Windows, you can install the Advanced IP Scanner (`www.advanced-ip-scanner.com`). All you have to do is click the Scan button.

- For Linux and Mac OS, you need to install nmap by using the command `sudo apt-get install nmap`. Then find your own IP address in your network by typing **ifconfig** in the terminal window. Below eth0, look for `inet addr`. You should see a number with four fields separated by dots. The first three fields are the same for all devices connected in the same network. Thus, if your IP address is something like `192.168.1.12`, all other IP addresses have the format `192.168.1.X`. To find all IP addresses in that format, type **nmap 192.168.1.0/24** in the terminal window. This command shows you all addresses on the network from `192.168.1.0` to `192.168.1.255`. One of those addresses is the BeagleBone's, and that's the IP you need to provide to connect to it.

Issue:

The BeagleBone crashed.

Solutions:

✔ Relax; it probably didn't crash. It's just too busy at the moment. Be patient, and let it finish its tasks.

✔ If you're controlling the BeagleBone remotely, try pressing Ctrl+C to terminate the currently running process. If you're running the Desktop environment, terminate a few programs. Otherwise, wait for a while.

✔ If your patience has run out, perhaps it really did crash. Reboot the BeagleBone by pressing the reboot button. It's a button close to the Ethernet dongle labeled RESET.

Things Not to Do

This section covers some things that you should avoid doing often, as they can be hazardous to your board:

✔ **Short-circuiting your board:** Short circuits are the bane of all electronic devices. Even though the BeagleBone features protection against short circuits — it immediately shuts down — some harm is always done. A short circuit happens whenever a voltage supply is connected directly to ground without anything in between. Be careful about doing the following things:

- *Connecting a 3.3V or 5V wire to a ground (GND) wire:* This one seems like something you wouldn't do, but it can happen if you're distracted and mix up your wires. Color coding helps you prevent this problem.

- *Misplacing a component:* Plugging a resistor into the wrong hole may be all it takes to have a 3.3V or 5V wire and GND with nothing in between, causing a short circuit.

- *Forgetting about pull-up resistors:* A button doesn't count as a component to place between a voltage source and ground. When you press a button and no pull-up resistor is present on your circuit, a short circuit happens.

- *Having random unconnected wires floating around:* When you walk past a black cat and break a mirror on a Friday the 13th, you may have the bad luck of two unattended wires causing a short circuit. It might seem like a long shot, but it can happen. It *has* happened. Make sure to keep your floating wires in check (or avoid having them at all).

✔ **Feeding the BeagleBone's digital pins with more than 3.3V and the Analog-to-Digital-Converters (ADCs) with more than 1.8V:** Often, for several applications, you will have 5V and 3.3V wires on your breadboard. You need to pay extra attention in order to never connect any of the 5V wires to the BeagleBone. Also, you have to keep in mind that the ADCs can only stand voltages up to 1.8V, so you have to ensure that the output voltage from the sensors you use don't surpass this value. Naturally, you have to be careful to not connect any of the 5V or 3.3V wires to any of the ADCs as well.

✔ **Turning power off abruptly:** The BeagleBone is a computer. Usually, you don't turn off a computer by pressing the power button or removing the battery or plug. The reason: The computer may be damaged when it loses power unexpectedly. In the specific case of the BeagleBone, abrupt power loss may corrupt the embedded MultiMediaCard (eMMC) memory, which isn't fun.

✔ **Powering off while installing or updating software:** *Never* turn off the BeagleBone when it's installing software or updates. You'll be left with half-processed operations that may lead to complications.

Miscellaneous

This section covers some useful things you can do on your BeagleBone to have a smoother experience with it.

Expanding the file system on your microSD card

Initially, when you're booting your operating system from your microSD card, you won't get all the space that the card provides — probably not even close. The reason is that you're still using an image of the operating system, so you still have to expand the file system to get all the space your microSD card claims to give you.

To do so, fire up a terminal window, and follow these steps:

1. **Log in as the superuser by typing** sudo su.

2. **Check available volumes with the following command:**

```
ls -l /dev/mmcb*
brw-rw---T 1 root floppy 179,  0 Jan  1  2000 /dev/mmcblk0
brw-rw---T 1 root floppy 179,  1 May 15 02:20 /dev/mmcblk0p1
brw-rw---T 1 root floppy 179,  2 Jan  1  2000 /dev/mmcblk0p2
brw-rw---T 1 root floppy 179,  8 Jan  1  2000 /dev/mmcblk1
brw-rw---T 1 root floppy 179, 16 Jan  1  2000 /dev/mmcblk1boot0
brw-rw---T 1 root floppy 179, 24 Jan  1  2000 /dev/mmcblk1boot1
brw-rw---T 1 root floppy 179,  9 Jan  1  2000 /dev/mmcblk1p1
brw-rw---T 1 root floppy 179, 10 Jan  1  2000 /dev/mmcblk1p2
```

3. **Find your microSD card in the list, and examine its partitioning with the following command:**

```
fdisk /dev/mmcblk0
```

Most of the time, that number should be 0.

4. **Type** p.

You see various details about the size partitions on your SD card. For our 16 GB card, for example, we see the following:

```
Disk /dev/mmcblk0: 16.0 GB, 16013852672 bytes
4 heads, 16 sectors/track, 488704 cylinders, total 31277056 sectors
Units = sectors of 1 * 512 = 512 bytes
Sector size (logical/physical): 512 bytes / 512 bytes
I/O size (minimum/optimal): 512 bytes / 512 bytes
Disk identifier: 0x00000000

        Device Boot      Start         End      Blocks   Id  System
/dev/mmcblk0p1   *         2048      198655       98304    e  W95 FAT16
        (LBA)
/dev/mmcblk0p2           198656     3481599     1641472   83  Linux
```

5. **Delete partition 2 by typing** d **and then typing** 2.

You delete partition 2 to create a new one that enables you to use all the space left in your SD card.

6. **Create a new partition by typing** n **for new,** p **for primary, and** 2 **for partition 2.**

7. **Press Enter or Return two times.**

8. **Type** p **again to see the new** /dev/mmcblk0p2, **with a lot more available space.**

9. **To commit to the changes you made, type** w.

If you're afraid that you messed up and want to start over, simply press Ctrl+Z.

10. **Reboot your BeagleBone with the** reboot **command.**

The partitions are created, but you still need to expand the file system.

11. **Log in as the superuser again by typing** sudo su **and then type** df.

The df command shows the available space in your file system:

```
Filesystem        1K-blocks      Used Available Use% Mounted on
rootfs           1582864  1499484      1308 100% /
udev                10240        0     10240   0% /dev
tmpfs              101700      640    101060   1% /run
/dev/mmcblk0p2   1582864  1499484      1308 100% /
(_)
```

12. **Run the following command to expand the file system:**

```
resize2fs /dev/mmcblk0p2
```

13. **Type** df **again to see the fruits of your labor.**

This command shows that you now have much more space available in the file system:

```
Filesystem        1K-blocks      Used Available Use% Mounted on
rootfs          15270256  1501100  13133688  11% /
udev                10240        0     10240   0% /dev
tmpfs              101700      644    101056   1% /run
/dev/mmcblk0p2  15270256  1501100  13133688  11% /
(...)
```

Accessing external storage devices when using the Linux Shell

Whenever you plug an external storage device, such as a USB key, into your BeagleBone, you can easily access it through the Linux Shell. Well, Access isn't as easy as it would be in a desktop environment, but it's no big deal.

Simply change to the /media directory and list it as shown in the following snippet. Remember to be logged in as root.

```
sudo su
cd /media
ls
```

Your external storage device should be listed. You can access the device and use it as though it were a regular directory. You're free to browse its files, copying, opening, and editing them as you like.

You may need to change the permissions by using the chmod command. This command is discussed in Chapter 4.

Appendix B

Controlling BeagleBone's GPIOs

● ●

*T*his appendix offers a handy reference to controlling and accessing your BeagleBone's general purpose input/output (GPIOs) with the file system, BoneScript, and Python.

Controlling the GPIO with the File System

You can use the following commands to control the GPIO with the file system.

Exporting a pin:

```
echo 40 > /sys/class/gpio/export
```

Setting a pin OUTPUT:

```
echo out > /sys/class/gpio/gpio40/direction
```

Writing a pin HIGH:

```
echo 1 > /sys/class/gpio/gpio40/value
```

Writing a pin LOW:

```
echo 0 > /sys/class/gpio/gpio40/value
```

Setting a pin INPUT:

```
echo in > /sys/class/gpio/gpio40/direction
```

Reading the value from an INPUT pin (returns 1 for HIGH and 0 for LOW):

```
cat /sys/class/gpio/gpio40/value
```

Controlling the GPIO with BoneScript

You can use the following BoneScript commands to control the GPIO.

Loading a BoneScript module:

```
var b = require('bonescript');
```

Setting a pin OUTPUT:

```
b.pinMode("P9_14", b.OUTPUT);
```

Writing a pin HIGH:

```
b.digitalWrite("P9_14", b.HIGH);
```

Writing a pin LOW:

```
b.digitalWrite("P9_14", b.LOW);
```

Setting a pin INPUT:

```
b.pinMode("P8_11", b.INPUT);
```

Reading the value from a digital INPUT pin (returns HIGH or LOW):

```
b.digitalRead("P8_11");
```

Setting a pin for pulse-width modulation (PWM) with 50 percent duty cycle:

```
b.pinMode('P9_14', b.OUTPUT);
b.analogWrite('P9_14', 0.5);
```

Reading the value from an analog INPUT pin (returns a value between 0 and 1):

```
b.analogRead('P9_40');
```

Controlling the GPIO with Python

You can use the following Python commands to control the GPIO.

Importing Adafruit's BeagleBone Input Output Library:

```
import Adafruit_BBIO.GPIO as GPIO
```

Setting a pin OUTPUT:

```
GPIO.setup("P9_14", GPIO.OUT)
```

Writing a pin HIGH:

```
GPIO.output("P9_14", GPIO.HIGH)
```

Writing a pin LOW:

```
GPIO.output("P9_14", GPIO.LOW)
```

Setting a pin INPUT:

```
GPIO.setup("P8_11", GPIO.IN)
```

Reading the value from a digital INPUT pin (returns HIGH or LOW):

```
GPIO.input("P8_11")
```

Setting a pin for PWM with 50 percent duty cycle:

```
import Adafruit_BBIO.PWM as PWM
PWM.start("P9_14", 50)
```

Setting an analog INPUT:

```
import Adafruit_BBIO.ADC as ADC
ADC.setup()
```

Reading the value from an analog INPUT pin (returns a value between 0 and 1):

```
analogReading = ADC.read("P9_40")
```

Appendix C
Guide to the BeagleBone's GPIOs

· ·

*T*he tables in this appendix provide you a quick way to see the signal name of each pin of your BeagleBone's expansion headers. Throughout this book, we use just a few general purpose input/output (GPIOs), but it's important to know that you can use the other GPIOs in your projects!

Table C-1	BeagleBone Expansion Header P8
Pin	**Signal Name**
1	GND
2	GND
3	GPIO1_6
4	GPIO1_7
5	GPIO1_2
6	GPIO1_3
7	TIMER4
8	TIMER7
9	TIMER5
10	TIMER6
11	GPIO1_13
12	GPIO1_12
13	EHRPWM2B
14	GPIO0_26
15	GPIO1_15
16	GPIO1_14
17	GPIO0_27
18	GPIO2_1

(continued)

Table C-1 *(continued)*

Pin	Signal Name
19	EHRPWM2A
20	GPIO1_31
21	GPIO1_30
22	GPIO1_5
23	GPIO1_4
24	GPIO1_1
25	GPIO1_0
26	GPIO1_29
27	GPIO2_22
28	GPIO2_24
29	GPIO2_23
30	GPIO2_25
31	UART5_CTSN
32	UART5_RTSN
33	UART4_RTSN
34	UART3_RTSN
35	UART4_CTSN
36	UART3_CTSN
37	UART5_TXD
38	UART5_RXD
39	GPIO2_12
40	GPIO2_13
41	GPIO2_10
42	GPIO2_11
43	GPIO2_8
44	GPIO2_9
45	GPIO2_6
46	GPIO2_7

Table C-2	BeagleBone Expansion Header P9
Pin	*Signal Name*
1	GND
2	GND
3	VDD_3V3
4	VDD_3V3
5	VDD_5V
6	VDD_5V
7	SYS_5V
8	SYS_5V
9	PWR_BUT
10	SYS_RESETn
11	UART4_RXD
12	GPIO1_28
13	UART4_TXD
14	EHRPWM1A
15	GPIO1_16
16	EHRPWM1B
17	I2C1_SCL
18	I2C1_SDA
19	I2C2_SCL
20	I2C2_SDA
21	UART2_TXD
22	UART2_RXD
23	GPIO1_17
24	UART1_TXD
25	GPIO3_21
26	UART1_RXD
27	GPIO3_19
28	SPI1_CS0
29	SPI1_D0
30	SPI1_D1
31	SPI1_SCLK

(continued)

Table C-2 (continued)

Pin	Signal Name
32	VDD_ADC
33	AIN4
34	GNDA_ADC
35	AIN6
36	AIN5
37	AIN2
38	AIN3
39	AIN0
40	AIN1
41	GPIO3_20
42	GPIO0_7
43	GND
44	GND
45	GND
46	GND

Index

• *X* •

About the Authors

Rui Santos is a popular electronics blogger known for sharing his knowledge through step-by-step video tutorials and articles that anyone can follow. He started studying electrical engineering in 2011, but his appetite for tinkering with electronics dates to long before that. Even today, most of his knowledge has been self-taught. He loves all things electronics. His work has been featured on Instructables (www.instructables.com) and Hackday (http://hackaday.com). You can find his projects at http://randomnerdtutorials.com.

Luís Perestrelo has been passionate about all things electrical ever since he started studying electrical engineering in 2011. Following his academic success in his freshman year, he was invited to work as a teaching assistant at his university in the areas of physics, math, and C programming. Luís is crazy about embedded systems, and he enthusiastically works alongside his colleagues and professors to build Autonomous Underwater Vehicles (AUVs) and Autonomous Sailboats.

Dedication

For Sara. — Rui

For Bingo, Óscar, and Zukta. — Luís

Author's Acknowledgments

We both want to thank Katie Mohr for giving us the opportunity to write this book; to Charlotte Kughen and Kathy Simpson for their editing support; and to Gerald Coley for offering his technical expertise.

Many thanks go to the Wiley Publishing team for their guidance throughout each step. Thank you to the BeagleBoard Foundation, not only because their work gave us something to write a book about, but also because both of us have done great and fun projects using the BeagleBone. We also want to acknowledge everyone who has developed software for the BeagleBone, especially Adafruit for their extensive and powerful Python library.

— Rui Santos and Luís Perestrelo

I'd like to say thank you to my parents and sister for their endless support; to my co-author Luís Perestrelo for accepting the invite to write this book; and to all my friends who followed me through this entire chapter in my life and heard me talking about the book nonstop. Thank you!

— Rui

I would like to thank my friends and family for providing support throughout this entire journey, and for always caring about the progress and asking me how the book was going. On that note, I'd like to send a special thanks to José Francisco Valente for providing cool project ideas and suggestions for the book and for bearing with me as I talked about it 24/7. Thanks also to João Salgado and Marco Moreira for helping out with image editing and photography in the initial chapters. Thank you to Rui Gomes, as well; I'm sure our colleagues will understand why. Saving the best for last, I would like to thank my friend and co-author Rui Santos for inviting me to tag along for this ride.

I'd also like to thank the teachers and professors that have both taught me and made me love digital electronics and embedded systems. Of special note is my professor José Carlos Alves, who started by teaching me basic binary algebra and ended up programming a BeagleBone side by side with me for our autonomous sailboat; he continuously provided support for the book in any way he could. You rock, Professor.

— Luís

Publisher's Acknowledgments

Senior Acquisitions Editor: Katie Mohr

Project Editor: Charlotte Kughen

Copy Editor: Kathy Simpson

Technical Editor: Gerald Coley

Editorial Assistant: Claire Brock

Sr. Editorial Assistant: Cherie Case

Project Coordinator: Emily Benford

Cover Image: Courtesy of Rui Santos

...ple & Mac

...ad For Dummies,
...h Edition
...8-1-118-72306-7

...hone For Dummies,
...h Edition
...8-1-118-69083-3

...acs All-in-One
...r Dummies, 4th Edition
...8-1-118-82210-4

...S X Mavericks
...r Dummies
...8-1-118-69188-5

...logging & Social Media

...acebook For Dummies,
...h Edition
...8-1-118-63312-0

...ocial Media Engagement
...or Dummies
...8-1-118-53019-1

...ordPress For Dummies,
...th Edition
...8-1-118-79161-5

...usiness

...tock Investing
...or Dummies, 4th Edition
...8-1-118-37678-2

...nvesting For Dummies,
...th Edition
...8-0-470-90545-6

Personal Finance
For Dummies, 7th Edition
978-1-118-11785-9

QuickBooks 2014
For Dummies
978-1-118-72005-9

Small Business Marketing
Kit For Dummies,
3rd Edition
978-1-118-31183-7

Careers

Job Interviews
For Dummies, 4th Edition
978-1-118-11290-8

Job Searching with Social
Media For Dummies,
2nd Edition
978-1-118-67856-5

Personal Branding
For Dummies
978-1-118-11792-7

Resumes For Dummies,
6th Edition
978-0-470-87361-8

Starting an Etsy Business
For Dummies, 2nd Edition
978-1-118-59024-9

Diet & Nutrition

Belly Fat Diet For Dummies
978-1-118-34585-6

Mediterranean Diet
For Dummies
978-1-118-71525-3

Nutrition For Dummies,
5th Edition
978-0-470-93231-5

Digital Photography

Digital SLR Photography
All-in-One For Dummies,
2nd Edition
978-1-118-59082-9

Digital SLR Video &
Filmmaking For Dummies
978-1-118-36598-4

Photoshop Elements 12
For Dummies
978-1-118-72714-0

Gardening

Herb Gardening
For Dummies, 2nd Edition
978-0-470-61778-6

Gardening with Free-Range
Chickens For Dummies
978-1-118-54754-0

Health

Boosting Your Immunity
For Dummies
978-1-118-40200-9

Diabetes For Dummies,
4th Edition
978-1-118-29447-5

Living Paleo For Dummies
978-1-118-29405-5

Big Data

Big Data For Dummies
978-1-118-50422-2

Data Visualization
For Dummies
978-1-118-50289-1

Hadoop For Dummies
978-1-118-60755-8

Language &
Foreign Language

500 Spanish Verbs
For Dummies
978-1-118-02382-2

English Grammar
For Dummies, 2nd Edition
978-0-470-54664-2

French All-in-One
For Dummies
978-1-118-22815-9

German Essentials
For Dummies
978-1-118-18422-6

Italian For Dummies,
2nd Edition
978-1-118-00465-4

 **Available in print and e-book formats.**

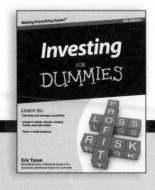

Available wherever books are sold. **For more information or to order direct visit www.dummies.com**

Math & Science

Algebra I For Dummies,
2nd Edition
978-0-470-55964-2

Anatomy and Physiology
For Dummies, 2nd Edition
978-0-470-92326-9

Astronomy For Dummies,
3rd Edition
978-1-118-37697-3

Biology For Dummies,
2nd Edition
978-0-470-59875-7

Chemistry For Dummies,
2nd Edition
978-1-118-00730-3

1001 Algebra II Practice
Problems For Dummies
978-1-118-44662-1

Microsoft Office

Excel 2013 For Dummies
978-1-118-51012-4

Office 2013 All-in-One
For Dummies
978-1-118-51636-2

PowerPoint 2013
For Dummies
978-1-118-50253-2

Word 2013 For Dummies
978-1-118-49123-2

Music

Blues Harmonica
For Dummies
978-1-118-25269-7

Guitar For Dummies,
3rd Edition
978-1-118-11554-1

iPod & iTunes
For Dummies, 10th Edition
978-1-118-50864-0

Programming

Beginning Programming
with C For Dummies
978-1-118-73763-7

Excel VBA Programming
For Dummies, 3rd Edition
978-1-118-49037-2

Java For Dummies,
6th Edition
978-1-118-40780-6

Religion & Inspiration

The Bible For Dummies
978-0-7645-5296-0

Buddhism For Dummies,
2nd Edition
978-1-118-02379-2

Catholicism For Dummies,
2nd Edition
978-1-118-07778-8

Self-Help & Relationships

Beating Sugar Addiction
For Dummies
978-1-118-54645-1

Meditation For Dummies,
3rd Edition
978-1-118-29144-3

Seniors

Laptops For Seniors
For Dummies, 3rd Edition
978-1-118-71105-7

Computers For Seniors
For Dummies, 3rd Edition
978-1-118-11553-4

iPad For Seniors
For Dummies, 6th Edition
978-1-118-72826-0

Social Security
For Dummies
978-1-118-20573-0

Smartphones & Tablets

Android Phones
For Dummies, 2nd Edition
978-1-118-72030-1

Nexus Tablets
For Dummies
978-1-118-77243-0

Samsung Galaxy S 4
For Dummies
978-1-118-64222-1

Samsung Galaxy Tabs
For Dummies
978-1-118-77294-2

Test Prep

ACT For Dummies,
5th Edition
978-1-118-01259-8

ASVAB For Dummies,
3rd Edition
978-0-470-63760-9

GRE For Dummies,
7th Edition
978-0-470-88921-3

Officer Candidate Tests
For Dummies
978-0-470-59876-4

Physician's Assistant Exam
For Dummies
978-1-118-11556-5

Series 7 Exam For Dummie
978-0-470-09932-2

Windows 8

Windows 8.1 All-in-One
For Dummies
978-1-118-82087-2

Windows 8.1 For Dummies
978-1-118-82121-3

Windows 8.1 For Dummies,
Book + DVD Bundle
978-1-118-82107-7

Available in print and e-book formats.

Available wherever books are sold. **For more information or to order direct visit www.dummies.com**

Take Dummies with you everywhere you go!

Whether you are excited about e-books, want more from the web, must have your mobile apps, or are swept up in social media, Dummies makes everything easier.

Leverage the Power

For Dummies is the global leader in the reference category and one of the most trusted and highly regarded brands in the world. No longer just focused on books, customers now have access to the For Dummies content they need in the format they want. Let us help you develop a solution that will fit your brand and help you connect with your customers.

Advertising & Sponsorships

Connect with an engaged audience on a powerful multimedia site, and position your message alongside expert how-to content.

Targeted ads • Video • Email marketing • Microsites • Sweepstakes sponsorship